The Quest For Meaning of Svāmī Vivekānanda

The Quest For Meaning of Svāmī Vivekānanda

a study of religious change

George M. Williams

New Horizons Press

Printed in the U.S.A.

First Printing 1974
Printed by Lawrence A. Brock
Chico, California

Library of Congress Cataloging Data
Williams, George Mason, 1940-
The Quest for Meaning of Swami Vivekananda
(The Religious quest, v. 1)
Bibliography: p. 141-44.
1. Vivekananda, Swami, 1863-1902.
I Title. II. Series
BL 1270.V5W54 294.5'6'4 [B] 74-10906
ISBN 0-914914-00-6 (pb)
ISBN 0-914914-02-2 (c)

New Horizons Press
P.O. Box 1758
Chico, California 95926

for each opportunity to learn
and to all who have shared
their learning, wisdom and help
--especially Marcia

THE RELIGIOUS QUEST

Volume One

Reappraisals of the religious foundations of mankind, both from within religious traditions and from outside of them.

CONSULTING EDITORS

Robert Baird
The University of Iowa

Alan Berger
Syracuse University

Willard Johnson
California State University, Long Beach

William Murnion
Ramapo College of New Jersey

Charles Winquist
California State University, Chico

TABLE OF CONTENTS

FOREWORD by Arvind Sharma ix

CHAPTER I. INTRODUCTION 1

The Definitional Problem. The Descriptive Procedure. The Type and Level of Understanding. The Object of Study. The Quotations, Transliterations and Appendices.

CHAPTER II. THREE CONVICTIONAL POSTURES DURING COLLEGE AND LAW SCHOOL 10

Brāhmo Samāji. Freemason. Sceptic.

CHAPTER III. HIS PATTERN OF ULTIMATE CONCERN AS ŚRĪ RĀMAKṚṢṆA'S DISCIPLE 22

The Questions and The Answers. Narendra's Internalization of Rāmakṛṣṇa's Teachings. Narendra's Renewed Doubts.

CHAPTER IV. THE SEARCH FOR THE TRUE AUTHORITY 38

Authority in The Scriptures. Help from Another Guru. A Pattern of Ultimacy in Spite of Uncertainty.

CHAPTER V. THE RELIGION ETERNAL 54

The Background of this Pattern of Ultimacy. The Principles of the Religion Eternal. Practical Vedānta.

CHAPTER VI. THE PLACE OF SVĀMĪ VIVEKĀNANDA IN THE RELIGIOUS HISTORY OF INDIA 105

NOTES 109

APPENDICES 131

BIBLIOGRAPHY 141

INDEX 145

FOREWORD

The modern Hindu is inclined to look upon the life of Svāmī Vivekānanda as a triumphant vindication of Hinduism. It was as if in him, Hinduism, struck dumb by the polemical attacks of other religions finally overcame nervous aphasia and found its lost voice—and a fiery one at that. Not only did he provide the words with which Hinduism could talk on terms of equality with other religions in a global context, in a national context he seemed to provide meaningfulness to the new educated Hindu who was being turned off alike by what appeared to be obsolete forms of his own tradition and by the importunate overtures of another. Such is the image of Svāmī Vivekānanda in Hindu eyes as it stands on the pedestal of history.

This book tries to tell us that this image is not a cast-iron image; that its feet, though not of clay, are human feet; that the life of Svāmī Vivekānanda was not merely a conquest; it was also a quest—a quest for meaning. It is fairly well-known that Svāmī Vivekānanda devoted himself to the cause of religion at the cost of great suffering to himself and to his family—a fact poignantly illustrated by the fact that his sister committed suicide. It is not so well-known, however, that the great devotion which sustained him through such crises was not free from moments of anguished doubt.

And by his doubts and the manner in which he faced them Svāmī Vivekānanda helped both to express and to stamp the spirit of Hinduism as much as by his convictions. This can be seen by raising a basic question: how does one face up to doubt in a belief system? One may prevent the doubt from emerging through dogmatism. Or one may suppress it (in oneself and in others) when it emerges through fanaticism. Or when doubt manifests itself with great force one can abandon the belief system and resort to scepticism. Or one may turn to other belief systems and become a convert (or at least a comparative religionist!). Or one may fashion one's faith out of doubt and turn agnostic. But in the life of Svāmī Vivekānanda doubt never gave way to despair—of which these above-mentioned reactions could be subtle forms. If anything becomes clear from this book it is that Svāmī Vivekānanda struggled with doubt throughout his life—but not as a crude dogmatist or a cynical sceptic or an agonised agnostic. He struggled with doubt as a Hindu. He searched for answers by going into the Scriptures, by going out to Gurus and by meditating on his experience. He also tried to face doubt by aiming at achieving that plenary experience by the alchemy of which doubt is transmuted into utter certitude. In doing all this he achieved, at different points in his life a different blend of beliefs, different flavours of faith; it was as if he was experimenting with different brands of Hinduism to the very end. Thus not only does it seem to be true now that there are as many

Hinduisms as there are Hindus, it seems to be equally true that the Hindu changes his brand of it at various points or stages in his life.

We all know of that Svāmī Vivekānanda who championed the cause of Hinduism in the external tensions in which it was historically caught; Dr. George Williams has now drawn for us a portrait of Svāmī Vivekānanda as caught in the internal tensions of Hinduism—of a religion which insists that there is a Reality but fights shy of saying what it is, which insists that the Reality can be reached (indeed there are many paths) but shrinks from indicating one exclusive road to it. And in seeing Svāmī Vivekānanda caught in these tensions one sees how the spokesmen of a tradition contribute as much to it by the honesty of their doubt as by the profundity of their faith.

Arvind Sharma
Center for the Study
of World Religions
Harvard University

Chapter 1

INTRODUCTION

Svāmī Vivekānanda, born Narendranath Datta (1863-1902), was the **kṣatriya-saṁnyāsin** (warrior-monk) who sought to awaken India to its mission to the world: the spreading of spirituality (**Sanātana Dharma**) as the world-conquering, socially active unity of all religions.

During his lifetime the **svāmī** was proclaimed by the world press as the hero of the Parliament of Religions held in Chicago in 1893. He had been the first modern Indian **saṁnyāsin** to cross the ocean—a religious offense according to the **Śāstras** which decreed the loss of caste and of religious privileges. He met this threat with the counter-attack that a **saṁnyāsin** had already renounced all and could not be outcasted. His speeches at the Parliament of Religions earned for him the position of interpreter of "Hinduism" in the West. He was offered professorships at both Harvard and Columbia Universities but turned them down to carry out "his plan" of preaching the Religion Eternal in the West in exchange for material help for India. He thereby became the embodiment of a new dimension in the modern period of an Indian religious tradition which was concerned with dissemination of the **Sanātana Dharma** (which the Svāmī termed "the Religion Eternal") to those who were not Aryan by birth.[1] He founded the Ramakrishna Mission upon the life and teachings of his **guru,** Rāmakṛṣṇa Paramahaṁsa (1836-1886). The Ramakrishna Mission has been regarded as the twentieth century's most potent religious force in India.[2]

Since 1902 the stature of Svāmī Vivekānanda has continued to grow until at the beginning of the seventies he has achieved the status of a cultural hero for a large number of present-day Indians.[3] The religious thought of the **svāmī** has been assimilated by thousands of believers. To understand religion in modern India and what has been called the "Hindu Renaissance," one must come to know the religious teachings of Svāmī Vivekānanda.

Because the methods of study not only influence the findings but also shape the questions which govern the direction and therefore the scope of a particular study, the preliminary task should begin with methodological considerations. These have been divided into the definitional problem, the descriptive procedure, the type and the level of understanding, and the object of study.

Some readers may choose to read Chapter VI next, passing over this section on methodology until later. Since this book assumes some knowledge of modern religious history in India, the reader studying India for the first time might wish to begin with "The Place of Svāmī Vivekānanda in the Religious History of India." Other readers may wish to begin with the content before looking at the methodology, thus skipping to the second chapter. Then one will return to this section on methodology when the connection between content and method is needed.

The Definitional Problem

When the historian of religions attempts to study the religion of a person or a community, semantic problems assert themselves immediately. What does he mean by "religion" as the object of study? What is meant not only will fix the direction of the study but also will suggest the values or norms "religion" will entail. This difficulty has become crucial in the history of religions because the historian is called upon to deal with more religions than one, which means that he risks assigning the values or norms of one "religion" to another.

Professor Robert Baird has suggested that two general approaches have been used in facing the task of defining "religion."[4] The first approach will be critically evaluated and left for others; the second will be chosen and followed in this study.

The "Essential-Intuitional Approach"

This implies "that religion is a something out there whose 'essence' can be apprehended by the historian of religions."[5] The clarifying question is "What is the nature of religion?" If the answer to the question is known at the beginning of the study, then the question is merely rhetorical, the nature of religion would have been posited at the start, and the work would be a matter of demonstrating the already known essence with the newly discovered data. This **a priori** approach (often referred to as "theologizing" the data of the religions of the world) is repudiated by all historians of religions, both of the "essential-intuitional approach" and the following "functional-definitional approach." If subordinating the perception of the nature of religion in one faith to that of another faith is to be avoided, then the answer to "What is the nature of religion?" must come at the end of the study. "Religion" must be studied so that it will present itself to the investigator and thereby its true nature may be discovered.

Phenomenologists of religion tend to use the "essential-intuitional approach." They begin without any preconceived notion of the essence of religion and allow "the religious" to present itself to the sensitive observer. Thus, when the true nature of religion is discovered, a definition of religion can be formulated.

The approach seemed straight-forward enough to a large number of scholars who have proceeded accordingly. Why was it, though, that as each phenomenologist of religion undertook the quest for the true nature of religion they have come to strikingly different configurations? The essence of religion presented itself as "the sacred," "power," "the numinous," and other conceptualizations with apparently dissimilar stuctures—a multiplicity of essences of religion (unless they should turn out to be semantic equivalents and partial structures relating to a greater unity).

Thus, the essence of religion is arrived at logically in a process of an inductive leap from the multiplicity of the phenomena to the "intuited" essence of its universal, "religion." The essential-intuitional approach" had begun without a definition of its object of study, "religion," had proceeded to examine the phenomena of "the religious," had drawn together a synthetic understanding of the essence of the manifested forms, and had presented this understanding as the very essence of "the religious"— as the **real** definition of religion, arrived at after the study. As I have argued previously, the logical procedure of the "intuitive approach" entails the fallacy of deducing what was previously induced.[6] In order to clarify this point, we might say it in the following way: One works with the multiplicity of phenomena and seeks to discover the one behind that multiplicity, the essence of "religion" behind its polyploidy: one intuits or induces the one in the many by making an "inductive leap;" and then, based upon the essence inductively arrived at, one boldly presents the real definition of "religion" as a deduction from an understanding of the essence and as the structure of "the religious." Professor Baird was correct in arguing that, as presently used, this approach is circular.[7] When such an uncritical use of the "inductive leap" to the whole or essence of religion is made, there can be no guarantee that the integrity of a particular religion will not be subverted. Whatever values or norms are seen in the "edetic vision" (technical term used to designate the inductive leap) of the essence of religion, thus becoming a part of the explanatory system in which a particular religious system will be interpreted, those values or norms will logically be derived deductively from the essence of religion or explanatory system later in accessing the relationship of a single religious phenomenon to the whole. (This approach resembles apologetic—although it discovers its explanatory system instead of beginning with it—rather than the physical sciences and their notion of models.)[8] This approach is therefore left for others whose interest is normative as they search for the true essence of religion.

The "Functional-Definitional Approach"

The development of the clarifying question is important, because it demonstrates the interest and thus the scope of this approach. Two scholars have contributed significantly to the approach. Professor Wilfred Cantwell Smith sought to solve the problem of not undercutting another man's religion with foreign norms and values by approaching "the religious" in a personal way. He denied the validity of the question "What is religion?" for the historian of religions. He stated that the goal should be an understanding of the "faith" of persons and, only secondarily the "cumulative tradition."[9] "The religious" was what the worshipper said it was for him. Smith discarded the question "What is the nature or essence of religion?" and chose as his goal "What is the faith of this man or community of believers?" He did not further the discussion of the definitional problem but only substituted his definition of religion as "faith of persons."[10] But an important advance for the historical study of religions had been made by separating the descriptive question "What is the faith of this particular person or group?" from the normative question "What is religion?"

Professor Robert Baird clarified the issue by distinguishing among the various types of definitions: **real** (truth statements about the essence of things); **lexical** (the various possibilities of meaning to which a single word is a sign; a historical record of the ambiguity of a single word with many meanings); **stipulative** or **functional** (the clarifying process of simply indicating which of the meanings is being used without asserting that this particular meaning is the true meaning of the word).[11]

Thus it followed that the historian of religions could begin his task by stipulating what he intended as his field of study. Since it was a stipulative or functional definition, he would not be concerned with the question "What is religion?"—the pursuit of essences. A definition would be chosen which was appropriate, adequate and comprehensive enough for a religio-historical investigation to proceed. Smith's limited question of "What is the faith of this person or group?" (which excluded any reified religion from study because reified religion, according to Smith, is not truly religious, the tautological fallacy of the real definition) had been changed by Baird to "What is the religion of this person or community?"[12] The **stipulative** definition of "religion" functioned to limit what was being studied from other interests of study. It intended no alien norms or evaluative critera from which might be deduced that the particular object of study was "truly religious," "quasi-religious" or "pseudo-religious." For this reason Baird's functional definition of "religion" included concerns which some believers considered religious, although they would have been excluded by Smith's normative definition of "faith" as the true type of religion.

The function of comparative evaluation among varying truth claims is recognized as a legitimate human interest which may be pursued by first paralleling functional equivalents, validating a normative or evaluative scale, demonstrating its applicability to the objects of comparison, and then effecting the ranking or evaluation. This normative endeavor is explicity excluded from this study, as will become evident in the following section.

It cannot be stated emphatically enough that the **stipulative** or **functional** definition is given in order that the field of study may be limited without imposing norms upon the object of study or excluding norms which are considered valid within the ontological system presupposed by a particular pattern of belief. The definition is useful if it suspends the truth question (whether or not this religion is really true) and allows the ''religio-historical description'' to proceed without hidden norms foreign to that religion.[13] It will assume as ''heuristically true'' the norms of the religious system since they govern its cohesion and coherence.

The definition of religion which stipulates the interest of this study is ''that which concerns a person or community ultimately.'' Its history as a formulation is twofold. As first formulated by Professor Paul Tillich, the interest or intention was that of suggesting the real essence of religion, whereby any particular form of religion might be judged.[14] Thus, as a normative formula ''religion as ultimate concern'' could be used to evaluate truth claims.[15] However, the formulation was seen by Professor Baird to be useful for a different interest and intention. Separated from its imputed essentialism of one pattern of ultimacy and its program to validate its own theological system, Tillich's definition could adequately serve the descriptive needs of the historian of religions who wished to present any pattern of ultimacy in its integrity. Baird has stated that other definitions are possible and that each stipulates the precise interest of the investigator, thus setting the boundaries around the intended object of study.[16]

In summary, this study begins with a stipulative definition of its object: The religious thought of Svāmī Vivekānanda is that pattern of ultimate concern which he has formulated and to which he has related his penultimate concerns at any period of belief.

The Descriptive Procedure

The object of study has been stipulated as that which concerns Svāmī Vivekānanda ultimately. It could be studied by numerous methods in order to attain equally numerous goals. The goal or intention of this study is the determinative factor for judging appropriate methods.

The ''religio-historical method'' has been articulated by Professor Baird in **Category Formation and the History of Religions.**[17] The goal of ''religio-historical'' study is an accurate description of the ultimate concern of a person or group as a part of the human past. The method is historical: it is concerned with what has happened in the human past, and what is being described is entirely within the historical realm. Whatever levels of transhistorical understanding there may be are left to other methods of inquiry. History is taken functionally to mean ''the descriptive study of the human past.''[18] Hence statements about religion are verified according to their accuracy by the canons of evidence, answering the question ''To what degree of probability did this happen, was this said, was this done?'' Historical evidence must be sufficient to support the degree of certainty indicated in the reporting of the event or saying. Selectivity and emphasis are submitted to the same verification, i.e. that the data support the presentation and is not violated by it. One must limit oneself to statements which are verifiable by documentation. Even the structure or ordering of a pattern of ultimate concern must not do violence to the integrity of the belief system. (Certain semantic variables are used for pattern of ultimate concern—ultimacy, belief system, religious system, truth system.)

Religio-historical description of a pattern of ultimate concern intends to do justice to the contribution of the individual or community. Therefore, it must exclude the historian of religions' notions and evaluations of ultimacy while presenting the subject's truth system in the manner he arrived at it. ''One would be hard pressed to hold that it is not of high importance to ascertain what has been most important to men individually and in community.''[19]

A ''pattern of ultimate concern,'' functionally defined, is the complex of beliefs as related to the subject's primary notion of ultimacy which was held for a demonstrable period to time. To pre-suppose that the subject had a pattern of ultimate concern which was singular or at least singularly emergent is to adopt an alternative prior to study which is both normative as well as formulative. A descriptive methodology must avoid this common error by describing the belief system with neutrality toward the number of belief systems held by the subject. The clarifying question would be ''What pattern of ultimate concern was held and when?'' However, at this juncture a normative interest could easily slip into the study undetected. The historian of religions may encounter a wide variety of changed patterns: the same category of ultimacy with different auxiliary beliefs, a partial pattern being emphasized at a given period, new questions and new answers being formulated in an emerging truth system, the same beliefs as in another period but reordered and revalued in such a way as to appear new, and so forth. The duration of any complex of emphases should become a conscious question so that the internal relationship of the various beliefs and the ways that they are valued will become evident. Any pattern of ultimacy may change, especially during times of personal or cultural crisis. This change can be continuous (evolutionary, developmental) or discontinuous (a radical break) or both.

How can one proceed in order to present adequately the new, the discarded, and the reordered in the subject's manner of believing without presupposing continuity, discontinuity, or both? It is proposed that the notion of "patterns" can be used functionally as a open term—open to all three interpretations equally. Therefore, the use of "patterns" of ultimacy is intended to function as a descriptive concept, including all types of reordered patterns but suspending judgment about continuity or discontinuity until after the data has been evaluated.

The Type and Level of Understanding

There are many kinds of understanding: psychological, economic, **ad infinitum.** Religio-historical understanding is functionally defined as "any valid knowledge about religion communicable in propositional form."[20] The propositions which contain knowledge about the religious past with varying degrees of accuracy are on two levels—the ideal and the **real.**[21] The **ideal level** refers to pattern of ultimacy as those profess it ought to be (usually the realm of conceptualization); while the **real level** refers to what can be verified in historical acts as that which concerns a man or group ultimately. This study stipulates that its interest is the **ideal level** of the pattern or patterns of ultimacy of Svāmī Vivekānanda.

Religio-historical understanding does not attempt to penetrate the realms of non-verbal communication, psychic states, and emotional or religious experiences except as they are articulated and valued by the subject. Then, what is of concern is the subject's explanation on the ideal level rather than how that phenomenon or state might be variously explained according to some norm or discipline. What the believer holds to be ineffable, either because of supposed innate ineffabality or because no one has yet acquired the means to express or signify the experience, is presented as ineffable, simply because it has been assigned this value or meaning in his pattern of ultimate concern.

The Object of Study

Since the goal is an accurate presentation of the pattern or patterns of ultimate concern of Svāmī Vivekānanda, the nature of the resources of that study is important.

The patterns of belief during the **svāmī's** college days must be pieced together from accounts other than from his own hand, except for his brief reflections. A clear distinction will be maintained between **contemporaneous documentation** and **later documentation** of beliefs and their assigned relationship to the **svāmī's** ultimate concern at a given time. **Contemporaneous documentation** of beliefs refers to records, either by Svāmī Vivekānanda (primary) or by a direct witness (secondary), which were made at the time when they were believed.

Later documentation of beliefs refers to records which were made after the period to which they refer. Later documention introduces a number of problems which must be handled and which lower the probability that the belief will be accurately represented. One is especially worth mentioning. When a pattern of belief has changed, consciously or unconsciously, the believer may project present beliefs into the past.

The problem of **secondary later documentation** is far more problematic. The reporter must have understood the first belief and its relation to the belief system sufficiently to have been able to overcome the problem of assimilating it with a second complex of beliefs. Further, the reporter's own interests and motives might influence his record. For this reason, a large body of secondary later documentation will be excluded from the body of this study; only in those rare instances when its inclusion appears to advance our goal will this type of documentation be included—but clearly indicated. Biographies, interpretation, and apologetic materials have been checked for leads to historical evidence and for insights but will be referred to only rarely. They are listed in the bibliography.

Mahendranath Gupta's **The Gospel of Sri Ramakrishna** (GRK) contains secondary contemporaneous documentation of the **svāmī's** beliefs from 1882 through 1887. **The Complete Works of Swami Vivekananda** (CW), volumes one through eight, contain the raw, unprocessed data for our study from 1888 to 1902. They are a compilation of writings, letters, lectures, extemporaneous speeches, remembered sayings and interviews. The unevenness of the compilation—writings by the **svāmī**, speeches recorded by stenographers, notes on speeches, notes on a significant saying, newspaper stories and interviews—will be used in accordance with the type of documentation and the logic of historical probability. There is a noticeable difference between what an American journalist might quote as the **svāmī's** main point in a particular lecture and what a well-informed disciple would cite. However, it is fortunate for the researcher that the Vedanta Society (as publisher of the complete works) did not alter these variations, while footnoting the obvious mistakes of the listener. One disturbing problem is the number of omissions which the Vedanta Society made in Svāmī Vivekānanda's private correspondence. Some of the deletions are readily understandable as references to persons, but others have to do with financial matters or omissions of everything except the religious saying in the letter.[22]

The Complete Works span only a portion of the **svāmī's** life. Although Svāmī Vivekānanda was born as Narendranath Datta on January 12, 1863, the first extant, primary document is dated August 12, 1888. Vivekānanda's master, Śrī Rāmakṛṣṇa, had been dead almost two years to the day and Vivekānanda, as yet not having settled upon his final monastic name, was wandering about India in the traditional manner of a begging **saṁnyāsin.** The last extant work of Vivekānanda was a letter dated June 14, 1902, several weeks prior to his death on July 4th. Thus all the documents of the collection date after the time of Vivekānanda's vow of **Saṁnyāsa**, December 24, 1886.

The Quotations, Transliterations and Appendices

The direct quotations of Svāmī Vivekānanda will maintain the British-influenced spellings of such words as "realisation" and "practicalisation" while the text of the study will follow American spellings. The **svāmī's** transliterations of Sanskrit terms will be maintained in direct quotations and will be italicized or will have diacritical marks only if they appear that way in the quotation.

Appendix A is a compilation of the chronological order of Svāmī Vivekānanda's extant writings. This was necessitated by the way the **svāmī's** writings have been arranged without any regard for chronology and by the need of this study to know what he believed and when. This compilation will facilitate future researchers so that they may add new materials to this corpus and then assess their influence upon the findings of this study.

Appendix B is a compilation of Sanskrit terms which the **svāmī** used with multiple English meanings. These meanings indicate the level of thought in which they were being used. This compilation reduces the complexity of the Sanskrit-English variables and often makes his intention for picking a particular meaning more apparent. Methodologically, a word study is the real beginning point in the study of a man's thought, for the way a man uses words in his own particular way must be bridged before his thought can be understood by another.

Chapter II

THREE CONVICTIONAL POSTURES DURING COLLEGE AND LAW SCHOOL 1878—1885

Narendranath Datta grew up in a period of religious turmoil, in which many conflicting truth claims were competing for allegiance. As if in a religious bazaar Narendra was confronted with a bewildering variety of wares—belief systems or even elements of them—which could be chosen or adapted to make one's life meaningful. He encountered and experimented with the teachings of traditional Indian faiths, of the reform-minded Brāhmo Samāj, of Christians, of Freemasons, of sceptics, of evolutionists, and of materialists.

The importance of Narendra's early religious development can be immediately appreciated. Each formulation of a pattern of ultimacy would represent the ideal of a particular period in his life and by which his activities, thought and values were integrated. Also questions unanswered by one conceptualization of ultimacy, as well as answers which were satisfactory and would remain unchanged, might reappear in later ones.

Primary contemporaneous documentation is not extant before 1888 for Narendra's patterns of ultimate concerns. Secondary contemporaneous accounts of his beliefs up to 1887 were recorded by Mahendranath Gupta in **The Gospel of Sri Ramakrishna.**

This chapter deals with the patterns of ultimacy for Narendra which roughly correspond to his years in college and in law school, 1878/9 until June 1885. During this period Narendra moved through a number of belief systems and their ways of ordering life: as a Brāhmo Samāji, a Freemason, a sceptic. From the end of 1881 or the beginning of 1882 Narendra visited a priest of Kālī, Śrī Rāmakṛṣṇa, but continued to worship as a Brāhmo Samāji until as late as March, 1885.[1] His membership in the Calcutta Masonic Lodge occured prior to his father's death in 1884.[2] Narendra's scepticism intertwined periods of affirmation until he had become a devotee of Rāmakṛṣṇa Paramahaṁsa.

Brāhmo Samāji

Narendra became a member of the Brāhmo Samāj in his youth. His brother, Bhupendranath Datta, stated that Narendra was a member of

Keshab Chandra Sen's "Band of Hope" which sought "to wean away the young men from the path of smoking, drinking, etc."[3] At the split of the Brāhmo Samāj in 1878 Narendra is said to have followed Paṇḍits Śivanath Śastri and Vijay Kṛṣṇa Gosvāmī in the Sādhāran Brāhmo Samāj, his name appearing on the original roll.[4] However, his family did not move back to Calcutta until 1879 and that is more probably the time he joined the Samāj, even though his parents may have discouraged it.[5]

Narendranath left no contemporaneous documents concerning his beliefs as a Samāji. His later references to the Brāhmo Samāj may be divided into four classes: (1) what he had believed, (2) why he no longer believed, (3) criticism, and (4) passing mention. Only one of thirteen references provided information on what he believed, only three on why he quit believing. (1) Looking back during a controversy with Pratap Chandra Mazumdar of the Brāhmo Samāj in 1894 as Svāmī Vivekānanda, he would list belief in the program of social reform and in renunciation of the world:

> P.S.--I had connection with Pundit Shiva Nath Shastri's party—but only on points of social reform. Mazoomdar and Chandra Sen—I always considered as not sincere, and I have no reason to change my opinion even now. Of course in religious matters even with my friends Punditji I differed much, the chief being, I thinking Sannyasa or (**giving up the world**) the highest ideal, and he, a sin. So the Brahmo Samajists consider becoming a monk a sin!! Yours, V.
>
> The Brahmo Samaj, like Christian Science in your country, spread in Calcutta for a certain time and then died out. I am not sorry, neither glad that it died. It has done its work—viz **social reform. Its religion was not worth a cent**, and so it must die out. If Mazoomdar thinks I was one of the causes of its death, he errs. **I am even now a great sympathiser of its reforms;** but the **"booby" religion** could not hold its own against the old "Vedanta." What shall I do? Is that my fault? Mazoomdar has become childish in his old age and takes to tactics not a whit better than some of your Christian missionaries. Lord bless him and show him better ways.[6]

(2) This class of references provided no insight into his beliefs (even those rejected) but will be treated later when his Samāji beliefs crumbled before the problems of suffering and doubt. The two other classes of references provide nothing to the point.[7]

The impression is left after an examination of later accounts by Svāmī Vivekānanda that the Brāhmo Samāj was of little consequence for him. However, quite the opposite impression comes from studying the contemporaneous documents left by those who knew his beliefs at the time. To present this evidence systematically, a device will be used. Each Brāhmo Samāji took an oath that he would practice the beliefs of the group. Although published in 1910, the following official statement of the beliefs of the Sādhāran Brāhmo Samāj can be demonstrated to sufficiently represent the beliefs of Narendra at this stage of his religious development. The beliefs will be presented separately to allow a presentation of how Narendra was observed to have internalized these principles.[8]

> (1) There is only one God, who is the Creator, Preserver and Savior of this world. He is spirit; He is infinite in power, wisdom, love, justice and holiness; He is omnipresent, eternal and blissful.

Narendra believed in a "formless God" to the degree that he ridiculed Rāmakṛṣṇa's belief in God with form and, more especially, in the idols at Dakshineswar.[9] In these contemporaneous accounts it can be seen that he, like the other Brāhmos, professed a belief in a beneficient **Brahman,** who was also addressed by the devotional name, **Hari.**[10]

> (2) The human soul is immortal, and capable of infinite progress, and is responsible to God for its doings.

A later remembrance of a fellow disciple would partially confirm that Narendra believed the human soul to be distinct from God.

> From the first it was Shri Ramakrishna's idea to initiate Narendra into the mysteries of the Advaita Vedanta. With that end in mind he would ask Naren to read aloud passages from **Ashtāvakra Samhitā** and other Advaita treatises in order to familiarize him with the philosophy. To Narendra, a staunch adherent of the Brahmo Samaj, these writings seemed heretical, and he would rebel saying, "It is blasphemous, for there is no difference between such philosophy and atheism. There is no greater sin in the world than to think of myself as identical with the Creator. I am God, you are God, these created things are God—what can be more absurd than this! The sages who wrote such things must have been insane." Shri Ramakrishna would be amused at this bluntness and would only remark, "You may not accept the views of these seers. But how can you abuse them or limit God's infinitude? Go on praying to the God of Truth and believe in any aspect of His which He reveals to you." But Naren did not surrender easily. Whatever did not tally with reason, he considered to be false, and it was his nature to stand against falsehood. Therefore he missed no opportunity to ridicule the Advaita philosophy.[11]

The account also suggests how the Brāhmo term for God, **Brahman,** was not being used; **Brahman** was distinct from human souls, unlike the **Brahman** of **Advaita Vedānta.**

> (3) God is to be worshipped in spirit and in truth. Divine worship is necessary for attaining true felicity and salvation.

Narendra joined in a style of worship that did not tolerate physical helps, which were regarded as idolatry. He even criticised Rāmakṛṣṇa for bowing down before the Brāhmo Samāj temple.[12] The depth of belief in a God of spirit who was worshipped in spirit can be inferred from Narendra's repulsion to the worship of Kālī.[13] He told Rāmakṛṣṇa on one occasion: "God with form is a mere idol."[14] Even as Keshab Chandra Sen had introduced the **bhakti** (devotion) practiced by followers of Chaitanya, so the Sādhāran Brāhmo Samāj used the **saṁkīrtana** (singing in chorus) and the **nagarkīrtaṇa** (town praise) in its worship.[15] Narendra was a member of this chorus.

(4) To love God and to carry out His will in all the concerns of life constitute true worship.

This belief referred to a positive valuation of life in the world and participation in it. Yet it was the most vulnerable belief of the reformers, as evidenced by the number of times they came to Rāmakṛṣṇa Paramahaṁsa and asked if a man could attain salvation in the world. Keshab Chandra Sen and Pratap Chandra Mazumdar of the Brāhmo Samāj, known after Janurary 1881, as "The Church of the New Dispensation," as well as Śiva Nath Śastri and Vijay Kṛṣṇa Gosvāmī of the Sādhāran Brāhmo Samāj went to Dakshineswar and listened to Rāmakṛṣṇa's call to renunciation.[16] Narendra went also, but it is important to remember that during these years he was actively pursuing an education for a degree in law. It may be inferred that prior to 1884 Narendra believed that one could love God and carry out his will in the world.

(5) Prayer and dependence on God and a constant realization of His presence are the means of attaining spiritual growth.

Narendra's belief in prayer to and depencence on God can be inferred from his later complaint that these were of no avail.

(6) No created object is to be worshipped as God, nor is any person or book to be considered as infallible and as the sole means of salvation; but truth is to be reverently accepted from all scriptures and from the teaching of all persons without distinction of creed or country.

This was an extremely complex belief which brought together elements that could lead to self-contradiction. Beginning with the last part of the belief, the Brāhmo Samāji affirmed a unity of all religions and would therefore accept "teaching of all persons without distinction of creed or country." Yet it also denied the validity of "idol worship" and called for its cessation in India. Persons and religious books were judged by reason and whatever was found to be true was accepted. Members of the Sādhāran Brāhmo Samāj were discouraged from even mixing with worshippers of "gods of form."[17] This openness toward all religions because they were true at their highest and most complex level (Keshab's teaching) and closure toward what they termed "idolatry" was affirmed by Narendra at this time.[18]

(7) The Fatherhood of God and the Brotherhood of man and

kindness to all living beings are the essence of true religion.

Because of its monotheistic stance, the brotherhood of all men was affirmed. That worked out to an attack on the existing social order comprised of the caste system and servitude of women. This was the area of belief that was acknowledged in the later documentation of Svāmī Vivekānanda.[19] Besides promoting the freedom and education of women and the abolition of caste, they carried out a program of philanthropy in the spirit of universal brotherhood.[20]

> (8) God rewards virtue, and punishes sin. His punishments are remedial and not eternal.

No documentary evidence is available to assess Narendra's internalization of this belief. However, it is not unrelated to the events which left him spiritually bankrupt and the reasons which he gave for leaving the Brāhmo Samāj. This belief hardly prepares one for a universal problem or crisis—the sufferings of a righteous man. It was not until after he had begun to experience such sufferings in 1884 that he seriously turned toward Śrī Rāmakṛṣṇa.

> (9) Cessation from sin accompanied by sincere repentance is the only atonement for it; and union with God is wisdom, goodness and holiness is true salvation.

Narendra's judgmental attitude toward his fellow students may account for his later criticism of the Brāhmo Samāj's teaching about sin.[21] While a Samāji he said of his generation of students: "They smoke cigarettes, indulge in frivolous talk, enjoy foppishness, play truant, and do everything of that sort. I have even seen them visiting questionable places."[22] His denunciation of the doctrine of sin later as Svāmī Vivekānanda might be explained in part because he once held it himself.

During this period his brother recounts a saying of their elder sister, Swarnamayi Devi: "While Narendranath was a fanatical Brahmo, he was a vegetarian in his diet."[23] Having been a Brāhmo at the very least for three years, Narendra adopted a belief in celibacy shortly before October 22, 1882.[24]

The depth of Narendra's participation in the Brāhmo Samāj can be partially suggested from several shreds of evidence. Besides his active part in the **Saṁkīrtaṇas**, Narendra cooperated, as did his fellow Sādhāran Brāhmo Samājis, with Keshab Chandra Sen's programs to influence the educated to undertake reforms. A few days prior to April 7, 1883, Narendra was a member of Keshab's play, **Nava-Vrindāvan.**[25] Keshab "played the role of Pāvhari Bābā" (of whom we will hear later).[26] (A Brāhmo Samāj source has the information that the play was originally performed in the middle of September, 1882, after a year's preparation.[27]) While the pages of **The Gospel of Sri Ramakrishna** reveal extensive cooperation and interchange between these two branches of the Brāhmo Samāj, little note has been taken about Keshab's influence on Narendra. The later documents of Svāmī

Vivekānanda suggest none. The similarity of Keshab's later views with some of Rāmakṛṣṇa's further obscure a conclusion. Narendra's brother provides a clue to the degree to which the future Svāmī had believed: "The late Haromohan Mitra used to repeatedly say to the writer, that Swamiji used to say: 'But for Ramakrishna I would have been a Brahmo missionary.' "[28]

Freemason

Sometime before his father's death in 1884, Narendra joined the Freemason's Lodge in Calcutta.[29] This membership may or may not have represented an altered belief system for him. Since Freemasonry sought to accept a membership of varying ultimate concerns, the area of possible alteration would have only been the penultimate concerns.

Primary later documentation valued this membership pejoratively; after having renounced the world Svāmī Vivekānanda would say that he had joined for purely social and financial advantages.[30] That might have meant that he was considering the economic possibilities the law degree would make possible. However, his continual sabotage of marital plans by this time demonstrated that he had not accepted the householder life in toto.[31] This assessment is further confirmed by his brother's account;

> Again, to give a further life in Narendranath's future career, his father made him enter Freemasonry as a member. On being asked by his uncle about the reason for this procedure, Narendranath's father answered that it will help him in his future life. (At that time it was the fashion with the Indians to become members of the Freemasonry. Lawyers, Judges and Government officials were its members. Thus, the membership gave a chance to mix with the high dignitaries and officials.) The writer has seen a piece of printed application form of Freemason's Lodge amongst the old household papers relating to Narendrantha's College certificates. (This paper has been sent to Belur Math.)[32]

Even if Narendra's motives were purely materialistic as his later valuation would suggest, Freemasonry in India contained a number of general notions which paralleled those he held as a Brāhmo Samāji—equality, social reform, philanthropy and a "common denominator" approach to religious unity.[33] The Stationary Lodge was established in Calcutta in 1730 and had become a force in the drive toward caste reform and the breaking of dietary laws.[34] Freemasons learned the charge that stated:

> 'tis now thought more expedient only to oblige them (Masons) to the Religion in which all men agree, leaving their particular Opinions to themselves; that is, to be **good Men and true,** or men of Honour and Honesty, by whatever Demoninations or

Persuasions they may be distinguished.[35]

In India there was a special appeal for those in commerce and in the professions to cast off the social restrictions of caste.[36] Working together in harmony in accord with the great plan of the Universal Architect had far reaching implications. Even so, these notions were general and in fact contained no special program of implementation.

Ten years later Svāmī Vivekānanda may have been in dialogue with this part of his past when he stated:

> The **grand plan** is to start a colony in Central India, where you can follow your own ideas independently, and then a little leaven will leaven all. In the meanwhile form a Central Association and go on branching off all over India. Start only on religious grounds now, and do not preach any violent social reform at present; only do not countenance **foolish superstitions.** Try to revive society on the old grounds of universal salvation and **equality** as laid down by the old Masters, such as Shankaracharya, Ramanuja, and Chaitanya.
>
> [...] No shilly-shanny, no **esoteric blackguardism,** no **secret humbug, nothing should be done in a corner.**[37]

This later document of Svāmī Vivekānanda may have been implicating Freemasonry's esoteric history and rituals and assigning them to the realm of "foolish superstitions." What can be seen clearly is that all these elements which might have possibly come from Freemasonry (or the next period of scepticism) have been consciously related to purely Indian religious sources.

Sceptic

Two paths—one existential, the other intellectual—converged by early 1884 to plunge Narendra into a sceptical pattern of ordering his concerns. Prior to this Narendra had been an active member of the Sādhāran Brāhmo Samāj, a member in the Masonic Lodge, a liberal arts student avidly studying Western thought, and a sporadic visitor to the Kālī **pūjāri** (priest of Kālī) at Dakshineswar, Śrī Rāmakṛṣṇa, without a recorded crisis of belief. Concerning the visits to Rāmakṛṣṇa, Narendra seemed to have been influenced, at least in part, to break several engagements for marriage.[38] He would later remember the following:

> One day my grandmother overheard my Master speaking in my room, about the efficacy of a celibate life. She told of this to my parents. They became greatly concerned lest I should renounce the world and were increasingly anxious that I should marry. My mother was especially fearful lest I should leave the family to take upon myself the vows of monastic life. She often spoke of the matter to me; but I would give a casual reply. But all their plannings for my marriage were frustrated by the strong will of the Master. On occasion all negotiations of marriage were

> settled, when a petty difference of opinion arose and the engagement was broken.[39]

But despite Rāmakṛṣṇa's influence on this matter Narendra had begun to reject him and ceased going to Dakshineswar around August 19, 1883. Secondary contemporaneous documentation suggests two reasons voiced by Narendra at the time—that Rāmakṛṣṇa was an "idolator" and that he and his devotees were intellectual inferiors.[40] When Narendra began staying away, Rāmakṛṣṇa first tried to visit him in Calcutta and then had him brought to Dakshineswar on August 19, 1883.[41] The results were evident and Rāmakṛṣṇa would ask a devotee a month later: "Narendra doesn't like even you, nowadays. Why didn't he come to me at Adhar's house?"[42] There remains no documentation of a further visit until after Narendra's existential framework was shaken apart.[43]

The Existential Crisis

The death of Narendra's father, Bisvanath Datta, submerged Narendra and his family in an ordeal from which they never recovered economically. This was in late February or early March, 1884, following the death of Keshab Chandra Sen by a few months.[44] Only a few days prior to his father's death Narendra had successfully completed the bachelor of arts examination.

Even before his father's death joint-family problems had become so intolerable that they had moved out of their ancestral home to temporary quarters.[45] At his death Narendra's great-aunt and -uncle retained possession of the home and forced a law suit. This would involve much of Narendra's energies for more than three years.[46]

If Narendra's brother has accurately connected the succeeding events, then what happened was

> that after graduation Narendranath was made by his father to enter the firm of Nemaichandra Basu, Attorney-at-Law as an articled-clerk to qualify himself for the attorneyship. The latter was a friend of his father. At the same time he studied law at the aforementioned Institution to prepare himself for B.L. Examination. Here, an interesting news is to be mentioned. We have already said that Narendranath previously showed his desire to go to England to study law. In this matter, the writer's elder brother, Mahendranath says, that Narendranath had the ambition to complete his law studies in England, and father was in agreement with this ambition. But the latter's sudden demise upset the plan.[47]

This arrangement evidently did not work out, as Bhupendranath added: "But after the death of Narendranath's father, he had to give up the articled-clerkship due to unexpectedly sudden family economic stringency, but continued to study law."[48]

Although Bisvanath Datta may have been one of the most successful "native lawyers" in Calcutta, the lawsuit concerning family property and an allegedly dishonest law-partner[49] borrowing money in Bisvanath's name left the family in poverty and Narendra as sole wage-earner. He found several small jobs, including a short time as a teacher in Vidyasagar's School, while he conducted the lawsuit and continued his studies.[50]

Marriage would have been the way out. All Narendra would have had to do was give up his belief in celibacy and marry. His brother recounted:

> Marriage-proposals from important parties came during Bisvanath's life-time. After his demise, proposals from quarters high up in society came as well. From the mother the writer heard that one of Bisvanath's friends from school days and latter-on, an attorney colleague of the High Court, proposed that he would bear the expenses of the family law-suit if Narendranath married his granddaughter. Again, right from the Ramakrishna circle, a householder devotee, the late Balaram Basu, a Zamindar of Cattack made a similar offer to Narendranath if he would marry his daughter. Further, the late Tulsiram Ghose, the eldest brother-in-law of Balaram Basu, brought a proposal for marriage with the convert-educated only daughter of R. Mitra a rich Calcutta Barrister. But all these proposals were of no avail. They fell on deaf ears.[51]

Is it hard to understand his family's violent reaction when he returned to Rāmakṛṣṇa? November 9, 1884, Rāmakṛṣṇa said: "His relatives beat him at home because he comes here. There is none to defend him."[52]

The Intellectual Crisis

Narendra entered Presidency College in Calcutta in 1880 but, according to his brother, was not permitted to take the Fine Arts examination because of poor attendance resulting from malaria.[53] So he transferred to what became known as the Scottish Church College. Study and ascetic practices seemed to have brought on a nervous breakdown, and he was forced to recuperate at Bodh-Gayā.[54] He returned and passed the First Arts examination in 1881. At college he was active in the philosophy club.[55] Even in his discussions with Rāmakṛṣṇa and his devotees Narendra cited Western authorities and used logical argumentation.[56] On one occasion, March 11, 1885, Narendra had quoted Hamilton, Spencer, Tyndall and Huxley; Rāmakṛṣṇa was reported to have said: "I don't enjoy these discussions." Later he said directly to Narendra: "As long as a man argues about God, he has not realised Him. You two were arguing. I didn't like it."[57]

Brajendra Nath Seal, a fellow student, witnessed Narendra's intellectual turmoil during this period. But his account was penned twenty-five years later, five years after Svāmī Vivekānanda's death. Seal began: "When I first met Vivekananda in 1881, we were fellow-students of Principal William Hastie, scholar, metaphysician, and poet, at the General Assembly's College."[58]

> This was the beginning of a critical period in his mental history, during which he awoke to self-consciousness and laid the foundation of his future personality. John Stuart Mill's **Three Essays on Religion** had upset his first boyish theism and easy optimism which he had imbibed from the outer circles of the Brahmo Samaj. The arguments from causality and design were for him broken reeds to lean upon, and he was haunted by the problem of the Evil in Nature and Man which he, by no means, could reconcile with the goodness of an All-wise and All-powerful Creator. A friend introduced him to the study of Hume's Scepticism and Herbert Spencer's doctrine of the Unknowable, and his unbelief gradually assumed the form of a settled philosophical scepticism.[59]

Narendra is reported to have translated some of Spencer's thought into Bengali.[60] (References to Spencer's evolutionary thought would later punctuate his speeches as Svāmī Vivekānanda.[61])

Seal observed that these studies destroyed his "old prayerful devotions" and were behind his "nonchalant air of habitual mocking and scoffing."[62] Seal continued:

> It was at this time that he came to me being brought by a common friend, the same who had introduced him to the study of Hume and Herbert Spencer. I had had a nodding acquaintance with him before, but now he opened himself to me and spoke of his harassing doubts and his despair of reaching certitude about the Ultimate Reality. He asked for a course of Theistic philosophic reading suited to a beginner in his situation. I named some authorities, but the stock arguments of the Intuitionists and the Scotch common-sense school only confirmed him in his unbelief. Besides, he did not appear to me to have sufficient patience for humdrum reading—his faculty was to imbibe not so much from books as from living communion and personal experience. With him it was life kindling life and thought kindling thought.[63]

Despite this accurate evaluation of Narendra's impatience with reading, Seal prescribed "a course of readings in Shelley. Shelley's Hymn to the spirit of a glorified millennial humanity moved him as the arguments of the philosophers had failed to move him."[64] A central belief was that the universe "contained a spiritual principle of unity."[65]

> I spoke to him now of a higher unity than Shelly had conceived, the unity of the Parabrahman as the Universal Reason. My own position at that time sought to fuse into one, three essential elements, the pure monism of the Vedanta, the dialectics of the Absolute idea of Hegel and the Gospel of Equality, Liberty and Fraternity of the French Revolution. The principle of individuation was with me the principle of Evil....
>
> The sovereignty of Universal Reason, and the negation of the individual as the principle of morals, were ideas that soon came to satisfy Vivekananda's intellect and gave him an assured conquest over scepticism and materialism.[66]

Yet Seal witnessed Narendra's struggle with a perceived duality of flesh and spirit and noted that a belief in the efficacy of "Pure Reason and the ineffable peace that comes of identifying the self with the Reason in the Universe" did not satisfy him.[67] The rest of Seal's account falls prey to the most common problem of secondary later documentation—reading back into the earlier period what becomes known later.[68] (A later assessment of this period by Svāmī Vivekānanda may best be presented in the following chapters, because its content has been given the values of a later period of belief.[69])

The Paths Converge

The existential crisis involved Narendra personally in the ancient conundrum—why the righteous suffer. His later explanation of why he left the Brāhmo Samāj can be deduced from his later criticisms. He stated that they believed "the world is full of happiness!" and he had learned this was untrue.[70] The Brāhmo belief in a just God rewarding the righteous failed him. The intellectual crisis had confronted him with the problem of verification. Again, his later criticisms of the Brāhmo Samāj confirms this conclusion, when he said: "The test of truth, for this Brāhmo Samāj is 'what our masters approve;' with us, what the Indian reasoning and experience approves."[71] Narendra questioned the validity of "the words of scripture" because of their contradictions and their lack of historicity.[72] He particularly focused his attack on the Rādhā-Kṛṣṇa episodes, which he considered "immoral and objectionable."[73] Further, he doubted the existence of God,[74] questioning those who professed belief in God as to whether or not they had seen him.[75] He even asked Debendra Nath Tāgore: "Sir, have you seen God?"[76] Only Rāmakṛṣṇa answered that he had seen God.

When Narendra turned to Rāmakṛṣṇa, he was instructed to turn to Kālī, the Divine Mother of the Universe. This episode merits careful reconstruction, because it initially deepened his scepticism. By separating contemporaneous accounts, even though incomplete, from later elaborations, two turnings to Kālī are found, the first in March 1885, and the second in June, 1885.[77] This is lost in Svāmī

Vivekānanda's later assessment, because he has not chosen to mention his initial loss of faith in Kālī and his return to scepticism.

In March, 1885, Narendra asked Rāmakṛṣṇa to pray to Kālī for him ("... the Master prayed to the Divine Mother to give me money").[78] Then he tried to meditate on Kālī, as Rāmakṛṣṇa suggested. When Rāmakṛṣṇa asked how he was (on March 11, 1885), Narendra replied: "Why, I have meditated on Kālī for three or four days, but nothing has come of it."[79] Narendra's intense scepticism would last until June, 1885.[80]

Chapter III

HIS PATTERN OF ULTIMATE CONCERN AS ŚRĪ RĀMAKṚṢṆA'S DISCIPLE 1885—1889

In a traditional framework **saṁnyāsa** would signify the attainment of a realization of the Absolute with consequent total renunciation of the phenomenal world. **Saṁnyāsa** is formalized by initiation from a **guru**, a **saṁnyāsin** whose initiation is believed to go back in an unbroken chain to the Vedic **ṛṣis.**[1]

Narendranath Datta's initiation differed from this traditional model. While Rāmakṛṣṇa had been initiated by the **advaita saṁnyāsin** Totapuri, he dressed as a **pūjāri** in white instead of as a **saṁnyāsin** in **geruā** (the ochre robe). Even though he seemed pleased that some of his young followers were wearing the **geruā** occasionally just prior to his death, he neither gave them a **mantra** nor a monastic name. More important Rāmakṛṣṇa refused to initiate Narendra and told him to wait and make the final renunciation of "woman and gold" after his impending death (August, 1886).[2]

The significance of not having received initiation from his **guru** may be seen as one of a complex of stresses which would cause this pattern of ultimate concern to be reordered after about four years. Narendra and his **gurubhāis** took **saṁnyāsa** on December 24, 1886, four months after Rāmakṛṣṇa's death.[3] If a traditional initiation had occurred, it would be logical to begin this period with this date. However, since this was not the case, Narendra's submission to Rāmakṛṣṇa as his **guru** would appear more important. That would place the **terminus a quo** about June, 1885; but this period of belief will be taken to include the process of instruction from Śrī Rāmakṛṣṇa, which had a slow, cumulative effect. The **terminus ad quom** of "Rāmakṛṣṇa's disciple" cannot be rigidly set, since the beginnings of doubt in this truth system occur as early as April, 1887.[4] But by August, 1889, a new period of ultimate concern had begun.

Contemporaneous documentation provides a wealth of data for this period of Narendra's conceptualization of ultimacy. This data will be organized to show which questions were carried over from Narendra's religious past and Rāmakṛṣṇa's answers to them, which teachings were internalized and the struggle involved, and which elements precipitated the quest for more adequate beliefs.

The Questions And The Answers

The problem of why the righteous suffer was brought to Rāmakṛṣṇa. Rāmakṛṣṇa's initial answer was recorded as follows:

> MASTER (to Trailokya and the other devotees): "The joys and sorrows of the body are inevitable. Look at Narendra. His father is dead, and his people have been put to extreme suffering. He can't find any way out of it. God places one sometimes in happiness and sometimes in misery."
>
> TRAILOKYA: "Revered sir, God will be gracious to Narendra."
>
> MASTER (with a smile): "But when? It is true that no one starves at the temple of Annapurna in Benares; but some must wait for food till evening."[6]

That his sufferings were God's doing and that he must wait patiently were answers which Narendra did not find immediately helpful. It would be a year before he would meditate on such a God.[7] Rāmakṛṣṇa was teaching about a God who was the sole doer,[8] whose acts were divine **līlā** (creating, sustaining and destroying),[9] and to whose will one must surrender.[10] Rāmakṛṣṇa taught that both God's absolute nature (**nitya**) and his relative aspect (**līlā**) must be accepted.[11] While it was true that the relative was illusory, it was also true that it was real "as long as God keeps the 'ego of a devotee' in man."[12] Narendra's belief in a God of love and of justice did not include the powerful and destructive side of God's nature, **Śakti.** It was the grace of **Śakti,** which was not different from **Brahman,**[13] that Rāmakṛṣṇa offered to Narendra to deliver him from his suffering. Besides his teachings, especially with stories, he sought to get Narendra to realize this aspect of God by two methods—meditation and **Śākta kīrtaṇas** (devotional songs to Kālī or Durgā).[14]

A second question was how can one know the truth—the problem of verification. Rāmakṛṣṇa countered by redirecting Narendra's question to the true question, for Rāmakṛṣṇa that being the realization of God. Narendra's earlier abhorrence of Kālī, a deity with form, and his period of "forced atheism"[15] made his **guru's** task difficult. Narendra expected to solve the question of verification with scripture or with reasoning. However, Rāmakṛṣṇa taught that both were but preliminary steps to real knowledge of Truth. Concerning scripture, he taught: "Too much study of the scriptures does more harm that good. The important thing is to know the essence of the scriptures. After that, what is the need of books? One should learn the essence and then dive deep in order to realize God."[16] The scriptures were not Truth; their relative value comprised of pointing men to the realization of God.[17] He stated:

> One should hear the scriptures during the early stages of spiritual discipline. After attaining God there is no lack of knowledge. Then the Divine Mother supplies it without fail.[18]

Nor could the test of truth be found in reason: He taught: "It is not good to reason too much. First comes God, and then the world. Realize God first; then you will know all about His world."[19] After Narendra's initial failure in meditation upon Kālī in March, 1884, Rāmakṛṣṇa instructed him how realization by the grace of God (**bhakti**) was higher than **jñāna** (knowledge) or **dhyāna** (meditation):

> I have observed that a man acquires one kind of knowledge about God through reasoning and another kind through meditation; but he acquires a third kind of Knowledge about God when God reveals Himself to him, His devotee. If God Himself reveals to His devotee the nature of Divine Incarnation—how He plays in human form—, then the devotee doesn't have to reason about the problem or need an explanation. . . .Likewise, if God gives us this flash of divine light, all our doubts are destroyed. Can one ever know God by mere reasoning?[20]

Since the scriptures were only preliminary for Rāmakṛṣṇa, the apparent problem of contradiction among the various religious texts would not lead to scepticism or agnosticism. Rāmakṛṣṇa taught:

> There are two interpretations of the scriptures: the literal and the real. One should accept the real meaning alone—what agrees with the words of God. There is a vast difference between the words written in a letter and the direct words of its writer. The scriptures are like the words of the letter; the words of God are direct words. I do not accept anything unless it agrees with the direct words of the Divine Mother.[21]

Rāmakṛṣṇa had turned Narendra's question about verification of truth to the source of truth which can be realized.[22] This realization comes from God the Doer, **Śakti,** and her grace.[23] In difficult times God's revelation becomes manifest as an **avatāra,** such as Rāma, Kṛṣṇa, Buddha, Christ, Chaitanya, and himself—Rāmakṛṣṇa. The highest realization of God would be **nirvikalpa samādhi** in which all consciousness of mind and body is lost into the One. Only an Incarnation of God can retain knowledge of the ego and return to the phenomenal world after such complete realization of God, and that for the good of mankind.[24]

Narendra also asked about the acceptance of duties in the world or the total renunciation of the world. Among the models of behavior were two which taught that duty was a positive requirement for all men. A traditional interpretation of **aśramadharma** (rules for the stages of life) stressed responsibilities for each of the four stages of life. According to this model sanctioned by the **Manuṣaśāstra** and presupposed in the **Purāṇas,** Narendra should next assume the duties of the householder, beginning with marriage. The other model was that of the Brāhmo Samāj which taught the positive value of service in the world. This question was treated by Rāmakṛṣṇa as a corollary to the question, how God can be realized. Rāmakṛṣṇa distinguished between those who had already touched **kāminikānchan** (Bengali: "woman and gold") and those who had not. To the former he would teach mental renunciation of the fruit of one's labors. Building upon Narendra's desire to be like his grandfather who had become a **saṁnyāsin** after he had been a householder, Rāmakṛṣṇa stressed the better path of total renunciation—never touching **kāminikānchan.**[25] He first taught Narendra who he was to be. This was done by positive affirmations of Narendra's qualities before him and others. He told Narendra that he was "ever-free,"[26] never to be bound by lust for woman or greed for gold. Further, Narendra was "ever-perfect."[27] Rāmakṛṣṇa interpreted his disregard of **varṇadharma** (caste law), even to the eating of meat,[28] as **nityasiddha** (eternally perfect). Rāmakṛṣṇa's descriptions of Narendra included "**Nārāyaṇa**" (a **Vaiṣṇava** term for God Incarnate), "**Ātman**" (**Vedānta** term denoting a vision of the Pure Soul), "**ākāśa**" (**Vedānta** term for subtlest form of matter into which all the elements are ultimately resolved), "manly," "virtuous beyond compare," "independent," "beloved" and "my intimate disciple."[29] Besides praising him with words, Rāmakṛṣṇa used mythological role-playing to demonstrate his conclusions about Narendra. He would caress Narendra's face or chest or would feed him as if "he was feeding Nārāyana Himself."[30] This at first embarrassed Narendra who would leave the room after one of these scenes.[31] Thus, Rāmakṛṣṇa's teaching converged into the twofold call for renunciation and realization:

> The essence of the **Gītā** is what you get by repeating the word ten times. The word becomes reversed. It is then **tāgi,** which refers to renunciation. The essence of the **Gītā** is: "O man, renounce everything and practice spiritual discipline for the realization of God!"[32]

Another question Narendra brought to Rāmakṛṣṇa was which religion was true. With whom would he serve God, if he could come to believe in God? Rāmakṛṣṇa taught that all paths (**yogas**), all disciplines (**sādhanās**), all sects (Tantric, Vaiṣṇava, Śaiva, et cetera), and all religions (Christian, Buddhist, Islamic, Hindu, et cetera), led to the realization of God. Having reached the highest realization of God from all these himself, he would teach the unity of all religions in their goal: the realization of God.[33] The formless **Brahman** and the Gods of form are all true, since they are different ways of referring to the same unity.[34] Thus **Brahman** and **Śakti** are one; **advaita** and **bhakti** are one. However, in the **Kaliyuga** (present world-cycle) **bhakti** is the best way.[35]

Narendra acquired another question only after he began going to Śrī Rāmakṛṣṇa. This involved the meaning of a variety of experiences which seemed to point beyond phenomenal explanations to something else. The experiences included mystical trances, occult powers, and other phenomena which were not satisfactorily explained for him according to his rationalistic **Weltanschauung** prior to **saṁnyāsa.** How was Narendra to understand the trance induced at Rāmakṛṣṇa's touch,[36] a vision on a Calcutta street,[37] a power to give an electric shock to a brother disciple,[38] an experience in which almost all his body vanished,[39] an electrical shock entering his body three or four days before Rāmakṛṣṇa's death,[40] or a vision of the Master in the Cossipore garden after his death?[41] Rāmakṛṣṇa's explanation for each of the experiences, except of course the last, was adopted by Narendra in his first pattern of belief as a **saṁnyāsin**—although they would be slightly modified later. On three occasions Rāmakṛṣṇa gave his explanation on the trance:

> At my first meeting with Narendra I found him completely indifferent to his body. When I touched his chest with my hand, he lost consciousness of the outer world. Regaining consciousness, Narendra said: "Oh, what have you done to me? I have my father and mother at home!"[42] (June 4, 1883)
>
> When I touched Narendra on the chest, he became unconscious; then he cried out: "Oh, what have you ḍone to me? don't you know that I have a father and mother?[43] (March 7, 1885)
>
> During one of Narendra's early visits I touched his chest and he became unconscious. Regaining consciousness, he wept and said: "Oh, why did you do that to me? I have a father! I have a mother!" This "I" and "mind" spring from ignorance.[44] (May 9, 1885)

There is no contemporaneous account of Narendra's valuing of this event, but a later account emphasized the monistic elements which were held at that period.[45] No contemporaneous account by either Rāmakṛṣṇa or Narendra has been found of the Calcutta street experience, but again the later account provides accurate information about a later valuation of the experience but provides data of low probability about the period in question.[46] The experience of giving an electrical shock to a brother disciple and the transmission of power from Rāmakṛṣṇa to Narendra may have been the same experience as valued differently in different belief systems or two separate experiences. The earlier account seemed to refer to a single experience, when Narendra stated:

> At Cossipore he transmitted his power to me.
>
> M (Mahendranath Gupta): Didn't it happen when you used to meditate before a lighted fire under a tree at the Cossipore garden house?
>
> NARENDRA: Yes, One day, while meditating, I asked (the fellow disciple) to hold my hand. Kali said to me, "When I touched your body I felt something like an electric shock coming to my body." But you must not tell this to anybody here. Give me your promise.
>
> M: There is a special purpose in his transmission of power to you. He will accomplish much work through you. One day the Master wrote on a piece of paper, "Naren will teach people."

> NARENDRA: But I said to him, "I won't do any such thing." Thereupon he said, "Your very bones will do it."[47]

Later documents by fellow disciples separated the two experiences, placing one in March, 1886 (on the night of the **Śivarātri**), and the other in August, 1886.[48] Narendra's other account, as Svāmī Vivekānanda in 1901, mentioned only the transmission of power from Rāmakṛṣṇa:

> Two or three days before Shri Ramakrishna's passing away, She whom he used to call "Kālī" entered this body. It is She who takes me here and there and makes me work, without letting me remain quiet or allowing me to look to my personal comforts.
>
> DISCIPLE: Are you speaking metaphorically?
>
> SWAMIJI: Oh, no; two or three days before his leaving the body, he called me to his side one day, and asking me to sit before him, looked steadfastly at me and fell into Samādhi. Then I really felt that a subtle force like an electric shock was entering my body! In a little while, I also lost outward consciousness and sat motionless. How long I stayed in that condition I do not remember; when consciousness returned I found Shri Ramakrishna shedding tears. On questioning him, he answered me affectionately, "Today, giving you my all, I have become a beggar. With this power you are to do many works for the world's good before you will return." I feel that that power is constantly directing me to this or that work. This body has not been made for remaining idle.[49]

The experience in which almost all of his body seemed to vanish was interpreted to him by Rāmakṛṣṇa as a realization of the Self. Such knowledge would normally cause a melting away of the body for all but an **avatāra,** but Rāmakṛṣṇa taught him that he had used his powers to prevent this. Narendra told what he had been taught a year later in 1887:

> M. Once you came to know about your true Self in nirvikalpa samadhi at the Cossipore garden house. Isn't that true?
>
> NARENDRA: Yes. In that experience I felt that I had no body. I could see only my face. The Master was in the upstairs room. I had that experience downstairs. I was weeping. I said, "What has happened to me?" The elder Gopal went to the Master's room and said, "Narendra is crying."
>
> When I saw the Master he said to me: "Now you have known. But I am going to keep the key with me."
>
> I said to him, "What is it that happened to me?"
>
> Turning to the devotees, he said: "He will not keep his body if he knows who he is. But I have put a veil over his eyes."[50]

Again there is a later version which emphasizes values of the later pattern of ultimacy.[51]

Rāmakṛṣṇa's answers were internalized in a new pattern of ultimate concern symbolized by the taking of **saṁnyāsa** on December 24, 1886.

Narendra's Internalization of Rāmakṛṣṇa's Teachings

The dynamic character of Narendra's quest for truth and meaningfulness could easily be obscured. The fact that Narendra left the circle of disciples and went in search of other **gurus** in 1889 to bring solace to his doubts would dictate that those elements of Rāmakṛṣṇa's teachings which were the most difficult to be assimilated be studied carefully. All extant contemporaneous documentation will be used to indicate what Narendra believed during this period (1883-1889).

The Acceptance of Kālī

Rāmakṛṣṇa taught that the formless **Brahman** and the God of form, **Śakti**, whose manifestation as Kālī was worshipped at Dakshineswar, were one. Rāmakṛṣṇa's initial attempt to get Narendra to accept this by worshipping Kālī as the Absolute ended in failure in March, 1885.[52] But in June 1885, Narendra had a religious experience in which he accepted the grace of the Divine Mother. There are three accounts of the experience—one is a secondary contemporaneous document, the other two are primary later accounts.

Vaikuntha Nath Sanyal visited Dakshineswar the morning after the event. He related that Narendra had come to Rāmakṛṣṇa "in straitened circumstances."[53] Rāmakṛṣṇa informed Sanyal:

> "So I advised him (Narendra) to pray to Mother for riches, but he couldn't. He said he was put to shame. Returning from the temple he asked me to teach him a song to the Mother, which I did. The whole of the last night he sang that song. So he is sleeping now." Then with an unfeigned delight he said, "Isn't it wonderful that Narendra has accepted Mother?"[54]

The only complete later version by the then Svāmī Vivekānanda, although quite long, will be quoted in full because of the number of details which vary from the Sanyal account.

> One day the idea struck me that God listened to Shri Ramakrishna's prayers; so why should I not **ask him to pray for me** for the removal of my pecuniary wants—a favour the Master would never deny me? I hurried to Dakshineswar and insisted on his making the appeal on behalf of my starving family. He said, "My boy, I can't make such demands. But why don't you go and ask the Mother yourself? **All your sufferings are due to your disregard of Her.**" I said, "I do not know the Mother, you please speak to Her on my behalf. You must." He replied tenderly, "My dear boy, I have done so again and again. **But you do not accept Her, so She does not grant my prayer.** All right, it is Tuesday— go to the Kali temple tonight, prostrate yourself before the Mother and ask Her any boon you like. It shall be granted. She is Knowledge Absolute, the Inscrutable Power of

Brahman, and by Her mere will has given birth to this world. Everything is in Her power to give.'' I believed every word and eagerly waited for the night. About 9 o'clock the Master commanded me to go to the temple. As I went, I was filled with a divine intoxication. My feet were unsteady. My heart was leaping in anticipation of the joy of beholding the living Goddess and hearing Her words. I was full of the idea. Reaching the temple, **as I cast my eyes upon the image, I actually found that the Divine Mother was living and conscious,** the Perennial Fountain of Divine Love and Beauty. I was caught in a surging wave of devotion and love. In an ecstasy of joy I prostrated myself again and again before the Mother and prayed, ''Mother, give me discrimination! Give me renunciation! Give me knowledge and devotion! Grant that I may have an uninterrupted vision of Thee!'' A serene peace reigned in my soul. The world was forgotten. Only the Divine Mother shone within my heart.

As soon as I returned, the Master asked if I had prayed to the Mother for the removal of my worldly wants. I was startled at this question and said, ''No, sir, I forgot all about it. But is there any remedy now?'' ''Go again,'' said he, ''and tell her about your wants.'' I again set out for the temple, but at the sight of the Mother again forgot my mission, bowed to Her repeatedly and prayed only for love and devotion. The Master asked me if I had done it the second time. I told him what had happened. He said, ''How thoughtless! Couldn't you restrain yourself enough to say those few words? Well, try once more and make that prayer to Her. Quick!'' I went for the third time, but on entering the temple a terrible shame overpowered me. I thought, ''What a trifle I have come to pray to the Mother about! It is like asking a gracious king for a few vegetables! What a fool I am!'' In shame and remorse I bowed to Her respectfully and said, ''Mother, I want nothing but knowledge and devotion.'' Coming out of the temple I understood that **all this was due to the Master's will.** Otherwise how could I fail in my object no less than thrice? I came to him and said, ''Sir, it is you who have cast a charm over my mind and made me forgetful. Now please grant me the boon that my people at home may no longer suffer the pinch of poverty.'' He said, **''Such a prayer never comes from my lips.** I asked you to pray for yourself. But you couldn't do it. It appears that you are not destined to enjoy worldly happiness. Well, I can't help it.'' But I wouldn't let him go. I insisted on his granting that prayer. At last he said, ''All right, your people at home will never be in want of plain food and clothing.''[55]

Another later account by Svāmī Vivekānanda in 1898 to Sister Nivedita indicated some of the difficulty of belief in Kālī:

"How I used to hate Kālī!" he said, "And all Her ways! That was the ground of my six years' fight,—that I would not accept Her. But I had to accept Her at last! Ramakrishna Paramahamsa dedicated me to Her, and now I believe that She guides me in every little thing I do, and does with me what She will. . .Yet I fought so long! I love him, you see, and that was what held me. I saw his marvelous purity. . .I felt his wonderful love. . .His greatness had not dawned on me then. All that came afterwards, when I had given in. At that time I thought him a brain-sick baby, always seeing visions and the rest. I hated it. And then I too had to accept Her!"

"No, **the thing that made me do it is a secret that will die with me.** I had great misfortunes at that time. . .It was an opportunity. . .She made a slave of me. Those were the very words—'a slave of you.' And Ramakrishna Paramahamsa made me over to Her."[56]

From the data it becomes evident that Narendra accepted Kālī in his belief system in June, 1885. There are frequent references to Rāmakṛṣṇa's joy over this in the months that follow.[57] Several references to the worship of Kālī were made by Narendra in his letters to Pramadadas Mitra during 1888 and 1889, the latter part of this period of belief,[58] but the primary period of her worship was the last year of Rāmakṛṣṇa's life; after that the worship of Śiva and even Rāmakṛṣṇa would share the devotion given by the young **saṁnyāsis.**[59] A **kīrtaṇa** sung by Narendra in July, 1885, might best summarize his belief in the Divine Mother:

Mother, thou art our sole Redeemer,
Thou the Support of the three gunas,
Higher than the most high.
Thou art compassionate, I know,
Who takest away our bitter grief.

Sandhya art Thou, and Gayatri;
Thou dost sustain this universe.
Mother, the Help art Thou
Of those that have no help but thee,
O Eternal Beloved of Siva!

Thou art in earth, in water Thou;
Thou liest at the root of all.
In me, in every creature,
Thou hast Thy home; though clothed with form,
Yet art Thou formless Reality.[60]

As late as March 11, 1885, Narendra had rejected the notion of Divine Incarnation from the position of a belief in the formless God. He had said: "God is infinite. How can infinity have parts?"[61] When pressed by Rāmakṛṣṇa's disciples, he went on to deny that God incarnates himself in human form, thus denying one of Rāmakṛṣṇa's basic teachings about himself.[62] As the argument progressed and it appeared that Narendra was defeating the **avatāra** proponents, Rāmakṛṣṇa stopped the discussion, stating that he did not enjoy it any longer.[63]

On May 9, 1885 Narendra asked: "How can I believe, without proof, that God incarnated Himself as a man?"[64] When others attempted to give proof from scripture, he pointed up the inconsistences of the scriptures. Finally he concluded: "It is enough to have faith in God. I don't care about what He is doing or what He hangs from. Infinite is the universe; infinite are the Incarnations."[65] This concession was immediately picked up by Rāmakṛṣṇa and cherished.

By October 27, 1885, after Narendra's acceptance of Kālī and during the onset of Rāmakṛṣṇa's final illness, Narendra had begun to move toward a belief in Rāmakṛṣṇa as an **avatāra.** He stated to the sceptical physician in attendance, Dr. Mahendra Lal Sarkar:

> We think of him as a person who is like God. Do you know, sir, what it is like? There is a point between the vegetable creation and the animal creation where it is very difficult to determine whether a particular thing is a vegetable or an animal. Likewise, there is a stage between the man-world and the God-world where it is extremely hard to say whether a person is a man or God.[66]

When pressed by the doctor, he reiterated that Rāmakṛṣṇa was "a god-like man."[67] Then he concluded: "We offer worship to him bordering on divine worship."[68] At this stage of his development of belief Narendra led those who followed Rāmakṛṣṇa as a great teacher, differing with those who already worshipped him as God Incarnate.[69]

In the closing months of Rāmakṛṣṇa's life, after Narendra had purposed to renounce the world in January, 1886,[70] Narendra was drawn to the **avatāra** doctrine to a greater degree. Then on March 15, 1886, he said to Rāmakṛṣṇa: "Your will and God's will have become one."[71] Then Rāmakṛṣṇa answered : "I see that all things—everything that exists—have come from this."[72] Asking Narendra with a sign what he understood, Narendra answered: "All created objects have come from you."[73] This confession at Cossipore identified Rāmakṛṣṇa as the **avatāra** of Śakti.

In August, 1886, Rāmakṛṣṇa's final self-revelation was made to Narendra on his deathbed. It is recalled in a later account derived from the community of devotees, but most likely reflects his beliefs at this time. The narrative reconstructs this last question:[74]

> He has said many times that he is an Incarnation of **God**. If I can make him say now as he is in the throes of death, in the midst of human anguish and physical pain, "I am God incarnate," then I will believe him!

The moment this thought came to Narendra's mind, it was stated that Rāmakṛṣṇa declared: "O my Naren, are you not yet convinced? He who was Rama and Krishna is now Ramakrishna in this body—but not from the standpoint of your Vedanta."[75]

It does not come as a surprise that Narendra and the **gurubhāis** worshipped Rāmakṛṣṇa after his **mahāsamādhi** as Deity.[76]

The Realization of God

Narendra accepted Rāmakṛṣṇa's teaching that the realization of God was the goal of life. Because he had experienced this in its highest form, Rāmakṛṣṇa was able to teach the ultimate unity of all beliefs and religions in the one goal—God.

While Narendra held this belief as central during this period, he differed from Rāmakṛṣṇa in one essential aspect: he had not experienced or attained that realization of God. Narendra openly confessed that he had not realized God in April, 1887, which included all the earlier trances and visions (one of which is later revalued as the highest realization of the Absolute, **nirvikalpa samādhi**).[77] He lamented: "We don't yet feel like giving up the body because we haven't realized God."[78] Again on May 7, 1887, he stated: "I shall fast to death for the realization of God." Then he continued:

> It seems there is no God. I pray so much, but there is no reply—none whatsoever. How many visions I have seen! How many mantras shining in letters of gold! How many visions of the Goddess Kālī! How many other divine forms! But still I have no peace.[79]

(This may mark the turning point in his approach to God-realization. Up to this time Narendra has been leading the other disciples with the use of severe **sādhanās** [spiritual disciplines], but from this time the study of scriptures, particularly **Advaita Vedānta,** becomes more evident.[80]

Renunciation of the World

For Rāmakṛṣṇa renunciation of the world was the necessary preparation to realization of God. No one could be bound to lust and greed—his **Kāminikānchan** doctrine—and realize God. That was the reason for the different **sādhanās** and **yogas.** Through them a person would give up the results of action, at least mentally. By having no desire for whatever followed from an act, which in itself was dedicated to God, no new **karma** would result—neither from desire for pleasure or gain nor from any other residual attachment to any aspect of the phenomenal world.[81] This renunciation acquired a special significance when one came to realize that all action was of God anyway.[82] God is the sole Doer and man must surrender to his will, dedicating whatever action to God and eradicating any attachment to its results. Even most of the effects of actions committed in past lives, **prārabdha karma**, could be "cancelled by the power of God's name."[83] The grace of God was waiting for those who turned to God in faith.

As has been shown, Rāmakṛṣṇa taught levels or stages of renunciation. He allowed for the fact that many would not be ready for total renunciation in their present life and would require of them only mental renunciation, allowing them to marry and to seek riches while practicing mental renunciation of them.

Narendra seemed to have accepted renunciation into his belief system but approached it more rigidly. In a conversation with Mahendranath Gupta on May 9, 1887, he said: "You may speak of leading a detached life in the world, and all that, but you will not attain anything unless you renounce 'woman and gold.' Don't you feel disgusted with your wife's body?"[84] Then he quoted some scripture which said: "Fools enjoy the contact of the body, filled with filth, peopled with worms, foul of smell by nature, made of flesh, blood, bone, and marrow; but the wise shun it." He continued: "Vain is the life of a person who does not take delight in the teachings of Vedānta and drink the Nectar of Divine Bliss."[85] So intense was his own quest through total renunciation at this time that Narendra offered no hope to the householder who remained in contact with **kāminikānchan**; it is not surprising that, when Mahendranath returned home from his visit at the Baranagore Math after a four day retreat, he did not return. The record of Rāmakṛṣṇa and his disciples, **The Gospel of Sri Ramakrishna**, ended with the entry on May 10, 1887.

The Scriptures

Although he was almost illiterate, Rāmakṛṣṇa used the scriptures in various ways. Most of his stories and illustrations came from the **Purāṇas.** But for him the essence of all scripture was the **Gītā.** The essence of the **Gītā** was renunciation of lust and greed, the primary barriors to spirituality, and realization of God. There could hardly be a problem of doubt in scripture, for scripture was only secondary while the direct experience of God was primary. During the training of his disciples Rāmakṛṣṇa had various texts read and often gave summaries of their meaning.

Rāmakṛṣṇa attempted to teach this belief to Narendra. On one occasion several months before he accepted Kālī, this pursuit of the experiential rather than the intellectual was brought out:

NARENDRA: How am I to believe in the words of scripture? The **Mahānirvāna Tantra** says, in one place, that unless a man attains the Knowledge of Brahman he goes to hell; and the same book says, in another place, that there is no salvation without the worship of Pārvati, the Divine Mother. Manu writes about himself in the **Manusamhita;** Moses describes his own death in the Pentateuch.

The Sāmkhya philosophy says that God does not exist, because there is no proof of His existence. Again, the same philosophy says that one must accept the Vedas and that they are eternal.

But I don't say that these are not true. I simply don't understand them. Please explain them to me. People have explained the scriptures according to their fancy. Which explanation shall we accept? White light coming through a red medium appears red, through a green medium, green.

A DEVOTEE: The **Gītā** contains the words of God.

MASTER: Yes, the **Gītā** is the essence of all scriptures. A sannyāsi may or may not keep with him another book, but he always carries a pocket **Gītā.**

A DEVOTEE: The **Gītā** contains the words of Krishna.

NARENDRA: Yes, Krishna or any fellow for that matter!

Sri Ramakrishna was amazed at these words of Narendra. [The editoral notation of Mahendranath Gupta.]

MASTER: This is a fine discussion. There are two interpretations of scriptures: the literal and the real. One should accept the real meaning alone— what agrees with the words of God. There is a vast difference between the words written in a letter and the direct words of its writer. The scriptures are like the words of the letter; the words of God are direct words. I do not accept anything unless it agrees with the direct words of the Divine Mother.[86]

After his acceptance of Kālī and during the lifetime of Rāmakṛṣṇa the method of the **bhakta**—experiential relationship to a living presence—took precedence over that of the **jñāna**—the intellectual search for knowledge and truth. After Rāmakṛṣṇa's death this attitude toward scripture was maintained by Narendra for about a year. Then he gradually began placing more importance on the study of scripture and less on **pūjā** and on the severe **sādhanās** which had characterized his quest for God-realization. After available texts were read, such as the **Gītā** and the **Yogavāśishṭa,**[87] Narendra wrote to Pramadadas Mitra for more in November, 1888. Upon their receipt Narendra expressed his appreciation:

> By sending your gift of the "Vedanta," you have laid under life-long obligation not only myself but the whole group of Shri Ramakrishna's Sannyasins. They all bow down to you in respect. It is not for my own sake alone that I asked of you the copy of Pāṇini's grammar; a good deal of study, in fact, is given to San-

skrit scriptures in this Math. The Vedas may well be said to have fallen out of vogue in Bengal. Many here in this Math are conversant with Sanskrit, and they have a mind to master the Samhitā portions of the Vedas. They are of opinion that what has to be done must be done to a finish. . . . This Math is not wanting in men of perseverance, talent, and penetrative intellect. I may hope that by the grace of our Master, they will acquire in a short time Pānini's system and then succeed in restoring the Vedas to Bengal.[88]

Without a realization of God, without the direct words of Kālī, and without a living **guru**—Narendra tried to lead in the study of scriptures which his **guru** had taught could be harmonized. By July, 1889, Narendra wrote to Pramadadas Mitra: "I have not lost faith in a benign Providence—nor am I going ever to lose it—my faith in the scriptures is unshaken."[89] However, the letter denied what would become a crisis only one month later.[90] (It is because of this shaken belief in the scriptures and of a search for a living **guru** that another period of belief is suggested.)

Advaita Vedānta

Rāmakṛṣṇa taught that **Advaita Vedānta** was the one **darśaṇa** (view) which must not be taught to householders.[91] He believed that its thought and its "aim to attain Nirvāna" was "beyond the reach of the ordinary man."[92] He reiterated this position shortly before his death.[93] He believed that only those who had completely renounced the world could be taught this philosophy. Thus he introduced Narendra to **Advaita Vedānta,** which he considered a step—among others—by which one might attain the realization of God. Rāmakṛṣṇa taught:

> First of all you must discriminate, following the method of "Neti, neti:" "He is not the five elements, nor the sense-organs, nor the mind, nor the intelligence, nor the ego. He is beyond all these cosmic principles." You want to climb to the roof; then you must eliminate and leave behind all the steps, one by one. The steps are by no means the roof. But after reaching the roof you find that the steps are made of the same materials—brick, lime, and brick-dust—as the roof.... It is the Supreme Brahman that has become the universe and its living beings and the twenty-four cosmic principles. That which is Ātman has become the five elements.[94]

He later added: "But the essence of Vedānta is: 'Brahman alone is real, and the world illusory; I have no separate existence; I am Brahman alone.' "[95] However he made it clear that this philosophy must not be taught to everyone:

> But for those who lead a householder's life, and those who identify themselves with the body, this attitude of "I am He" is

> not good. It is not good for householders to read Vedānta or the **Yogavāśishtha**. It is very harmful for them to read these books. Householders should look on God as their Master and on themselves as His servants. They should think, "O God, You are the master and Lord, and I am your servant." People who identify themselves with the body should not have the attitude of "I am He."[96]

While **advaita** may have contributed to the undermining of Narendra's theistic beliefs of the Brāhmo Samāji period, Rāmakṛṣṇa tried in numerous ways to make him a **bhakta** (devotionalist). Besides having him do **Kālī pūjā** he told Narendra a few months before his death: "Your face and hands show that you are a bhakta. But the jnāni has different features; they are dry."[97]

Even before Rāmakṛṣṇa's death Narendra had begun to study **advaita** thought more seriously. By January, 1886, he had read Śaṁkara's **Vivekachudāmani**.[98] In April Narendra was meditating on the "Six Stanzas on **Nirvāna**" by Śaṁkara.[99] After his **guru's** death Narendra and the other **saṁnyāsis** at Barānagore used a number of **advaita** chants and hymns.[100]

Narendra's enthusiasm for **Advaita Vedānta** manifested itself in an unusual way: he taught the philosophy forbidden to householders by Rāmakṛṣṇa to Mahendranath Gupta and other householder devotees.[101]

Narendra's Renewed Doubts

Rāmakṛṣṇa had left Narendra with two instructions for the future: (1) "Naren, take care of the boys." (2) "Naren will teach others." Narendra believed that something of a monastic life had been forseen so that the "boys" could be kept together. But even with all the many teachings of Rāmakṛṣṇa about God-realization and renunciation of "Woman and gold," little had been said about the practical problems of the next steps. It was over four months before they took **saṁnyāsa.** While no contemporaneous account of the event was made, the official version—even while maintaining its orthodoxy—reveals its unusual nature:

> When a break was made Naren began to tell the story of the Lord Jesus, beginning with the wondrous mystery of his birth through his death on to the resurrection. Through the eloquence of Narendra, the boys were admitted into the apostolic world wherein Paul had preached the gospel of the Arisen Christ and spread Christianity far and wide. Naren made his plea to them to become Christ themselves, to aid in the redemption of the world; to realize God and to deny themselves as the Lord Jesus had done. Standing there before the Dhuni, with the flames lighting up their countenances and with the crackling of the wood the sole

disturbance of their thought, they took the vows of Sannyāsa before God and one another. The very air seemed to vibrate with their ecstatic fervour. Strangely, the monks discovered afterwards that it was Christmas Eve! Before returning to Baranagore they went on pilgrimage to the famous temple of Tārakeswar Shiva to worship the Lord of Monks.[102]

Certain aspects of Narendra's past were being brought toward a synthesis: Keshab Chandra Sen's love of Christ and the imitation of him in his self denial, the total renunciation of the **saṁnyāsin,** the realization of God, and many others. The catholicity of this longed-for synthesis embraced "the teachings of Sri Ramakrishna, Śankarāchārya, Rāmānuja, and Jesus Christ, and of Hindu philosophy, European philosophy, the Vedas, the Purānas, and the Tantras."[103] Among their resources were included **The Imitation of Christ,** to which Narendra wrote a preface and eventually translated six chapters into Bengali, and two books by Girish Ghosh, **Life of Buddha** and **Life of Chaitanya.**[104]

However the synthesis did not occur; it was not as easy for Narendra as it had been for Rāmakṛṣṇa Paramahaṁsa to homologize these diverse perspectives and teachings. Not only did Narendra continue to go through deep periods of doubt in which he denied the very existence of God,[105] but he also underwent frequent change in the way he put these things together. After one such occurrence the following exchange took place.

PRASANNA: Sometimes you say that God does not exist, and now you are saying all these things! You are not consistent. You keep changing your opinions.

All laughed.

NARENDRA: All right! I shall never change what I have just said. As long as one has desires and cravings, so long one doubts the existence of God. A man cherishes some desire or other. Perhaps he has the desire to study or pass the university examination or become a scholar, and so forth and so on.[106]

Not only was it difficult for him to know what to teach, but there remained some question as to why he should teach. Rāmakṛṣṇa had forbidden them to form a sect and he had told them that "those who go about making disciples belong to a very inferior level. So also do those who want occult powers to walk over the Ganges and to report what a person says in a far-off country and so on."[107] All that Rāmakṛṣṇa had taught converged into two principles: the realization of God and the renunciation of the world. He had even consigned doing good to others to the action of the two lesser natures, **rajas** and **tamas.**[108] While he did teach service to all beings, these disciples had been told that **bhakti,** and not **karmayoga,** was the path of this age, the **Kaliyuga.**[109]

No longer able to teach what he had not realized, Narendra left the Baranagore Math in search of a new **guru** for himself.

Chapter IV

THE SEARCH FOR THE TRUE AUTHORITY

1889-1890

August 1889, through mid-May, 1890, comprised a period in the religious development of Narendranath Datta which has received little or no attention in previous studies. When treated at all, it has been passed over briefly as a parenthesis in the future **svāmī's** religious achievement.[1] Narendra's own description at the time viewed these nine and a half months as a period in which he was "driven mad with mental agonies."[2]

When we ask "What was the pattern of ultimate concern of Narendra during this period?," we are confronted with the fact that it resembled neither the previous pattern nor the following one in several important ways. First, Narendra doubted his previous role as **guru**, for implicitly he had been functioning as the **guru** of the order for almost three years. Even though he had been charged with the responsibility for the disciples' spiritual training, this alone did not overcome his own sense of inadequacy in assuming the role. We have already discovered his basic honesty when confronted with a difficult question—he did not feel bound to a past answer. But for the same reason he disturbed rather than taught his fellow **gurubhāis**. He had cherished the freedom to search for truth without regard to persons or institutions. He had often and openly questioned anything which did not seem true to him, subjecting even Rāmakṛṣṇa to scrutinizing inquiry. That he could neither supply answers to their doubts nor his own directly contributed to his sense of frustration at his incomplete training. Second, Narendra began to raise questions which Rāmakṛṣṇa's answers would have quelled before. But in this period of belief and doubt he asked questions which implied an inadequacy in Rāmakṛṣṇa's teachings.

This period differed from what followed in an extremely important facet. During 1889-1890 Narendra sought help from others—first from Pramadādās Mitra and then from Pavhāri Bābā. In the following period there would be much less emphasis on external grace or on the formal submission to the teachings of others and more on **puruṣakāra** (personal exertion), **svadharma** (personal doctrine), and **parivrājaka** (the stage of solitary wanderings), until he was able to share with others the external message—the **Sanātana Dharma.**

The search for adequate authority pushed Narendra inward in an agonizing study of the scriptures and outward for another **guru** who would direct his quest. The search of the scriptures became qualitatively different in August, 1889, in relation to the previous period of study as that pattern of meaning was pointedly rejected and new answers sought out. He temporarily suspended his doubts of the scriptures in September, 1889, in an exertion of faith.[3] Consequently, he later raised the problems which he had uncovered in the scriptures and solved them by a principle which he had by then learned and which replaced the "faith" solution.[4]

In January 1890, Narendra left the Baranagore Math in quest of a **guru.** No more significant act could have been taken to symbolize his break with the pattern of belief as Rāmakṛṣṇa's disciple. Although some external factors confused the issues,[5] by mid-May, 1890, Narendra would renounce his search for another **guru** who could show him a way to realize God and legitimatize his teachings.

Thus, "The Search" will be used to designate that pattern of ultimacy which Narendra later called his period of "mental agonies"—August, 1889, through mid-May, 1890. This brief period may be designated as another pattern of ultimacy because it contained an integrative focus of concerns—for which all else was secondary. The primary contemporaneous documentation for this period would seem to necessitate a threefold examination: authority in the scriptures, help from the **guru,** and a pattern of ultimacy in spite of uncertainty.

Authority in the Scriptures

During 1888 Narendra corresponded with Pramadādās Mitra, the well known Sanskrit scholar of Vārānasī. He acquired from him a number of texts, which were chiefly of **Advaita Vedānta** philosophy. By 1889 these studies began to affect Narendra's belief system. The **advaita** philosophy of Śaṁkara seemed to be in conflict with Rāmakṛṣṇa's teachings particularly on the problem of caste (**varṇadharma**). But this should not have been the case as Rāmakṛṣṇa taught the harmony of all views; thus none should be truly in conflict. When Narendra raised the possibility of such conflict, he had already suspended, if not temporarily rejected, his belief in the adequacy of Rāmakṛṣṇa's synthesis of all views. (Later he would be able to return to a belief in a higher synthesis.)

On August 7, 1889, Narendra asked the renowned **paṇḍit** to answer the following questions for him:

1. Does any narrative occur about Satyakāma, son of Jabālā, and about Jānashruti, anywhere else in the **Vedas** excepting the **Upanishads**?

2. In most cases where Shankaracharya quotes Smriti in his commentary on the **Vedānta-Sutras,** he cites the authority of the

Mahābhārata. But seeing that we find clear proofs about caste being based on qualification both in the Bhishmaparva of the **Mahābhārata** and in the stories there of the Ajagara and of Umā and Maheshvara, has he made any mention in his writings of this fact?

3. The doctrine of caste in the **Purusha-Sukta** of the **Vedas** does not make it hereditary—so what are those instances in the **Vedas** where caste has been made a matter of hereditary transmission?

4. The Acharya could not adduce any proof from the **Vedas** to the effect that the Shudra should not study the **Vedas.** He only quotes **"yajñe 'navakḷptah** (Tai. Saṁhitā, Vii, i.6) to maintain that when he is not entitled to perform Yajnas, he has neither any right to study the **Upanishads** and the like. But the same Acharya contends with reference to **"athāto brahmajijñāsā,"** (**Vedānta-Sutras,** I.i.1) that the word **atha** here does not mean "subsequent to the study of the Vedas," because it is contrary to proof that the study of the **Upanishad** is not permissible without the previous study of the **Vedic Mantras** and **Brāhmanas** and because there is no intrinsic sequence between the **Vedic Karma-kānda** and **Vedic Jñāna-kānda.** It is evident, therefore, that one may attain to the knowledge of Brahman without having studied the ceremonial parts of the **Vedas.** So if there is no sequence between the sacrificial practices and **Jñāna,** why does the Ācharyā contradict his own statement when it is a case of the Shudras, by inserting the clause "by force of the same logic?" Why should the Shudra not study the **Upanishad?**[6]

The first question doubted Śaṁkara's interpretation of the text, **Vedānta Sūtras,** I.iii.34-37. Narendra understood Śaṁkara to be saying that Satyakāma and Jānashruti were given Upanishadic wisdom specifically because they were not **śudras;** he understood Śaṁkara to teach that the members of the fourth caste were not entitled to receive these teachings. Narendra directly questioned his handling of the text. The issue was who could study the **Vedas;** its contemporary implications were great in countering the charges that caste was an integral part of the religious documents themselves and thus of the religion of those who accepted the texts as authoritative.

The second question to **Paṇḍit** Mitra challenged Śaṁkara's use of sources. Narendra pointed out that Śaṁkara cited **smṛti**, in most cases the **Mahābhārata.** Even in the **smṛti** which he used, there were "clear proofs about caste being based on qualificiation" rather than on heredity.[7] And if caste were based on spiritual qualities, then the social rigidity of caste based on heredity for which Śaṁkara was arguing would be wrong. (This was the question of a potential reformer, and its divisive possibilities at that moment in history should not be underestimated.)

The third question concerning the doctrine of caste in the **Puruṣa Sūkta** of the **Ṛgveda** (X.90) went to the heart of the problem of the hierarchy of authority in the scriptures. If the **Vedas** were primary and one **Veda** clearly taught a non-hereditary doctrine of caste, then where could another passage be found "in the **Vedas** where caste has been made a matter of hereditary transmission?"[8] The power of the question rested upon the shared assumption that the **Vedas** were eternal, infallible, and thus without contradiction. Narendra was arguing that there would be no other passage— a deduction which was self-evident for those holding Vedic infallibility. Further he was using **śruti** which had primacy in Śaṁkara's system of scriptural authority to refute his purported finding in **smṛti** of an example of hereditary caste.

Narendra's fourth question is preceded by an intricate discussion. He found Śaṁkara basing his argument against allowing the **śudras** to study the **Upaniṣads** upon the **Taittirīya Saṁhitā's** rejection of the **yajñas** (sacrifices) of the **śudras.** But this argument would require that Śaṁkara had been able to find a necessary connection between the unsuitability of the **śudra's** sacrifice and his study of the **Upaniṣads.** Narendra pointed to Śaṁkara's handling of the initial passage of the **Vedānta Sūtras** in which he did not require the seeker after the knowledge of **Brahman** to begin with the sacrifices. Thus, if there were no intrinsic sequence between the Vedic **karma kānda** (the sacrificial system with its **mantras** and ritual worship) and the Vedic **jñāna kānda** (the pursuit of the knowledge of **Brahman** without external ritual), then it was "evident, therefore, that one may attain to the knowledge of Brahman without having studied the ceremonial parts of the Vedas."[9] Triumphantly, Narendra then asked:

> So if there is no sequence between the sacrificial practices and Jnana, why does the Acharya contradict his own statement when it is a case of the Shudras, by inserting the clause "by force of same logic?" Why should the Shudra not study the Upanishad?[10]

From the context of Narendra's next letter, August 17th, Paramadādās Mitra's attempt to answer one of the four questions can hardly be reconstructed.[11] Narendra stated: "About one amongst my several questions to which you sent your replies, my wrong idea is corrected. For that I shall remain indebted to you for ever."[12]

The August 17th letter began anew with the caste question. However, Narendra then proceeded to give his conviction that caste "is a social law and is based on diversity of Guna and Karma."[13] Reminding the **paṇḍit** of the questions he did not answer, Narendra probed further:

> Another of these questions was: Whether Acharya Shankara gives any conclusion regarding caste based on Gunas as mentioned in **Puranas** like the **Mahabharata.** If he does, where is it to be found? I have no doubt that according to the ancient

view in this country, caste was hereditary, and it cannot also be doubted that sometimes the Shudras used to be oppressed more than the helots among the Spartans and the negroes among the Americans! As for myself, I have no partiality for any party in this caste question, because I know it is a social law and is based on diversity of Guna and Karma. It also means grave harm if one bent on going beyond Guna and Karma cherishes in mind any caste distinctions. In these matters, I have got some settled ideas through the grace of my Guru, but if I come to know of your views, I may just confirm some point or rectify others in them.[14]

The new series of questions to **Paṇḍit** Mitra demonstrated Narendra's mental powers. He began:[15]

1. Is the Mukti, which the Vedanta-Sutras speaks of, one and the same with the Nirvana of the Avadhuta-Gita and other texts?

This question struck at the heart of Rāmakṛṣṇa's teachings. How could the ultimate goals of each of these respective texts be reconciled? (The form of the question shows that he presumes it more likely that a reconciliation of goals can be made than not.)

But the second question boldly formulated the perceived differences between the two ideals of **mukti** and **nirvāṇa.** While Narendra understood the **Vedānta-Sūtras** to teach total merger in an absolute without distinctions, he found a possible contradiction with the **Avadhūta Gītā** which seemed to suggest that in **nirvāṇa** one acquired the capacity to create, preserve or destroy the universe.

2. What is really meant by Nirvana if, according to the aphorism, "Without the function of creating, etc." (**Avadhuta-Gītā,** IV.iv.7), none can attain to the fullest Godhead?

Unless this apparent contradiction could be reconciled by a higher principle, Narendra's acceptance of the ultimate unity of all religious quests would be compromised.

Narendra's third question probed another direction: Can **sūtras** be of one system and the commentary which purports to interpret them be of another? He asked the **paṇḍit:**

3. Chaitanya-deva is said to have told Sārvabhauma at Puri, "I understand the Sutras (aphorisms) of Vyasa, they are dualistic; but the commentator makes them monistic, which I don't understand." Is this true? Tradition says, Chaitanya-deva had a dispute with Prakashananda Sarasvati on the point, and Chaitanya-deva won. One commentary by Chaitanya-deva was rumored to have been existing in Prakashananda's Math.

This question demonstrated real metaphysical sophistication as well as a perspective which was addressing the differences in the systems rather than attempting to obtain a synthesis. (It is true that he would later use the differences to explain a higher synthesis, but this concern for a homologized system is not being asserted here because of his present interest in metaphysical contradiction—a possibility denied by **advaita.**)

Is there essential unity between the Buddhist ideal of **Śūnyatā** and the **Advaita Vedānta** ideal of **Brahman?** This was Narendra's fourth question.

> 4. In the Tantra, Acharya Shankara has been called a crypto-Buddhist; views expressed in **Pranjāpāramitā** [sic.: **Prajñāpāramitā**], the Buddhist Mahayana book, perfectly tally with the Vedantic views propounded by the Acharya. The author of **Panchadashi** also says, "What we call Brahman is the same truth as the Shunya [sic.: **Śūnyatā**] of the Buddhists." What does all this mean?

This question was loaded. Besides the obvious "unity of religious ideals" there was a problem of Śaṁkara's being dependent on Buddhist thought for his teaching—an intolerable idea for an **advaitan!** (How to interpret Buddhism involved a great deal of his later efforts, and the answers given most often involved the question of historical development.)

Next Narendra turned to the question: Is there no foundation for the authority of the **Vedas** other than the circular argument that they are the breath of God (i.e., that they are dependent upon the existence of the One whose existence they seek to prove)? He hit the **paṇḍit** with what must have been for him a mind-boggler:

> 5. Why has no foundation for the authority of the **Vedas** been adduced in the **Vedanta-Sutras?** First, it has been said that the **Vedas** are the authority for the existence of God, and then it has been argued that the authority for the **Vedas** is the text: "It is the breath of God." Now, is this statement not vitiated by what in Western logic is called an argument in a circle?

With no pause or elaboration Narendra raised another dilemma: If faith is required for conclusiveness in **Advaita Vedānta,** why is it denied in the proofs of other schools?

> 6. The Vedanta requires of us faith, for conclusiveness cannot be reached by mere argumentation. Then why has the slightest flaw, detected in the position of the schools of Sānkhya and Nyāya, been overwhelmed with a fusillade of dialectics? In whom, moreover, are we to put our faith? Everybody seems to be made over establishing his own view; if, according to Vyasa, even the great Muni Kapila, "the greatest among perfected souls," is himself deeply involved in error, then who would say that Vyasa may not be so involved in a greater measure? Did Kapila fail to understand the **Vedas**?

This attack on the use of faith as the foundation of knowledge was a dual attack both on **Advaita Vedānta** and on the teachings of his **guru,** Śrī Rāmakṛṣṇa.[16]

Turning to yet another source of doubt, Narendra questioned how the findings of those who claimed knowledge of the highest truths could be believed when their teachings about the cosmos were filled with inaccuracies.

> 7. According to the Nyaya, "Shabda or Veda (the criterion of truth), is the word of those who have realized the highest," so the Rishis as such are omniscient. Then how are they proved, according to the **Surya-siddhānta,** to be ignorant of such simple astronomical truths? How can we accept their intelligence as the refuge to ferry us across the ocean of transmigratory existence, seeing that they speak of the earth as triangular, of the serpent Vasuki as the support of the earth and so on?

Their claim to "all-knowledge" [**Sarvajñā**] seemed to be vitiated by superstitions and ignorance. Their teaching was that, with the highest realization of God, one also acquired full knowledge of the cosmos.

Narendra next turned to question a tenet he had been taught concerning the omnipotence of **śakti:** Does everything happen according to a fixed order?

> 8. If in His acts of creation God is dependent on good and evil Karmas, then what does it avail us to worship Him? There is a fine song of Nareshchandra, where occurs the following: "If what lies in one's destiny is to happen anyhow, O Mother, then what good is all this invoking by the holy name of Durgā?"

If **karma** were the fixed order of the universe and each cause has a necessary effect, then the belief that a deity will be able to perform an act of grace would not logically follow. This question would strike at the heart of **bhakti**—and specifically at the teachings of Rāmakṛṣṇa about **prasāda,** help or grace from the deity.

Paṇḍit Mitra was then asked: If **dharma** is eternal, what is the value of temporary requirements?

> 9. True, it is improper to hold many texts on the same subject to be contradicted by one or two. But why then are the long continued customs of Madhuparka and the like repealed by one or two such texts as "the horse sacrifice, the cow sacrifice, **Sannyāsa,** meat-offerings in Shraddha," etc.? If the Vedas are eternal, then what are the meaning and justification of such specifications as "this rule of Dharma is for the age of Dvapāra," "this for the age of Kali," and so forth?

Narendra's question was examining the possibility that the **Vedas** were not eternal at all because the aspects which he had mentioned were already understood to have been for an earlier **yuga** (age, dispensation). But if there were dispensations (**yugas**), which one was be obeyed?

> 10. The same God who gives out the Vedas becomes Buddha again to annul them; which of these dispensations is to be obeyed? What of these remains authoritative, the earlier or the later one?

If the earlier, then one would be required to return to the sacrificial system of the **Vedas**—what Narendra called the Vedic **karma kānda**; but if the later, then one would be required to follow the teachings for the **Kaliyuga.** But there were many competing claims as to which deity and system of commitment was authoritative for the **Kaliyuga.** So Narendra asked **Paṇḍit** Mitra:

> 11. The Tantra says, in the Kali-Yuga the Veda mantras are futile. So which behest of God, the Shiva, is to be followed?

Integral to Narendra's continued acceptance of the teachings of Rāmakṛṣṇa was the **yuga** doctrine. The **yuga** doctrine had been depended upon to account for religious change. Behind Narendra's question was the doubt in immutability and fear that all was changing so that nothing could be found that was eternal. Thus, no **Sanātana Dharma!**

The final question to the **paṇḍit** combined accurate observation with scepticism. The scriptures record Vyasa saying contradictory things; is it the scripture or Vyāsa that is in contradiction?

> 12. Vyasa makes out in the **Vedanta-Sutras** that it is wrong to worship the tetrad of divine manifestation, Vasudeva, Sankarshana, etc., and again that very Vyasa expatiates on the great merits of that worship in the Bhāgavata! Is this Vyasa a madman?

Narendra's concluding remarks to this important letter demonstrated his quandary. He still believed in external grace which would help him solve his doubts. He also knew that the **paṇḍit** would most likely suggest less reasoning about and more practice of religion in order to overcome his doubts. Yet he admitted,

> I have many doubts besides these, and, hoping to have them dispelled from my mind through your kindness, I shall lay them before you in future. Such questions cannot be all set forth except in a personal interview; neither can as much satisfaction be obtained as one expects to. So I have a mind to lay before you all these facts when presenting myself to you, which I expect will be very soon, by the grace of the Guru.
>
> I have heard it said without inner progress in the practice of religion, no true conclusions can be reached concerning these matters, simply by means of reasoning; but satisfaction, at least to some extent, seems to be necessary at the outset.[17]

Paṇḍit Mitra responded with "two kind letters." After some days Narendra replied to what he felt was their main point: that he "give up arguing and disputing"—the solution of overcoming doubt in the adequacy of a belief system by giving up doubt. The complete body of the September 2nd, 1889 reply stated:

> Some days ago I received your kind letters. I am very much pleased to find in you a wonderful harmony of Jnāna and Bhakti. Your advice to me to give up arguing and disputing is very true

indeed, and that is really the goal of life for the individual—"Sundered are the knots of the heart, torn off are all the doubts, and the seeds of his Karma wear off, when the sight of the Transcendent One is gained." But then, as my Master used to say, when a pitcher is being filled (by immersion), it gurgles, but when full, it is noiseless; know my condition to be the same. Within two or three weeks, perhaps, I shall be able to meet you—may God fulfill that wish![18]

From the extant evidence Narendra's lack of correspondence would suggest several equally possible interpretations. First, the advice of the **paṇḍit** may have been temporarily satisfactory. Second, he may have been silenced in his doubt; then three and a half months later the doubts returned after he had nursed a fellow monk back to health in Allahabad. Third, he ceased to write for answers from a respondent whose comprehensive answer was not to question. But whatever his reasons for remaining silent for three months, he resumed correspondence to ask for the **paṇḍit's** help for two **gurubhāis,** Rakhal and Subodh, who would be visiting Vārānasī. **Paṇḍit** Mitra sent a pamphlet on "scientific Advaitism" and appears to have invited Narendra to visit him in Vārānasī. Narendra's reply revealed a few more threads in the fabric of his religious transactions.

I have all particulars from your letter; and from Rakhal's which followed, I came to know of your meeting. I have received the pamphlet written by you. A kind of **scientific Advaitism** has been spreading in Europe ever since the theory of the conservation of energy was discovered, but **all that is Pariṇāmavāda, evolution by real modification.** It is good you have shown **the difference between this and Shankara's Vivartavāda [progressive manifestation by unreal superimposition].** I can't appreciate your citing Spencer's parody on the German transcendentalists; he himself is fed much on their doles. It is doubtful whether your opponent Gough understands his Hegel sufficiently. Anyway, your rejoinder is very pointed and thrashing.[19]

(This passage would hardly be worth noting if it were not for Narendra's usage of "evolution" three years later in his speeches before the World Parliament of Religions in Chicago. There the distinction between **pariṇāmavāda** and **vivartavāda** was not maintained, but rather the antiquity of the Hindu concept of evolution as recently verified by modern science was presented.[20]

The letter Narendra sent to Yajneshwar Bhattacharya on January 5, 1890, revealed the degree to which he had gone in retreating from his earlier questioning—if what he advised for another can be taken as indicative of what he would advise for himself. He wrote:

> ...A word for you. Remember always, I may not see you again. Be moral. Be brave. Be a heart-whole man. Strictly moral, brave unto desperation. Don't bother your head with religious theories. Cowards only sin, brave men never, no not even in mind. Try to love anybody and everybody. Be a **man** and try to make those immediately under your care, namely Ram, Krishnamayi, and Indu, brave, moral, and sympathizing. No cowardice, no sin, no crime, no weakness—the rest will come of itself....And don't take Ram with you ever or ever allow him to visit a theatre or any enervating entertainment whatever.[21]

Not bothering with religious theories would have been the position for one who valued action over dogma. Renouncing "religion" for "morality and bravery" included aspects of Narendra's past which had rejected the superstitious and had been ambivalent about the place of ritual.

Before he could go up to Vārānasī to visit with **Paṇḍit** Mitra, whose "soul-affinity" had become "so pleasing and agreeable,"[22] circumstances took Narendra to Allahabad to tend to a sick **gurubhāi,** Yogan. He stayed a while longer for part of the holy month of **Māgha.**[23] Then he stopped at Vārānasī for several days while suffering from fever and then went to Ghāzīpur in order to fulfill a new purpose—to "Interview Pavhāri Bābā."[24]

Help From Another Guru

After Narendra reached Ghāzīpur on January 18, 1890, he wrote twenty-two letters which have been saved. These chronicle a visit which subtly but significantly changed his life.

Narendra's letters contained much that would deny that he was seeking help from another **guru.** While he wrote **Paṇḍit** Mitra that the object of his visit was "an interview with the Babaji," Pavhāri Bābā, this need not have been more than that.[25] His speaking of the **paramahaṁsa,** Śrī Rāmakṛṣṇa, while at Ghāzīpur would be further evidence of his continued loyalty to his master.[26] He professed only openness to truth when he wrote a fellow disciple of Rāmakṛṣṇa:

> "My motto is to learn whatever good things I may come across anywhere. This leads many friends to think that it will take away from my devotion to the Guru. These ideas I count as those of lunatics and bigots. For all Gurus are one and are fragments and radiations of God, the Universal Guru."[27]

Behind these denials of disloyalty to Rāmakṛṣṇa, however, Narendra was struggling in a major spiritual crisis.

Narendra had been drawn to a **sādhu** made famous by Keshab Chandra Sen's play, **Nava-Vrindāvan,** which he had performed with Keshab. As Narendra was to learn first-hand, Pavhāri Bābā was an ascetic of the first order. His ability to live on practically nothing earned him the name "**Pav + āhāri** (air-eater) **Bābā** (father)."[28] Narendra even later would thrill at his total renunciation celebrated in the story of the thief. Upon returning to his home the **sādhu** surprised a thief who in his flight left the objects which he sought to steal.[29] Running after the thief, **bābājī** fell at his feet and said: "O Lord, I knew not that Thou wert there! Take them! They are Thine! Pardon me, Thy child!"[30] So seeing divinity in the thief, he had demonstrated to Narendra his own.

Pavhāri Bābā was an interesting synthesis of religious systems. He was a **brāhman,** raised in the **Śrī** sect of Rāmānuja.[31] He had been tutored in **Vyākaraṇa** and **Nyāya** and in the theology of the sect.[32] Becoming a celibate, he took the style of the **parivrājaka,** the wandering monk. At Mount Girnār he was "initiated into the mysteries of practical Yoga."[33] Then on the banks of the Ganges near Vārānasī he became a "disciple of a Sannyasin who practices Yoga and lived in a hole dug in the high bank of the river."[34] Later he studied "the Advaita system under a Sannyasin in Varanasi."[35] At Ghāzīpur he lived within a walled compound, having allowed no one to see him for some time. Narendra described the situation:

> His dwelling has walls on all sides with a few doors in them. Inside these walls, there is one long underground burrow wherein he lays himself up in Samādhi. He talks to others, only when he comes out of the hole. Nobody knows what he eats, and so they call him Pavhāri Bābā. Once he did not come out of the hole for five years, and people thought he had given up his body. But now again he is out. But this time he does not show himself to people and talks from behind the door.[36]

Externally the **sādhu** was a **Vaiṣṇava.** He followed strict dietary discipline, worshipped Rāmachandra and the image of Śrī Raghunāthji, and performed **pūjā** with sacrificial oblations.[37] Narendra observed:

> He is a learned man no doubt, but nothing in the line betrays itself. He performs scriptural ceremonials, for from the full-moon day to the last day of the month, sacrificial oblations go on. So it is sure, he is not retiring into the hole during this period.[38]

What he had to offer Narendra was **Rāja yoga,** a system of belief which taught **puruṣakāra,** personal exertion, rather than **prasāda,** help or grace from the Lord.

The direct evidence that Narendra was involved in a contest of religious loyalties is worth noting. Ten of the twenty-two letters distributed over the three and a half months mentioned that he would be leaving Ghāzīpur shortly. While Svāmī Akhanānanda (Kali) knew that he was in Ghāzīpur he requested that he not pass this information on to the **gurubhāis** of Rāmakṛṣṇa: "Don't, please, write to anyone at Baranagore that I am staying at Ghazipur."[39] Then in late March, when Narendra had been in Ghāzīpur for over two months, he wrote **Paṇḍit** Mitra about an incident for which he expressed deep regret:

> Another brother of mine had been with me, but has left for Abhedananda's place. The news of his arrival has not yet been received, and his health being bad, I am rather anxious for his sake. I have behaved very cruelly towards him—that is, I have harassed him much to make him leave my company.[40]

Then he confessed: "My Gurubhāis must be thinking me very cruel and selfish."[41]

While all of his letters attempted to reassure his brothers that his loyalty to Śrī Rāmakṛṣṇa had not left, the depth of the struggle came out only at the end of his life. In 1902 he recalled that he had been ready to receive **dīkṣā** (initiation) from Pavhāri Bābā and become his disciple.[42] In this light his lament of "so many misdoings of a man driven mad with mental agonies" takes on added significance.[43]

> I have obtained an interview with Babaji. A great sage indeed! —It is all very wonderful, and in this atheistic age, a towering representation of marvellous power born of Bhakti and Yoga! I have sought refuge in his grace; and he has given me hope— a thing very few may be fortunate enough to obtain. . . **Unless one is face to face with the life of such men, faith in the scriptures does not grow in all its real integrity.**[44]

From this initial encounter, Narendra began to receive instruction in **Rāja yoga,** practicing austerities in the lemon grove of his host, Babu Satish Chandra Mukherji.[45] Narendra's longing to realize the absolute had been repeatedly thwarted by his inner conflicts. Here was a **sādhu** whose serenity was remarkable. He wrote in March 1890:

> It is rumoured that he remains in a state of Samādhi for months together. His fortitude is most wonderful. Our Bengal is the land of Bhakti and of Jnāna, where Yoga is scarcely so much as talked of even. What little there is, is but the queer breathing exercises of the Hatha-Yoga—which is nothing but a kind of gymnastics. Therefore I am staying with this wonderful Raja-Yogi—and he has given me some hopes, too.[46]

From a later account (1902) we know that Narendra was seeking initiation: he wished to take Pavhāri Bābā as his **guru.** However, the

bābājī had adopted the life of a solitary monk, working out his own salvation. But his attraction to Narendra was great. Narendra had been receiving instructions from him for only a month when illness kept him away. He observed:

> For the last few days I haven't been able to go to see Pavhariji, but out of his kindness he sends every day for my report. But now I see the whole matter is inverted in its bearings! While I myself have come, a beggar, at his door, he turns round and wants to learn of me! This saint perhaps is not yet perfected—too much of rites, vows, observations, and too much of self-concealment. The ocean in its fullness cannot be contained within its shores, I am sure. So it is not good, I have decided not to disturb this Sadhu for nothing, and very soon I shall ask leave of him to go. No help, you see; Providence has dealt my death to make me so tender![47]

His struggle had only just begun when he wrote on March 8, somewhat prematurely,

> So the great conclusion is that Ramakrishna has no peer; nowhere else in this world exists that unprecedented perfection, that wonderful kindness for all that does not stop to justify itself, that intense sympathy for man in bondage. Either he must be the Avatāra as he himself used to say, or else the ever-perfected divine man, whom the Vedanta speaks of as the free one who assumes a body for the good of humanity. This is my conviction sure and certain; and the worship of such a divine man has been referred to by Patanjali in the aphorism: "Or the goal may be attained by meditating on a saint."[48]

Toward the end of the second months' stay with Pavhāri Bābā, Narendra was visited by one of his brother-disciples. So upset was he by the visit that, even though the disciple was ill, he hid from him to make him leave.[49] Did the presence of a disciple of Rāmakṛṣṇa intensify his conflict and necessitate privacy so that a decision about the absolute would not be influenced by relative matters? Whatever one might speculate about motives, Narendra wrote **Paṇḍit** Mitra in Vārāṇasī to have him help the disciple.[50]

Although Narendra's last two letters from Ghāzīpur at the beginning of April still indicated a tentativeness about his own commitment to stay with Pavhāri Bābā,[51] it was only when two mundane circumstances forced his leaving that he returned to the order. He recalled: "I had no wish to leave Ghazipur this time, and certainly not to come to Calcutta, but Kali's illness made me go to Varanasi, and Balaram's sudden death brought me to Calcutta."[52] Neither having found true renunciation nor having realized the absolute, he returned to the Baranagore Math in May

1890, in the midst of its financial crisis. It was remembered later that he said many times "that whenever he desired to retire into the life of silence and austerity, he was compelled by the pressure of circumstances to give it up."[53]

By the end of May, 1890, Narendra was able to write from the **Math** to the **paṇḍit** reaffirming his loyalty to Rāmakṛṣṇa, which from the context of Narendra's reply, Pramadādās Mitra seemed to have reason to doubt:

> Dear Sir,
>
> I write this to you while caught in a vortex of many untoward circumstances and great agitation of mind; with a prayer to Vishvanatha, please think of the propriety and possibility, or otherwise, of all that I set forth below and then oblige me greatly by a reply.
>
> 1. I already told you at the outset that **I am Ramakrishna's slave,** having laid my body at his feet "with Til and Tulasi leaves," I cannot disregard his behest. If it is in failure that that great sage laid down his life after having attained to super-human heights of Jnana, Bhakti, Love, and powers, and after having practised for forty years stern renunciation, non-attachment, holiness, and great austerities, then where is there anything for us to count on? **So I am obliged to trust his words as the words of one identified with truth.**
>
> 2. Now **his behest** to me was **that I should devote myself to the service of the order of all-renouncing devotees founded by him,** and in this I have to persevere, come what may, being ready to take heaven, hell, salvation, or anything that may happen to me.
>
> 3. His command was that his all-renouncing devotees should group themselves together, and I am entrusted with seeing to this.[54]

Narendra proceeded to solicit funds for a temple to shelter **Bhagavān** Rāmakṛṣṇa's "sacred remains" near Calcutta.[55] This reaffirmation of loyalty to Rāmakṛṣṇa and his **gurubhāis** brought to a close the external aspects of this period.

A Pattern of Ultimacy In Spite Of Uncertainty

During this period Narendra held firm to the goal of realization of the absolute. He sought **brahmajñā.** It was not the goal that had changed but the means. As we have seen, Narendra had not attained this realization under Rāmakṛṣṇa nor during the following years of 1885-1889. He then turned to the scriptures but found contradictions, to Śaṁkara's **Advaita Vedānta,** but found unacceptable teachings with regard to caste and blind (or circular) faith, and to Pavhāri Bābā's **Rāja yoga** but found a conflict in loyalties. Yet the total impact of the period can only be assessed in retrospect. In the next period of his religious development he emphasized **puruṣakāra** (personal exertion) and not **prasāda** (grace), **Advaita Vedānta** and not **śakti pūjā** or Rāmakṛṣṇa **pūjā**, **svadharma** and not religious ceremonies or rituals. Thus the period was immensely important to bring about changes toward those patterns which would become the hallmark of the Ramakrishna Order.

The penultimate concerns during "The Search" filled out Narendra's belief system. It was at this time that renunciation and service, **vairāgya** and **dāsya-bhakti**, were first combined in his writings, the occasion being the recommendation of the **"Imitation of Christ** written by a Christian Sannyasin."[56] But it was his interest in Buddhism and his fascination for the Buddha that would suggest later motifs. He believed that

> What Buddha did was to break wide open the gates of that very religion which was confined in the Upanishads to a particular caste. What special greatness does his theory of Nirvana confer on him? His greatness lies in his unrivalled sympathy. The high orders of Samadhi, etc., that lend gravity to his religion, are almost all there in the Vedas; what are absent there are his intellect and heart, which have never since been paralleled throughout the history of the world.[57]

"Everything for others" exemplified the superior Buddhist ethic.[58] His widesweeping generalizations and the implied contradictories of the period can be captured in several representative passages.

> (1) The Vedic doctrine of Karma is the same as in Judaism and all other religions, that is to say, the purification of the mind through sacrifices and such other external means—and Buddha was the first man who stood against it.[59]
>
> (2) Caste also remained as of old (caste was not wholly obsolete at the time of Buddha), but it was not determined by personal qualifications; and those that were not believers in his religion were declared as heretics, all in the old style. 'Heretic' was a very ancient word with the Buddhists, but then they never had recourse to the word (good souls!) and had great toleration. Argument blew up the Vedas. But what is the proof of your religion? Well, put faith in it!——the same procedure as in all religions.[60]
>
> (3) The Lord Buddha is my Ishta—my God. He preached no theory about Godhead—he was himself God, I fully believe it. But no one has the power to put a limit to God's infinite glory. No, not even God himself has the

power to make Himself limited.[61]

(4) It is my belief that the Tantras, in vogue amongst us, were the creation of the Buddhists themselves. Those Tantrika rites are even more dreadful than our doctrine of Vāmāchāra; for in them adultery got a free rein, and it was only when the Buddhist became demoralized through immorality that they were driven away by Kumārila Bhatta.[62]

Thus, Narendra greatly admired the Buddha's religionless, selfless concern for others; but for the degradation (his assessment of Buddhism's subsequent history in India) into which his followers quickly led Buddhism, Narendra had nothing but scorn. The strong emphasis on morality over religion and on service over doctrine were implicit here but explicit in the letter of January 5, 1890.[63]

Chapter V

THE RELIGION ETERNAL
1890-1902

Svāmī Vivekānanda's actions from 1890-1902 would not suggest an integrated belief system. He broke with the **gurubhāis** of Śrī Rāmakṛṣṇa in 1890, leaving them to follow their paths of **pūjā** (devotional worship of the **guru**) or of **dhyāna** (meditation). He wandered about India trying to start religious and social reforms. Then he turned to America and Europe. First seeking help from abroad, he later began to give help from India to those hungering for spirituality. Eventually winning the **gurubhāis** of Śrī Rāmakṛṣṇa to his understanding of the mission of Rāmakṛṣṇa, he founded the Ramakrishna Mission as an active instrument for bringing a religious awakening to India and, through India, to the world.

The external actions of the **svāmī** need to be studied in greater detail to understand their relationship to the ideals which he both professed and taught during 1890 to 1902. Once the context has been presented, we will turn to the pattern of ultimacy in its absolute ("The Principles of the Religion Eternal") and its relative conceptions ("Practical **Vedānta**").

The Background of This Pattern of Ultimacy

Narendra returned to the Baranagore Math in May, 1890, and stayed until July. Shortly after, he began a pilgrimage with Kali (later known to the world as Svāmī Akhandānanda) but soon demanded solitude from all his brother monks. They later remembered that:

> He had received the command of God regarding his future and told the monks that he was going to leave them in order to become the solitary monk. When Akhandananda begged to be taken along with him he said, "The attachment of Gurubhais is also Māyā! If you fall ill I must look after you, and in case of my illness you must attend me. Thus one is hindered in one's resolutions and attainment of the goal. I am determined to have no longer any form of Māyā about me!"[1]

Even when he came into contact with them accidently at Delhi in January 1891, he told them pointedly to leave him alone:

My brethren, I have said that I desire to be left alone. I have asked you not to follow me. This I repeat once more. I do not want to be followed. Herewith I leave Delhi. No one must follow me or try to know my whereabouts. I demand that you obey me. I am going to cut myself off from all old associations. Whithersoever the spirit leads, there shall I wander. It matters not whether it is a forest or a desert waste, a mountain region or a densely populated city. I am off. I wish every one to strive for his own goal according to his light.[2]

During his wanderings he paused in the months of 1891-92 at Probandar where he helped Shankar Pāndurang translate a portion of the **Vedas.**[3] The **paṇḍit** reportedly suggested to him: "Swami, I am afraid you cannot do much in this country. Few will appreciate you here. You ought to go to the West where people will understand you and your worth. Surely you can throw a great light upon Western culture by preaching the Sanātana Dharma!"[4] (This idea had also been expressed almost two years earlier in January, 1890, by the district judge at Ghāzīpur, a Mr. Pennington.[5] Later in 1891, the **svāmī** told C. H. Pandya of Junagad of the idea.[6])

Since he had not been given a monastic name by his **guru** the **svāmī** searched for a number of years before finding the name which expressed his quest and his realization. During 1891-93 he assumed several different names: Sachchidānanda, Vividiśānanda, et cetera.[7] These seem to have been for the purpose of protecting the privacy of his quest and of renouncing the attachment even to a name.

Except for his separation from the order, later accounts present the picture of a remarkable continuity in his teachings while on pilgrimage with those of the rest of his life.[8] The **svāmī** was trying to find a means by which he could accomplish his task. Driven by the knowledge that he must accomplish what Rāmakṛṣṇa had called "the work of Kālī," he first determined to find laborers in every region of India, **especially** among the **rājas** of India whose traditional duty it had been to effect the divine will in the world. In October, 1892, he summarized his plan:

Just compare the results one can achieve by instructing thousands of poor people and inducing them to adopt a certain line of action on the one hand, and by converting a prince to that point of view on the other. Where will they get the means for accomplishing a good project even if the poor subjects have a will to do it? A prince has the power of doing good to his subjects already in his hands. Only he lacks the will to do it. If you can once wake up that will in him, then, along with it, the fortune of his subject will take a turn for the better, and society will be immensely benefited thereby.[9]

In his attempt to influence Indian rulers to help in the awakening of India (**Prabuddha Bhārata**), the **svāmī** sought and obtained audiences with at least the following **rājas** and **dewans** (prime ministers): Major Ramchandra, **dewan** of Alwar; **Mahārāja** Manga Singh of Alwar; Hari Singh, Commander-in-Chief of the State at Jaipur; **Mahārāja** of Khetri, Rajputana; a **rāja** at Limbdi; **Dewan** Haridās Vihāridas at Junagad; a **dewan** at Bhooj; **Mahārāja** of Cutch; **Dewan** Shankar Pāndurang at Porbandar; **Dewan** Bahadur Manibhai J. of Borodā; **Mahārāja** of Kolhāpur; **Mahārāja** of Baunager; Sir K. Seshadri Iyer, **dewan** of Mysore; **Mahārāja** Chamarajendra Wadiyar of Mysore; **Rāja** Martanda Varma of Trivandrum; **Mahārāja** of Trivandrum; **Rāja** Bhaskara Setupati of Rāmnād.[10] In these visits, when he was allowed the chance, he told of "his mission" to awaken India and its masses to the heights of its past glories. In contradiction of the Brāhmo Samāj and of the Christian missionaries, he asserted that India's present condition was not the fault of its religion but of India's having abandoned its religious identity. He defended "Hinduism" by pointing to lost depths of meaning in her criticized practices, such as image worship. He stated that India must take science from the West and in return give of its spirituality. It must educate women and the masses, improve agricultural conditions, end child marriage. The message of the **Vedānta** was the key.[11] But when the Indian rulers, all under British hegemony, did not perform their **svadharma**—their duty according to the **śāstras,** the **svāmī** began considering a trip to the West to ask for material help so that India could recover its former greatness.

By May, 1892, the **svāmī** had learned of the Parliament of Religions to be held in connection with the Columbian Exposition at Chicago in 1893. At that time he stated to Haridās Chatterjee, "If someone can help me with the passage money, all will be well, and I shall go."[12] Whenever the opportunity arose thereafter, he mentioned the need for **Vedānta** to be preached in the West. In October at Belgaum he said to Haripada Mitra, "But they are holding a parliament of Religions at Chicago and I shall go there if I get an opportunity."[13] When the lawyer offered to raise a subscription, the **svāmī** refused the offer. Later he described his mission to the **Mahārāja** of Mysore; the prince promised the money for the trip—but the **svāmī** again refused.[14] The **svāmī's** internal conflict centered upon the renunciation of money as a **saṁnyāsin** and upon the example of his **guru**, Śrī Rāmakṛṣṇa, who did not touch **kāminikānchan** (women and gold). A trip to the West would certainly involve his handling of money. There was also the further complication that the **Śāstras** (religious texts of the middle ages of India) decreed the loss of caste and of religious privileges to anyone crossing the ocean. Until these issues were resolved in his mind, he continued on the traditional path followed by many **saṁnyāsis** visiting the four corners of India.

By late December, 1892, Svāmī Sachchidānanda (the name he was using at the time) reached the southern tip of India at Kanyākumāri (Cape Comorin), completing his journey to the cardinal points of India. There he seems to have had an experience that brought together and focused into a plan of action all that he had witnessed during his travels. He describes his remembrance of the experience in a letter to a brother at the **Math** about a year later (and after his arrival in America). A number of things had transpired between the event and the account of it to influence the way in which it was valued—the tremendous reception at the Parliament of Religions, almost five months of paid lecturing, and international attention from the press.

> My brother, in view of all this, specially of the poverty and ignorance, I had no sleep. At Cape Comorin sitting in Mother Kumari's temple, sitting on the last bit of Indian rock—**I hit upon a plan:** We are so many Sannyasins wandering about, and teaching the people metaphysics—it is all madness. Did not our Gurudeva use to say, "An empty stomach is no good for religion?" That those poor people are leading the life of brutes is simply due to ignorance. We have for all ages been sucking their blood and trampling them underfoot.
>
> [....] Suppose some disinterested Sannyasins, bent on **doing good to others,** go from village to village, disseminating education and seeking in various ways to better the condition of all down to the Chandala, through oral teaching, and by means of maps, cameras, globes, and such other accessories—can't that **bring forth good** in time? All these plans I cannot write out in this short letter. The long and the short of it—if the mountain does not come to Mohammed, Mohammed must go to the mountain. The poor are too poor to come to schools and Pathashalas, and they will gain nothing by reading poetry and all that sort of thing. We, as a nation, have **lost our individuality,** and that is the cause of all mischief in India. **We have to give back to the nation its lost individuality and raise the masses.** The Hindu, the Mohammedan, the Christian, all have trampled them underfoot. Again the force to raise them must come from inside, that is, **from orthodox Hindus.** In every country the evils exist not with, but against, religion. Religion, therefore is not to blame, but men.
>
> To effect this, the first thing we need is men, and the next is funds. Through the grace of our Guru I was sure to get from ten to fifteen men in every town. I next travelled in search of funds, but do you think the people of India were going to spend money! [....] Selfishness personified—are

> they to spend anything? **Therefore I have come to America, to earn money myself, and then return to my country and devote the rest of my days to the realization of this one aim of my life.**
>
> As our country is poor in social virtues, so this country is lacking in **spirituality. I give them spirituality, and they give me money. . . .**
>
> You may perhaps think what **Utopian nonsense** all this is! You little know what is in me. **If any of you help me in my plans, all right, or Gurudeva will show me the way out.**[15]

Significantly, his plan was arrived at and begun without reference to the disciples of Śrī Rāmakṛṣṇa. Four months after the Kanyākumāri decision, as he was on his way to Bombay to board the ship for America, he met two of his former brothers with whom he had renounced ties at Delhi, Svāmīs Brahmānanda and Turiyānanda. To Turiyānanda, he said, "Haribhāi, I am still unable to understand anything of your so-called religion."[16] (His criticism about **saṁnyāsis** wandering India doing nothing for the suffering masses was applied also to his "former" brothers.)

Thus having come to the definite decision at Kanyākumāri that he would go to Chicago, he turned northeast to find support. At Pondicherry he was denounced by an orthodox **paṇḍit** for his desire to cross the sea.[17] But in Madras he found both moral and financial support. His quickly-won disciples raised five hundred rupees. But then doubt came. He reportedly turned in prayer to Kālī: "Am I following my own will? Am I being carried away by enthusiasm? Or is there a deep meaning in all that I have thought and planned? O Mother, show me Thy will! It is Thou who are the Doer. Let me be only Thy instrument."[18] Then he decided, "My boys, I am determined to force the Mother's will. She must prove that it is Her intention that I should go, for it is a step in the dark. If it be Her will, then money will come again of itself. Therefore, take this money and distribute it amongst the poor."[19] He then resumed teaching, until he was asked to visit Hyderābād. After arriving in Hyderābād on February 10, 1893, Svāmī Sachchidānanda wrote of his lack of success in obtaining financial support.

> So all my plans have been dashed to the ground. That is why I wanted to hurry off from Madras early. In that case I would have months left in my hands to seek out for somebody amongst our northern princes to send me over to America. But alas, it is too late. First, I cannot wander about in this heat—I would die. Secondly, my fast friends in Rajputana would keep me bound down to their sides if they get hold of me and would not let me go over to Europe. So my plan was to get hold of some new person without my friends' knowledge. But this delay at Madras has dashed all

my hopes to the ground, and with a deep sigh I give it up, and the Lord's will be done! However, you may be almost sure that I shall see you in a few days for a day or two in Madras and then go to Bangalore and thence to Ootacamund to see "if" the M-Mahārāja sends me up. "If"—because you see I cannot be sure of any promise of a Dakshini (southern) Raja. They are not Rajputs. A Rajput would rather die than break his promise. However, man learns as he lives, and experience is the greatest teacher in the world.

"Thy will be done on earth as it is in heaven, for Thine is the glory and the Kingdom for ever and ever."[20]

Before leaving Hyderābād, the **svāmī** spoke on "My Mission to the West," but it did not produce a sponsor. He then traveled back to Madras, where, during March and April, his followers again raised the money for his passage. The **svāmī** had told them: "If it is the Mother's will that I go, then let me receive the money from the people! Because it is **for the people of India that I am going to the West**—for the people and the poor!"[21] All arrangements had been made, when the private secetary of the **Mahārāja** of Khetri arrived and pleaded with Svāmī Sachchidānanda to postpone his departure long enough to participate in the celebration in Khetri over the birth of a son to the **Mahārāja.**[22] After a short visit with the **Mahārāja,** whom he had blessed two years before "so that a son might be born to him," he hurried to Bombay. The **Mahārāja** had given him a first class ticket, the attire of a **rāja** and a new name.

On May 31, 1893, Svāmī Vivekānanda—the name suggested by the **Mahārāja** of Khetri—left Bombay by the Steamer Peninsular. Arriving in the United States months before the beginning of the Parliament of Religions and without credentials that would allow his participation, he soon exhausted his funds. Part of his later denunciation of the Brāmho Samāj and of the Theosophical Society resulted from their rejection of his requests for certification.[23] But he was befriended by some wealthy Americans and by Harvard Professor John Henry Wright who was able to pull strings so that the **svāmī** could participate even though he was not the approved representative of any religious body.

From his first speech on September 11, 1893, at the World's Parliament of Religions, he received international press coverage. After the parliament closed, he began working for a lecture bureau, drawing large crowds, earning fairly large sums of money and speaking in the major cities of the east, south and midwest. Possibly because of his ambivalence toward earning money—something he had foresworn after the practice of Srī Rāmakṛṣṇa—he had the lecture bureau reduce his share per lecture. Later he saw that he had been cheated and quit in July, 1894.[24] He then delivered a series of lectures at the Greenacre Conferences in Elliot, Maine, sponsored by Christian Scientists.[25] The fall of 1894 was spent in Boston, Chicago and New York, responding to the invitations of the wealthy. He finally saw that most were using him as a conversation piece and were hardly serious about practicing Indian spirituality. He settled in Brooklyn and began to give regular classes. Out of these classes came the first Americans to take **saṁnyāsa** and his first book, **Rāja-Yoga.**[26] Other major works followed when stenographer J.J. Goodwin joined "the cause," as the **svami** termed it, and transformed lectures into treatises (**Karma-Yoga, Jnana-Yoga, Bhakti-Yoga**).[27] Unfortunately, Vivekānanda never completed any of his plans to write a major work on **Vedānta,** so only through the dedicated efforts of others were his ideas compiled.[28]

Some of the **svāmī's** letters indicated that he at first believed that he would be able to earn enough money in America to effect his plans for India. But when he left the lecture bureau, he saw his hopes dashed. He then concentrated on establishing self-supporting **Vedānta** societies in America and eventually in England. The changes in his conception of his mission and his reason for being in the West, especially after the Parliament of Religions, started with the idea of representing (defending) "Hinduism"[29] and developed, through making money for his plans for India,[30] to establishing the **Sanātana Dharma** as a worldwide movement.[31]

To accomplish his goals for India he believed he needed (Western) organization. His householder disciples in Madras responded more quickly than did his **gurubhāis** in Calcutta. Vivekānanda was striving "to set in motion a machinery which will bring noble ideas to the door of everybody"—a desire expressed in January, 1894.[32] In April of that year he wrote: "I believe the Satya Yuga (Golden Age) will come when there will be one caste, one Veda, and peace and harmony. This idea of Satya Yuga is what would revivify India."[33] His calls to work for the cause of reviving the greatness of India was heady stuff, as easily capable of arousing the passions of Indian nationalism as of spirituality. As early as September, 1894, the **svāmī's** speeches were being published for their political power, and Vivekānanda responded:

> One thing I find in the books of my speeches and sayings published in Calcutta. Some of them are printed in such a way as to savour of political views; whereas I am no politician or political agitator. I care only for the Spirit—when that is right everything will be righted by itself.[34]

His struggle to organize his householder disciples and to get them to do anything besides writing "empty words" demonstrated an exceptional talent as well as the effort needed to infuse social concern into their religious conceptions.[35] The struggle to get the disciples of Rāmakṛṣṇa to join him in "his plans" was no less difficult.[36]

The mission of establishing **Vedānta** in the West was hampered by his lack of credentials. For one long year after the Parliament of Religions he waited for some official recognition of his representation of "Hinduism." When it finally came—saving the work in America—it was the direct result of his pleadings to his **gurubhāis** in Calcutta, his disciples in Madras, and his close friend, the **Mahārāja** of Khetri.[37]

The **svāmī's** active phase of preaching **Vedānta** and initiating disciples in the West comprised two periods—November 1894 to December 1896, and August 1899 to October 1900. His first return to India in January 1897 was triumphal. He labored in India, founding the Ramakrishna Mission on May 1, 1897, after having won over the disciples of Śrī Rāmakṛṣṇa to the ideal of working in the world for the good of mankind as a means to **mukti.**[38]

Just prior to his second return to India in 1900 he began to struggle again with his responsibility for his family. In taking **saṁnyāsa** he had left his family in poverty. His sister committed suicide. One brother ran away from home. His mother, grandmother and younger brother were left. He considered going back to the life of a householder:

> It is becoming clearer to me that I lay down all the concerns of the Math and for a time go back to my mother. She has suffered much through me. I must try to smooth her last days. Do you know, this was just exactly what the great Shankarāchārya himself had to do!...leaving my mother was a great renunciation in 1894—it is **a greater renunciation to go back to my mother now.**[39]

As it worked out later, he did not have to return to the world to provide for his mother. He died a year and a half after his return to India.

Besides the active periods as organizer and preacher during which his American friends referred to him as the "cyclonic Hindu," there were passive, contemplative periods. There were times when he was able to teach and to meditate, as on the Thousand Island Park retreat in June 1895.[40] At other times, however, the balance between work and meditation was lost, and work was devalued. One such period was April, 1900.

> The sweetest moments of my life have been when I was drifting; I am drifting again—with the bright sun ahead and masses of vegetation around—and in the heat everything is so still, so calm—and I am drifting languidly—in the warm heart of the river! I dare not make a splash with my hands or feet—for fear of breaking the marvelous stillness, stillness that makes you feel sure it is an illusion!

> Behind my work was ambition, behind my guidance the thirst of power! Now they are vanishing, and I drift. I come! Mother, I come![41]

During these periods of quietude, Kālī, the Mother of the universe, brought him peace. He was in one of these periods—over a year without any work in the world for others, broken only by a trip to Buddha Gayā—when he died on July 4, 1902, the very day that he had predicted.[42]

The relationship between the external events (the real level of his religious behavior) and the value or belief system of this period involves not two but at least four components: the flux of external events, the way the events are interpreted or valued later, the messages that were preached to particular audiences, and the belief system itself. We have just considered enough of the first three components to suggest their complex relationship to the belief system. It is a simple matter to distinguish between the real level of behavior and the ideal level of belief. However, the way events are interpreted, the message and the belief system are often felt to be synonymous. Such a mixture could eventuate in misunderstanding Svāmī Vivekānanda's pattern of ultimacy from 1890-1902. He valued his actions in the light of his pattern of ultimacy. These valuings are not to be mistaken for the belief system but are an expression of it under varying circumstances. Similarly, the messages to various types of audiences were an application of the pattern of belief to the occasion. His struggle was to apply a complex system with actions and words to a set of problems which had not been tackled before. He had no example to follow, not even that of his **guru**. If his **guru** had taught the same pattern of ultimacy, and the **svāmī** stresses that Śrī Rāmakṛṣṇa had done so, he had not applied it to the situation which Vivekānanda did.

Therefore, the events from 1890-1902 provide the context for the pattern in which he perceived ultimate meaning. The **svāmī** was seeking to live out the implications of his apprehension of eternal principles. Despite the marked differences in his religious moods (**bhakti**, **karma**, or **jñāna**) and in his practices (ranging from **advaita dhyāna** to Kālī **pūjā**) or in his active and passive periods, there was but one pattern of ultimacy articulated on the ideal level during this twelve year span.[43] So, the pattern of ultimacy of "The Religion Eternal" will be presented under the following divisions: the eternal principles, "The Principles of the Religion Eternal," and the application of them in the world, "Practical **Vedānta**."

The viewpoint will be that of the **svāmī**, as drawn from his extant teachings. This is a significant departure from procedures which have placed him in a tradition (i.e. **Vedānta**) and have then expounded the basic tenets of that tradition, procedures that have failed to discover Svāmī Vivekānanda's unique place in Indian thought. The structure of the presentation will arise, therefore, from the way Svāmī Vivekānanda appears to have related the beliefs and values which he found ultimately meaningful. The quotations will provide a first hand appreciation of the intellectual depth of the **svāmī** as well as an insight into his areas of weakness. For this reason each quotation should be given careful attention.

The Principles of the Religion Eternal

"The principles of religion that are in the Vedānta are unchangeable. Why? Because they are all built upon the eternal principles that are in man and nature; they never change."[44] This set of principles

> is that which abides forever, being built upon the nature of man, the nature of the soul, the soul's relation to God, the nature of God, perfection, and so on; there are also the principles of cosmology of the infinitude of creation, or more correctly speaking—projection, the wonderful law of cyclical procession, and so on—these are the eternal principles founded upon the universal laws of nature.[45]

Even so,

> It is true that we create a system, but we have to admit that it is not perfect, because the reality must be beyond all systems. We are ready to compare it with other systems and are ready to show that this is the only rational system that can be; but it is not perfect, because reason is not perfect. It is, however, the only possible rational system that the human mind can conceive.[46]

The paradox that the principles of Vedānta are both external/changeless/uncreated, and temporal/changing/created derives from a juxtaposition of truths which are on different levels of perception and realization. Understanding how this realization of the levels of truth came to be perceived is the starting point. The search for eternal principles (ultimate truth) will proceed according to Svāmī Vivekānanda's schema from epistemology, to the process of perception, then the process of projection, and finally to the realization of absolute unity.

Epistemology

Vivekānanda's pattern of ultimacy presupposed the following (prior to the formulation of his epistemological question): (1) that the phenomenal world consists of change (taken as a self-evident), (2) that change is finitude, weakness, suffering and misery,[47] and

(3) that something beyond change (the absolute) can be known and will provide meaning and purpose to all this (apparent) change.[48] As he put it, the direction is from pessimism to optimism. True knowledge or **vijñāna** ("all-knowingness") must, therefore, be knowledge which does not change and is beyond the phenomenal world.

How can man know what is changeless, pure, infinite, absolute? This question forms the epistemological goal. The goal resolves the crisis of purposeless change. Knowledge of that which lies beyond all change is the appropriate answer of life when the preconditioning question has been accepted as entailing the problem.

Epistemological Foundations. Vivekānanda analyzed the traditional foundations of knowledge (**pramāṇas**) and found them unable to sustain belief in the Absolute. He found that the primary **pramāṇas—pratyakṣa** (perception), **anumāna** (inference or reason, the term he favored most) and **sṛuti** (revelation or intuition)—were insufficient in and of themselves to provide direct perception of the absolute, **Nirguṇa Brahman.** If the goal is that unity of knowledge which is beyond all multiplicity (which is thus beyond all change and is therefore eternal and infinite), then the foundation of knowledge must lie beyond the bondage of change, the **keśa-kāla-nimitta** (space-time-causation) complex. This radical departure from the traditional starting-point of Indian metaphysics[49] was necessitated by his perception of two fundamental weaknesses in the traditional starting-point. If the **Vedas** were to prove the existence of God (i.e., knowledge of the Absolute) but must first be accepted, any argument from that which has not been proved to that which would be proved would never yield certainty.[50] Further, the **Vedas** were not infallible, since they contained errors like a triangular earth.[51] Since everything which is manifested is within the phenomenal world of appearance (**vivarta**) and limited by **deśa-kāla-nimitta,** then even the **Vedas** which have been written down are **vivarta.**

> All philosophy and scriptures have come from the plane of relative knowledge of subject and object. But no thought or language of the human mind can fully express the Reality which lies beyond the plane of relative knowledge! Science, philosophy, etc. are only partial truths. So they can never be the adequate channels of expression for the transcendent Reality. Hence viewed from the transcendent standpoint, everything appears to be unreal—religious creeds, and works, I and thou, and the universe—everything is unreal! Then only it is perceived: "I am the only reality ; I am the all-prevading Atman, and I am the proof of my own existence."[52]

However, the sources of truth and knowledge within sensate existence are not error. They are merely lower levels of truth and participate in true knowledge (**paramārtha**).[53] **Vyāvahārika** (ordinary knowledge), because it relates to the nature of man and the universe and thus to the source of both, aids in the realization of the absolute. Each of the bases of knowledge are able to do this because they point beyond themselves. They point to a level of knowledge which is direct, without multiplicity, and without change. As direct knowledge there is no external authority or source. The absolute must be one, for there cannot be two absolutes. Neither can there be duality in absolute knowledge, as this would limit its infinity. (Thus, there is no room for an extended discussion of the **pramāṇas** on the transcendent level since their function is to point beyond themselves.[54] We will encounter the **pramānas** in "Practical **Vedānta**.")

If there is no knowledge of the absolute through the senses (and this would include the mind), then is one left with silence? No, direct perception of the absolute is possible because of the structure of the mind. There are three states of mind—subconscious, conscious and superconscious. Just as knowledge on the conscious level comes from experience, so knowledge on the superconscious level comes from experience.[55] Knowledge of the absolute is not based on anything beyond the self nor upon any outside authority.[56] The structure of the self is such that direct perception of the absolute lies within.[57] This direct perception of the absolute is called **aparokṣānubhūti.**[58] By degrees the self is able to know the absolute which is beyond all conscious thought. The personal verification of true knowledge (**paramārtha**) is in **samādhi**, the highest state of which is **nirvikalpa samādhi** (complete oneness with the absolute).[59]

This conception would be merely speculative if it were not proven by the realizations of **ṛṣis** and **avatāras.** Through them the structure of knowledge is known. Moreover, there was one in the present age whose **aparokṣānubhūti** (transcendental perception) was complete. Śrī Rāmakṛṣṇa experienced **nirvikalpa samādhi** (waveless unity with the absolute) and, being an **avatāra** (divine incarnation), was able to retain a memory of the ego in order that, for the good of mankind, he could return from that state and help others with his knowledge.[60]

Epistemology and Unity. Svāmī Vivekānanda's **Vedānta**[61] proceeded from the epistemological question: "What is that by realizing which everything is realized?" (**kasmittu bhagavo vijāte servamidaḥ vijātaḥ bhavati**).[62] This question set the goal of the belief system as directed toward a special kind of knowledge. It denied that the goal of life would be found in multiplicity and thus is an analysis of the cosmos bound in **deśa-kāla-nimitta.** It affirmed that the goal is that unity in which everything is realized.

This special knowledge is **aparokṣānubhūti,** transcendental realization, which sees the absolute unity of subject and object, and of mind and matter by going beyond them to their unitary source. True knowledge is, therefore, knowledge of unity (**ekaṁ**). " 'One Brahman there is without a second,' 'There is nothing manifold in existence' (Brihadāranyaka, IV.iv.19)."[63] The object of knowledge is

> to find unity in the midst of diversity.... In reality, the metaphysical and the physical universe are one, and the name of this One is Brahman; and the perception of separateness is an error—they called it Māyā, Avidyā, or nescience. This is the end of knowledge.[64]

The personal realization of unity is aided by the epistemological process of generalization. All knowledge requires generalization, which is the bringing together of observations—the facts known by the senses—and then drawing the conclusion or principle.[65]

> The limited always requires a higher generalization of the unlimited to explain itself. The bound can only be explained by the free, the caused by the uncaused.... It is the duty of science to explain facts by bringing them to a higher generalization.[66]

Consequently, the search is directed to "the last possible generalization" which would be that by which everything else is explained (realized).[67] The random multiplicity of sense experience is given meaning by perceiving the next higher generalization. This process eventually leads to **aparokṣānubhūti,** the realization of the final unity of all generalizations.

> Again generalization, the essence of sense-knowledge, is impossible without something upon which the detached facts of perception unite. The whole world of external perceptions requires something upon which to unite in order to form a concept of the world, as painting must have its canvas.[68]

Thus, true knowledge or Truth is oneness, unity. The test of truth is oneness.[69] The principle by which truth is judged, which Svāmī Vivekānanda has designated "reason,"[70] is unity. "Unity is the goal of Religion and of Science."[71] Unity or "Absolute Truth is God alone."[72] "Truth is to be judged by truth and by nothing else."[73]

The epistemological framework of absolute truth and knowledge would be diagrammed as follows: God (**Brahman**) = Truth (**satya**) = True Knowledge (**aparokṣānubhūti**) = Oneness (**ekaṁ**) = Love (**bhāva,** the ethical dimension of unity and the reason for all morality). All this would be mere speculation if it could not be personally verified.[74] Final verification is **nirvikalpa samādhi.**

Summary of Vivekānanda's Epistemology. The **svāmī's** quest for meaning has as its goal nothing less than absolute truth. To be absolute is to be unaffected by change. The absolute cannot be part of an order limited by space, time, and causation (**deśa-kāla-nimitta**). Yet all that confronted the senses is necessarily within the phenomenal realm, even the written **Vedas.** So one cannot begin with the scriptures (**Vedas**) as the foundation for the realization of changless knowledge. The scriptures had first been accepted "on faith" in order that they might be used to prove the existence of the Absolute. This could never grant certainty. Therefore, the traditional starting point had to be discarded.

Svāmī Vivekānanda found that the foundation of every level of knowledge is personal experience. True knowledge must never be accepted "on faith" in an outside authority. If it is universally true, it must be capable of verification by each seeker after truth when he has reached that level of understanding.

The discoveries of **ṛṣis** and **avatāras,** which are repeatable when one reaches that stage of spirituality, have shown that the foundations of knowledge (**pramāṇas**) in the sensate world are not untrue but actually lower levels of truth which point beyond themselves to the direct experience of the Absolute (**aparokṣānubhūti**). Because of this structure of true knowledge all relative knowledge must be judged by the highest principle. That principle is unity. According to the process of generalization, which was seen by Svāmī Vivekānanda as the scientific way of acquiring knowledge all lower apprehensions of truth depend upon each higher synthesis, until, at last, the highest generalization is reached—the unity or oneness of all the universe.

This is further demonstrated by an understanding of the processes of perception ("Hindu" psychology) and of projection (**Vedānta** cosmology).

Sāṁkhya Psychology: the Process of Perception

According to Svāmī Vivekānanda all philosophy must rest upon psychology, i.e. the process of perception. **Sāṁkhya** was seen by the **svāmī** as constituting this foundation, even though its conclusions maintained a basic dualism between soul and matter as well as perceptual dualism between subject and object.

> The system of the **Sānkhya** [**Sāṁkhya**] philosophy is one of the most ancient in India, or in fact in the world. Its great exponent Kapila is the father of all Hindu psychology; and the ancient system that he taught is still the foundation of all accepted systems of philosophy in India today which are known as Darshanas. They all adopt his psychology, however widely they differ in other respects.
>
> The **Vedānta,** as the logical outcome of the **Sānkhya,** pushes its conclusions yet further. While its cosmology agrees with that taught by Kapila, the **Vedānta** is not

> satisfied to end in dualism, but continues its search for the final unity which is alike the goal science and religion.[75]

Even more, the "Hindu" understanding of perception was seen as the basis of all philosophy, whether admitted or not. This claim by the **svāmī** was founded less upon historical evidence than upon what he deemed epistemological necessity. The structure of knowledge was perceived to require the eventual unity of all particulars in order that the gap between subject and object might be bridged. Thus all philosophy or science must be based upon an adequate analysis of perception. This reason allowed him to say:

> Wherever there is any philosophy or rational thought, it owes something or other to Kapila. Pythagoras learnt it in India, and taught it in Greece. Later on Plato got an inkling of it; and still later the Gnostics carried the thought to Alexandria, and from there it came to Europe. So wherever there is any attempt at psychology or philosophy, the great father of it is this man, Kapila. So far we see that his psychology is wonderful; but we shall have to differ with him on some points as we go on. We find that the basic principle on which Kapila works is evolution. He makes one thing evolve out of another, because his very definition of causation is "the cause reproduced in another form" and because the whole universe, so far as we see it, is progressive and evolving.[76]

It should be noted that Svāmī Vivekānanda evaluated Kapila's contribution in two ways. Kapila was praised for constructing an evolutionary philosophy. However, in each estimate there is an indication that Kapila's analysis of the process of perception would be assimilated by a higher generalization discovered by **Vedānta. Sāṁkhya's** contribution was assessed from two directions: the process of perception and the nature of the perceiver.

The Process of Perception. Since the epistemological goal is knowledge of that by which everything is realized, how one realizes is of supreme importance. The process of perception is therefore analyzed by Svāmī Vivekānanda to determine where true knowledge lies. This analysis follows the epistemological principle of generalization by proceeding from perceptions of multiplicity to the perception of that which lies beyond and which is the highest abstraction which will explain all.[77] Thus, the Truth is the capstone that holds all truths together.

How can anything be known in itself? "When you want to know a thing, it immediately becomes limited by your mind."[78] Knowing the essence of something would mean having true knowledge. Why? Precisely because the limitations of sense knowledge based on sense perceptions would have been transcended. The **svāmī** explained this as follows:

> For instance, let us examine our perceptions. I see a blackboard. How does the knowledge come? What the German philosophers call "the thing-in-itself" of the blackboard is unknown, I can never know it. Let us call it **x.** The black board **x** acts on my mind, and the mind reacts. The mind is like a lake. Throw a stone in a lake and a reactionary wave comes towards the stone; this wave is not like the stone at all, it is a wave. The black-board **x** is like a stone which strikes the mind and the mind throws up a wave towards it, and this wave is what we call the blackboard. I see you. You as reality are unknown and unknowable. You are **x** and you act upon my mind, and the mind throws a wave in the direction from which the impact comes, and that wave is what I call Mr. or Mrs. So-and-so. There are two elements in the perception, one coming from outside and the other from inside, and the combination of these two, **x** + mind, is our external universe. All knowledge is by reaction. In the case of a whale it has been determined by calcuation how long after its tail is struck, its mind reacts and the whale feels the pain. Similar is the case with internal perception. The real self within me is also unknown and unknowable. Let us call it **y**. When I know myself as so-and-so, it is **y** + the mind. That **y** strikes a blow on the mind. So our whole world is **x** + mind (external), and **y** + mind (internal), **x** and **y** standing for the thing-in-itself behind the external and the internal worlds respectively.[79]

What we take to be ourselves then, is "**y** + mind" and what we take to be an object of perception is "**x** + mind," the wave of reaction to the impression coming towards our minds. (This fundamental split between subject and object is made even more radical by the denial of the subject's knowledge of itself.)

The analysis of **Sāṁkhya** philosophy destroys any certainty about knowledge gained by the senses about the phenomenal realm. It probes the mind of the individual, searching to find the faculty capable of true knowledge, but finds instead an unintelligent state being acted upon from beyond. **Sāṁkhya** exhausts the entire content of phenomenal reality without finding the knower. Svāmī Vivekānanda felt that its categories for and its analysis of perception were correct.

How does perception occur? First a vibration (**spandana**) comes from an object. It is picked up by a particular instrument of sense. In the case of vision it would be the eyes. The external instrument (**sthūla śarīra**) transmits the vibrations to the particular organ (**indriya**), the organ of vision in this case, the optic nerve and its centers. The mind (**manas**) collects these forces and presents them to the intellect (**buddhi**). The **indriyas,** the **manas,** and the **buddhi** all manufacture the life-force (**prāṇa**) into the finer forces of perception. The **buddhi** is the determinative faculty and it reacts, forming the impressions (**saṁskāras**). But behind the **buddhi** lies the egoism (**ahaṁkāra**) which is self-conscious, which says "I am." And behind that lies the intelligence (**mahat**). **Sāṁkhya** philosophy makes a mistake here by assigning all manifestation to **prakṛti** (matter, nature) and conceiving of that as eternal and as separate from **puruṣa** (soul, spirit). All manifestation would therefore be the blows of **prakṛti** upon **puruṣa.** This would leave an eternal duality, a duality without an absolute.[80]

Advaita Vedānta's analysis corrected this mistake in **Sāṁkhya.** It discovered that behind the **mahat**, the universal intelligence, was "the Self of man, the Purusha, the Atman, the pure, the perfect, who alone is the seer, and for whom is all this change."[81]

Thus, the analysis of the process of perception had demonstrated that knowledge on the plane of sense experience is dependent knowledge. Nowhere had a center of changeless knowledge of others (knowledge of the object-in-itself) been found. Without finding a center where permanence, lack of change and lack of composition reside, there can be no true knowledge—knowledge that is changeless, uncomposed, eternal, absolute. Since this center was not found in the process of phenomenal perception, Vivekānanda then turned to the perceiver. Does changeless knowledge reside there?

The Nature of the Perceiver. Man as an individual **jīva** exists relatively on a plane of becoming which limits his awareness to one level of consciousness. As the analysis of the process of perception has demonstrated, true knowledge does not lie in the conscious plane. That means the conscious or sensate plane must be transcended so that consciousness can be known.

Is it possible to transcend the limitations of the process of perception within the perceiver itself? If such could be the case, then the **jīva** as perceiver would be its own foundation of true knowledge. However, Svāmī Vivekānanda's analysis of perception has already cut off the possibility of the **jīva's** knowing an object-in-itself. Without knowledge of the true essence of an object, phenomenal perception remains ultimately meaningless. The **svāmī** stated this quite radically when he said: "Now as each individual can only see **his own** universe, that universe is created with his bondage and goes away with his liberation, although it remains for others who are in bondage."[82] Yet the **jīva** also is without knowledge of its own true essence. Since it is bound in a state of becoming (and this is apparently the case when all that is known is that which is perceived by the senses), the **jīva's** knowledge of itself as perceiver is an infinite regress in flux and becoming.

Thus, the **jīva** is not the true perceiver but merely a lower plane of phenomenal and relative existence.

On the conscious plane of the senses the **jīva** is limited within itself to a limited knowledge of what amounts to its own universe. No way is found open, when only sense experience is considered, to bridge the gulf among the (apparent) perceivers. How can it be known that in their particularity and subjectivity the reactions of the impressions (**saṁskāras**) of objects upon their minds have any correspondence to true knowledge? Without a posited solution which would have to be taken "on faith" Svāmī Vivekānanda maintained that there was no solution on the conscious plane.

What has been maintained is that no true knowledge (i.e. changeless, infinite, absolute) can be found in the apparent perceivers (**jīvas**). However from a higher viewpoint the **jīvas** are found not to be perceivers at all. True perception would involve consciousness (**vijñāna**). Consciousness entails real existence, real knowledge and real bliss (**sat-cit-ānanda**). The **svāmī** described **vijñāna** in his non-linear way:

> According to Vedānta, the three fundamental factors of consciousness are, I exist, I know, and I am blessed. The idea that I have no want, that I am restful, peaceful, that nothing can disturb me, which comes from time to time, is the central fact of our being, the basic principle of our life; and when it becomes limited, and becomes a compound, it manifests itself as existence phenomenal, knowledge phenomenal, and love. Every man exists, and every man must know, and every man is mad for love. He cannot help loving. Through all existence, from the lowest to the highest, all must love. The **y,** the internal thing-in-itself, which combining with mind, manufactures existence, knowledge, and love, is called by the Vedantists Existence absolute, Knowledge absolute, Bliss absolute. That real existence is limitless, unmixed, uncombined, knows no change, is the free soul; when it gets mixed up, muddled up, as it were, with the mind, it becomes what we call individual existence. It is plant life, animal life, human life, just as universal space is cut off in a room, in a jar, and so on. And that real knowledge is not what we know, not intuition, nor reason, nor instinct. When that degenerates and is confused, we call it intuition; when it degenerates more, we call it reason; and when it degenerates still more, we call it instinct. That knowledge itself is **vijñāna,** neither intuition, nor reason nor instinct. The nearest expression for it is all-knowingness. There is no limit to it, no combination in it.[83]

Returning to the symbols of one's perception of the external world ("**x** + mind") and the internal world ("**y** + mind"), both of which were unknowable on the phenomenal plane—the plane of the conscious, Svāmī Vivekānanda suggests the solution.

> All difference is due to time, space, and causation. These are the constituent elements of the mind. No mentality is possible without them. You can never think without time, you can never imagine anything without space, and you can never have anything without causation. These are the forms of the mind. Take them away, and the mind itself does not exist. All difference is, therefore, due to the mind. According to Vedānta, it is the mind, its forms, that have limited **x** and **y** apparently and made them appear as external and internal worlds. But **x** and **y**, being both beyond the mind, are without difference and hence one. We cannot attribute any quality to them, because qualities are born of the mind. That which is qualityless must be one; **x** is without qualities, it only takes qualities of the mind; so does **y**; therefore these **x** and **y** are one. The whole universe is one. There is only one Self in the universe, only One Existence, and that One Existence, when it passes through the forms of time, space, and causation, is called by different names, Buddhi, fine matter, gross matter, all mental and physical forms. Everything in the universe is that One, appearing in various forms.[84]

Behind the multiplicity of apparent perceptions on the conscious plane, lies the true Self, the only perceiver, the supreme "Unit Abstraction" of the internal sphere, the **Ātman.**

"So the personal man is broken down, and man as principle is built up. The person is only a phenomenon, the principle is behind it."[85] The individual **jīva** is known for what it is, ultimately without intelligence, perception or consciousness. In transcendent realization (**aparokṣānubhūti**) the true perceiver, the **Ātman,** perceives as the eternal subject, infinite, immortal, perfect and free.[86]

Summary of Vivekānanda's Psychology. Svāmī Vivekānanda has identified the changeless, infinite, eternal unity as the most meaningful concern of life. But even as the sources of knowledge were found to yield impermanent knowledge, so also the process of perception was found to leave a radical break between the impression of an object upon the mind and the knowledge of the object-in-itself. That which was external to the individual (**jīva**) was found to be unknowable in its essence. The **jīva** merely reacted to what came from beyond its mind (**manas**) and was limited to its created visions—its own illusory universe.

Not only was the **jīva's** knowledge of objects incomplete and ever changing, it also suffered from the impossibility of true knowledge of itself. The mind (**manas**) of the individual (**jīva**) was limited by **deśa-kāla-nimitta** (space, time and causation) and because of this differentiates that which is really one as a multiplicity by **nāma-rupa** (name and form). The **jīva** cannot know the true perceiver because the **jīva** has relative existence on the sensate plane where true perception does not occur. The real is beyond the mind (**manas**). It is beyond differentiation.

This analysis has led the **svāmī** through the sources of knowledge to the process of perception. Each analysis has pointed beyond itself. He next analyzes what is perceived as the cosmos.

Vedānta Cosmology: The Process of Projection

Sāṁkhya psychology has reduced the apparent multiplicity of perceivers, **jīvas**, to the sole and eternal subjectivity, the **Ātman.** But what about the (apparent) manifestations which are perceived? Can it be that their multiplicity will be resolved in unity? According to the epistemological decision which the **svāmī** already made, that the principle of truth is unity, the multiplicity of the universe stands in contradiction to unity unless that very multiplicity can be brought into question.

Just as the **svāmī** had found the multiplicity of perceivers being questioned by **Sāṁkhya** and resolved in **Vedānta,** so he also found the multiplicity of the perceived being questioned by "modern science" and resolved by **Vedānta.** He believed that the scientific notions of evolution and of the conservation of energy and matter not only refuted dualistic conceptions of the nature of the universe but also would eventually lead science to discover the unity behind the cosmos. This coincidence between science and **Vedānta** made it "the only scientific religion,"[87] incorporating within its teachings the law of evolution and the law of the conservation of energy and matter.[88] He predicted:

> When the modern tremendous theories of evolution and conservation of energy and so forth are dealing death blows to all sorts of crude theologies, what can hold any more the allegiance of cultured humanity but the wonderful, convincing, broadening, and ennobling ideas that can be found only in that most marvellous product of the soul of man, the wonderful voice of God, the Vedānta.[89]

Vedānta had already discovered the law of conservation of energy and matter when it taught "that the cause is the same as the effect, and the effect is only the cause in another form. Therefore, this whole universe cannot be produced out of nothing."[90] Disproving the doctrine of creation **ex nihilo,** science, stated the **svāmī**, pointed toward the external unity of the universe. "Modern physics also has demonstrated that the sum total of the energies in the universe is the same throughout."[91] **Vedānta** and science agreed that, in the manifestation of the cosmos, "the sum total of the energy remains the same, whatever the forms it may take."[92] This meant that the primitive belief in creation from nothing "would be laughed at by modern scientists."[93] Therefore, the **svāmī** maintained that modern science and **Vedānta** were not only in agreement but were also seeking the same unity.[94]

Vedānta's understanding of the cosmos, to which science pointed but had not yet arrived, is known as the Law of Projection, the Law of Cyclical Procession, and the Fact of **Māyā**.[95]

The Law of Projection. Svāmī Vivekānanda used many cosmological schemes to express the **Vedānta** conception of the projection (**sṛṣṭi**) of the cosmos: **prakṛti-puruṣa** (Primal nature and soul of **Sāṁkhya** dualism);[96] **akāśa-prāṇa** (Primal matter and energy);[97] self-hypnotism of the cosmos;[98] unfolding, infinite, cosmic intelligence;[99] or **māyā**.[100] In this way he touched base with many schools of thought, teaching that, although they varied in detail, they were the same in essence.

The cosmos is within **deśa-kāla-nimitta,** space-time-causation. Since nothing is produced without a cause, it must be understood that the cosmos was caused and is subject to the limitations of time and space. Yet the effect is but the cause reproduced.[101] The cosmos is merely a projection (**sṛṣṭi**), a manifestation, or a contraction of the unmanifested in its "vain attempt [...] to manifest itself."[102] This transformation (**pariṇāma**) of the cause into its effects is the secret of the law of causation. "Everything in this universe has been projected, Prana vibrating."[103] The Eternal Subject is attempting to objectify Itself.[104]

In this way the **svāmī** has found basic agreement, between both science and **Vedānta,** about the nature of causation. The equation has been constructed between the kind of causation entailed in the law of the conservation of energy and matter and a similar kind of causation found in Indian thought. This latter theory of causation is the **pariṇāma** of **Sāṁkhya** thought, transformation by real modification. (We have already seen how in **"The Search"** the **svāmī** had held that this conception of **Sāṁkhya** was opposed to Śaṁkara's **vivarta,** "progressive manifestation by unreal superimposition."[105] This departure from strict **Advaita Vedānta** will become more apparent when the **svāmī's** ethics of service in the world necessitate a cosmology which does not value the world as illusion. The other factor which influenced the apparent reversal is the growing role that science comes to play in buttressing his thought.) However, the significance of this conception of causation as projection (**sṛṣṭi**) is that, since the cause is the effect in another form, unity has not been compromised. If the cause were different from the effect, then duality would exist according to the nature of causation. Since cause and effect are the same, multiplicity can again be transcended.

The Law of Cyclical Procession. This law combines with the law of projection to form Vivekānanda's cosmogony. It involves these conceptual elements; **pralaya-pariṇāma, kalpa-yuga,** and **karma-saṁsāra.**

Within **deśa-kāla-nimitta** there is an eternal process of **pralaya** and **pariṇāma,** (involution and evolution) of the cosmos. The **pralaya** (involution or atavism—the contracting of the higher existence into a more primitive one) precedes the **pariṇāma** (the expansion of the continuity of life as it evolves upward toward realizing its true nature).[106] **Jātis** (species) change from one to another through the evolutionary process (**pariṇāma**) by "the infilling of nature" (**prakṛtyāpurāt**).[107]

> The whole of this life which slowly manifests itself evolves itself from the protoplasm to the perfected human being—the Incarnation of God on earth—the whole of this series is but one life, and the whole of this manifestation must have been involved in that very protoplasm. This whole life, this very God on earth, was involved in it and slowly came out, manifesting itself slowly, slowly, slowly. The highest expression must have been there in the germ state in minute form; therefore this one force this whole chain, is the involution of that cosmic life which is everywhere. It is this one mass of intelligence which, from the protoplasm up to the most perfected man, is slowly and slowly uncoiling itself.[108]

This could also be expressed according to the steady state theory of the universe.

> The sum total is the same always. Only the manifestation varies, being involved and evolved. So this cycle is the evolution out of the involution of the previous cycle, and this cycle will again be involved, getting finer and finer, and out of that will come the next cycle. The whole universe is going on in this fashion. Thus we find that there is no creation in the sense that something is created out of nothing. To use a better word, there is manifestation, and God is the manifester of the universe. The universe, as it were, is being breathed out of Him, and again it shrinks into Him, and again He throws it out.[109]

This eternal process of **pralaya-pariṇāma** occurs within **kāla** (time) according to **kalpas** and **yugas** (cosmic cycles and ages). Accordingly, there was no beginning at which time there was a creation. "Time and space are infinite, and therefore have neither beginning nor end."[110] Each **kalpa** (cosmic cycle) has four ages—the **satya yuga,** the **tretā yuga,** the **dvāpara yuga,** and the **kali yuga.**[111] Within this temporal structure, which is ever worsening, the **jīva** (individual soul) must strive toward perfection. (Svāmī Vivekānanda seems to have sensed a contradiction in maintaining an evolution in time of man toward perfection while holding to a theory of the ages, which saw man becoming worse. He once called the **yuga** doctrine one of the "arbitrary assumptions of Pauranika times."[112])

Linked to **pralaya-pariṇāma** and to **kalpa-yuga** within the eternal procession of nature are the laws or processes of **karma** and **saṁsāra.** **Karma** prescribes that one must ultimately be responsible for every action. Any action, whether good or bad, and "each thought we think, produces an impression called in Sanskrit Samskara, upon the mind and the sum total of these impressions becomes the tremendous force which is called 'character.' "[113] Good **karma** produces good **saṁskāras** (impressions), while bad produces bad. But both are "bondages of the soul."[114]

> The character of a man is what he has created for himself; it is the result of the mental and physical actions that he has done in his life. The sum total of the Samskaras is the force which give a man the next direction after death. A man dies; the body falls away and goes back to the elements; but the Samskaras remain, adhering to the mind which, being made of fine material, does not dissolve, because the finer the material, the more persistent it is. But the mind also dissolves in the long run, and that is what we are struggling for.[115]

There is a continuity of life forms in which any **jīva** will become manifested, according to past **karma.**

> In the Deva form they make no Karma at all; only man makes Karma. Karma means work which will produce effect. When a man dies and becomes a Deva, he has only a period of pleasure, and during that time, makes no fresh Karma; it is simply a reward for his past good Karma. When the good Karma is worked out, then the remaining Karma begins to take effect, and he comes down to earth. He becomes man again, and if he does very good works, and purifies himself, he goes to Brahmaloka, and comes back no more.
>
> The animal is a state of sojourn for the Jiva evolving from lower forms. In course of time the animal becomes man. It is a significant fact that as the human population is increasing, the animal population is decreasing. The animal souls are all becoming men. So many species of animals have become men already. Where else have they gone?[116]

Directed by the result of past action, a **jīva** evolves or "devolves" in an eternal series of births and rebirths (**saṁsāra**). It is without beginning and end; it is the law of manifestation in its sphere (**karmabhumi**).[117] Thus, the law of Cyclical Procession teaches

> that the true secret of evolution is the manifestation of the perfection which is already in every being; that this perfection has been barred and the infinite tide behind is struggling to express itself. These struggles and competitions are but the results of our ignorance, because we do not know the proper way to unlock the gate and let the water in.[118]

This struggle for perfection has resulted from an ignorance of the true nature, and therefore the true purpose, of the universe. That ignorance is overcome when the universe is known as **māyā.**

The Fact of Māyā. The projection (**sṛṣṭi**) of the universe (**virāt**) in its multiplicity seems to admit the existence of something besides the One. Yet **Vedānta** maintains that

> "This world has no existence." What is meant by that? It means that it has no absolute existence. It exists only in relation to my mind, to your mind, and to the mind of everyone else. We see this world with the five senses but if we had another sense, we would see in it something more. If we had yet another sense, it would appear as something still different. It has, therefore, no real existence; it has no unchangeable, immovable, infinite existence. Nor can it be called non-existence, seeing that it exists, and we have to work in and through it. It is a mixture of existence and non-existence.[119]

Ignorance of the true nature of the perceiver and the perceived is **māyā.**[120] "All that binds us is Māyā—delusion."[121] Yet numerous questions occur: "What is the cause of Māyā?"[122] "How is it that this One Principle becomes manifold?"[123] "How can the uncaused cause?"[124] "What makes the undifferentiated appear differentiated to mind?"[125] "How does this Perfect Being become mixed up with will, mind, thought?"[126] The **svāmī** addressed these questions in the following discussion.

> God is the material cause of this universe, but not really, only apparently. The celebrated illustration used is that of the rope and the snake, where the rope appeared to be the snake, but was not really so. The rope did not really change into the snake. Even so this whole universe as it exists is that Being. It is unchanged, and all the changes we see in it are only apparent. These changes are caused by Desha, Kāla, and Nimitta (space, time, and causation), or, according to a higher psychological generalisation, by Nāma and Rupa (name and form). It is by name and form that one thing is differentiated from another. The name and form alone cause the difference. In reality they are one and the same. Again, it is not, the Vedantists say, that there is something as phenomenon and something as noumenon. The rope is changed into the snake apparently only; and when the delusion ceases, the snake vanishes. When one is in ignorance, he sees the phenomenon and does not see God. When he sees God, this universe vanishes entirely for him. Ignorance or Māyā, as it is called, is the cause of all this phenomenon—the Absolute, the Unchangeable, being taken as this manifested universe. His Māyā is not absolute zero, nor non-existence. It is defined as neither existence nor non-existence. It is not existence, because that can be said only of the

> Absolute, the Unchangeable, and in this Māyā is non-existence. Again, it cannot be said it is non-existence; for if it were, it could never produce the phenomenon. So it is something which is neither; and in the Vedānta philosophy it is called Anirachaniya or inexpressible. Māyā, then, is the real cause of this universe. Māyā gives the name and form to what Brahman or God gives the material; and the latter seems to have been transformed into all this.[127]

Thus, the mistake of all the questions asked about the cause of **māyā** or the manifestation of the unmanifested is that they erroneously attempt to place upon the Absolute the limitations of **deśa** and **kāla** as well as that of **nimitta** (causation). Since all of these questions evidence wrong cognition (**avidyā**), they not only cannot, but they also should not be answered. The **svāmī** exposed this impossibility with the question: "What makes the undifferentiated appear differentiated to mind?" Then he analyzed the nature of questions which assume that the Absolute comes within **deśa-kāla-nimitta.**

> This is the same kind of question as what is the origin of evil and free will? The question itself is contradictory and impossible, because the question takes for granted cause and effect. There is no cause and effect in the undifferentiated; the question assumes that the undifferentiated is in the same condition as the differentiated. "Whys" and "wherefores" are in mind only. The Self is beyond causation, and It alone is free.[128]

Svāmī Vivekānanda attempted to illustrate this paradoxical teaching with a diagram and an explanation. The conception begins with **pariṇāma** ("The Absolute has become the universe.") but ends with **vivarta** (". . .in the Absolute there is neither time, space, nor causation." ". . .there is no mind, no thought.").

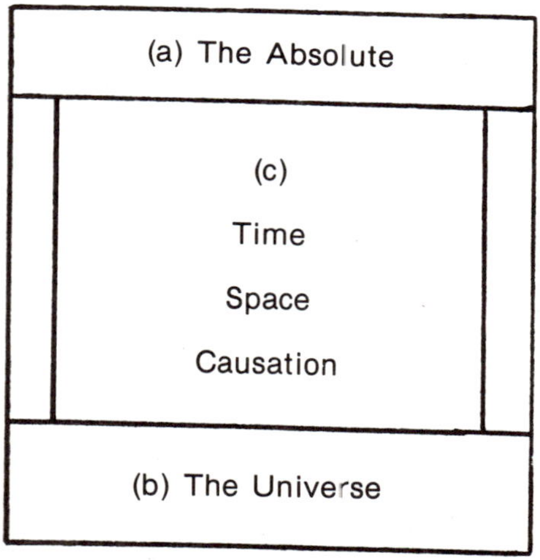

> Here is the Absolute (a) and this is the universe (b). **The Absolute has become the universe.** By this is not only meant the material world, but the mental world, the spiritual world—heavens and earths, and in fact, everything that exists. Mind is the name of a change, and body the name of another change, and so on, and all these changes compose our universe. This Absolute (a) has become the universe (b) by coming through time, space, and causation (c). This is the central idea of Advaita. Time, space and causation are like the glass through which the Absolute is seen, and when It is seen on the lower side, It appears as the universe. Now we at once gather from this that **in the Absolute there is neither time, space, nor causation.** The idea of time cannot be there, seeing that **there is no mind, no thought.** The idea of space cannot be there, seeing that there is no external change. What you call motion and causation cannot exist where there is only One.[129]

The illustration depicts the apparent manifestations (b) which the mind perceives as it attempts to see the Absolute (a) from beneath through **deśa-kāla-nimitta** (c). True reality—true existence (**sat**)— is beyond its multiplicity in the universe. The illustration further demonstrates why all the preceding questions have no logical basis for being asked. One cannot expect to ask questions bound in **māyā** and to receive answers which aid in the realization of the Absolute. Therefore, all activity in **pariṇāma** (the modifications by evolution of all mind and matter) is bondage to relative reality. The soul (**jīva**) must seek freedom (**mukti**) from all this. Knowledge of the nature of the apparent covering (**āvaraṇa**) is stripped away and only the Absolute (**Brahman**) is left. Thus, **Vedānta** paradoxically maintains: "God has not become this universe: the universe is not."[130] This knowledge leads the soul (**jīva**) to renunciation (**vairāgya**) of the relative for the absolute, for freedom in the realization of its true nature.[131]

Summary of Vivekānanda's Cosmology: The unique aspect of the **svāmī's** teaching about the cosmos is not that the cosmos lacks ultimate reality. While he says this, it is commonplace among **advaitans.** Nor does his usage of the notions of **māyā** and **avidyā** suggest originality. Through these notions, he was able to demonstrate, like those before him, that the world which we see is **vivarta** (appearance). What is unique is the **svāmī's** combination of two theories of causation and their corollary views of the universe. He combined **pariṇāma** from **Sāṁkhya** with **vivarta** from **Advaita Vedānta** and made them refer to two complimentary, but distinct realms of reality. Accordingly, **pariṇāma** referred to a real transformation of the cause into a multiplicity of effects. But this was viewing the universe from beneath, within **māyā** and bound by **deśa-kāla-nimitta.** According to **vivarta** the relative view is transcended and the apparent multiplicity of objects can no longer be found. For beyond the bonds of time, space and causation there is only **Brahman.**

Vedānta Eschatology[132]

Vedānta eschatology completes the principles of the Religion Eternal. The epistemological question was "What is that by realising which everything is realised?" This determined that true knowledge would yield knowledge of the unitive principle beyond the (apparent) multiplicity. **Sāṁkhya** psychology, in analyzing perception, determined that true knowledge and consciousness lies beyond the (apparent) multiplicity of perceivers (**jīvas**) in the unity of the **Ātman.** Then **Vedānta** cosmology determined that the (apparent) multiplicity of the perceived, the manifestations, were caused by **māyā** or **avidyā** (ignorance). The universe uses but an apparent projection from **Brahman** (the one reality beyond all causation).

In this way all seeming multiplicity has been transcended and the true nature of being (**sat**) as **advaita** (non-dual) has been apprehended. The only component of the belief system that remains to be explicated is the nature of the absolute. Svāmī Vivekānanda taught that once the **jīva** renounced the relative reality of the world, it could proceed according to "the great law of spirit evolution" in "moving onwards and upwards" to unity with the One.[133] Thus, **Vedānta** eschatology teaches the final freedom of the real Soul, the **Ātman,** from bondage in relative existence, i.e. multiplicity, ignorance, suffering and finitude.

> When man has been sufficiently buffeted by the world, he awakes to a desire for freedom; and searching for means of escape from the dreary round of earthly existence, he seeks knowledge, learns what he really is, and is free.[134]

This freedom (**mukti**) is attained by the enormous efforts of saints striving throughout many lives. Yet by retracing their findings it is possible to realize the absolute in a single lifetime by renouncing the relative, working out past **karma**, and following a path (**yoga**) to its culmination in the one. "The Vedanta teaches that Nirvana can be attained here and now, that we do not have to wait for death to reach it. Nirvana is the realisation of the Self...."[135] This freedom comes when one realizes that the true soul (**Ātman**) and the cosmic process (**Brahman**) are one. It proceeds through stages of realizing the complete incomprehensibility of **Brahman**—the Absolute beyond the absolute conceived by men. All this is "proved only by realisation. When one realises Brahman, for him Maya exists no longer, just as once the identity of the rope is found out, the illusion of the serpent comes no more."[136]

The **svāmī** taught two views or levels of the Absolute (**Brahman**), **Saguṇa Brahman** and **Nirguṇa Brahman.** Since we are limited to the extant data, we must discover what the **svāmī** left as his teaching. There is some ambiguity or even some confusion of the levels when judged by the strict **advaita** (non-dualism) of Śaṁkara. But our expectation of affinity with Śaṁkara must not prevent us from viewing the documents as they come to us.

Saguṇa Brahman. Svāmī Vivekānanda taught that the absolute is perceived in the first stage of non-dual realization with attritubes (**sa** + **guṇa**). As **Saguṇa Brahman** the Real is manifested to the mind "in Its highest in Iśvara, or the Supreme Ruler, as the highest and omnipotent Life or Energy."[137] The mind, being within **deśa-kāla-nimitta** and being a function of **māyā** can only come to the idea of a Personal God with attributes.

> Now whatever is reality in nature is this Absolute, and nature comes to us in three forms, God, conscious, and unconscious, i.e. God, personal souls, and unconscious beings. The reality of all these is the Absolute; through Māyā it is seen to be diverse. But the vision of God is the nearest to the reality and the highest. The idea of a Personal God is the highest idea which man can have. All the attributes attributed to God are true in the same sense as are the attributes of nature. Yet we must never forget that the Personal God is the very Absolute seen through Maya.[138]

However, the idea of God as "personal does not mean that God has a body, sits on a throne somewhere, and rules this world, but means Saguna, with qualities."[139] This perception of the absolute through the categories of the mind leads to certain descriptions of the activities of the Personal God, as "the Ruler, the Creator, the Preserver, and the Destroyer of this universe."[140] But **advaita** goes beyond this idea of the Personal God to "a still higher phrase of this Personal God, which is personal-impersonal."[141] Yet, even before the higher stage of realization of the Absolute as "personal-impersonal" is attained, the non-duality of the Absolute and the universe can be realized in **Saguṇa Brahman**. Thus, the Supreme Ruler, **Īśvara**, is manifested as "the Living" ("the highest and omnipotent Life or Energy"), "the Loving" ("Infinite Love, in the Supreme Lord"), and "the Beautiful" ("the greatest attraction of the soul"), **Satyaṁ-Shivaṁ-Sundavaṁ.**[142]

> Every existence from the highest to the lowest, all manifest according to their degree as—energy (in the higher life), attraction (in the higher love), and struggle for equilibrium (in the higher happiness). This highest Energy-Love-Beauty is a person, an individual, the Infinite Mother of this universe—the God of gods—the Lord of lords, omnipresent yet separate from the universe—the Soul of souls, yet separate from every soul—the Mother of this universe, because She has produced it—its Ruler, because She guides it with the greatest love and in the long run brings everything back to Herself. Through Her command the sun and moon shine, the clouds rain, and death stalks upon the earth.
>
> She is the power of all causation. She energises every cause unmistakably to produce the effect. Her will is the only law, and as She cannot make a mistake, nature's laws—Her

will—can never be changed. She is the life of the Law of Karma or causation. She is the fructifier of every action. Under Her guidance we are manufacturing our lives through our deeds or Karma.

> Freedom is the motive of the universe, freedom its goal. The laws of nature are the methods through which we are struggling to reach that freedom, under the guidance of Mother. This universal struggle for freedom attains its highest expression in man in the conscious desire to be free.[143]

Īśvara becomes manifest to the mind as a person, but more especially as the Infinite Mother of the universe. (Formulations like this one constitute the reason why the **svāmī** has been viewed by some Indians as a sectarian devotee of **Śakti,** the Divine Mother. He maintained that She was his particular "fad," his **Iṣṭadeva** or chosen deity.) This ground of all existence as oneness with qualities is affirmed by the **svāmī** in the prospectus of the Advaita Ashrama—an institution which would teach "nothing but the Doctrine of Unity," which was "dedicated to Advaita and Advaita alone," and which would "preach this Noble Truth entirely free from the setting of dualistic weakness."[144] The **advaita** evidenced in the prospectus does not transcend the level of **viśiṣṭādvaita**—the identification of cause and effect, of **Brahman** and **virāt** (universe). The prospectus stated:

> In Whom is the Universe, Who is in the Universe, Who is the Universe; in Whom is the Soul, Who is in the Soul, Who is the soul of Man; knowing Him—and therefore the Universe—as our Self, alone extinguishes all fear, brings an end to misery and leads to Infinite Freedom. Wherever there has been expansion in love or progress in well-being, of individuals or numbers, it has been through the perception, realisation, and the practicalisation of the Eternal Truth—THE ONENESS OF ALL BEINGS.[145]

(What is strange about the **svāmī's** formulation is that its perspective is **viśiṣṭādvaita** rather than the pure **advaita** to which the document pointed as the solution to the problem of "dualistic weakness." It is quite possible to keep the phases of the Absolute, **Saguṇa Brahman** and **Nirguṇa Brahman**, separate. This formulation could be passed over as a slip, if it were not for the significance of the Advaita Ashrama in the program of the Ramakrishna Mission. The reasons why the phases of the Absolute have been compromised in the prospectus will become more apparent after the presentation of the **svāmī's** "Practical **Vedānta**." At this point it is sufficient to note that Svāmī Vivekānanda did not maintain an unambiguous notion of the phases of **Brahman**.)

Svāmī Vivekānanda taught that the realizations of the Absolute with qualities, as the omnipotent and omniscient Personal God (**Īśvara**), must be transcended so that the last traces of dualism would be left behind and that true existence and freedom would be known.

Nirguṇa Brahman. The realization of the Absolute as **nirguṇa** (without qualities) can be formulated positively, i.e. **Nirguṇa Brahman** is **Sat-Cit-Ānanda,** but in the end all formulations must be negated. The **svāmī** expressed this distinction as follows:

> No adjective can illustrate where there is no qualification, and the Advaitist would not give Him any qualities except the three—Sat-Chit-Ānanda, Existence, Knowledge, and Bliss Absolute. This is what Shankara did. But in the Upanishads themselves you find they penetrate even further, and say, nothing can be predicated of it except Neti, Neti, "Not this, Not this."[146]

The **svāmī** began positively, teaching that **Nirguṇa Brahman** can be realized as **Oṁ Tat Sat, Sat-Cit-Ānanda**, and **Tattvamasi**. Among the **svāmī's** papers were some notes on one of the books he intended to write entitled "The Message of Divine Wisdom."[147] The third chapter intended to treat "The Absolute and the Attainment of Freedom." It began with these sketchy notes.

> 1. Om Tat Sat—that Being—Knowing—Bliss.
>
> (a) The only real Existence, which alone is—everything else exists inasmuch as it reflects that real Existence.
>
> (b) It is the only Knower—the only Self-luminous—the Light of consciousness. Everything else shines by light borrowed from It. Everything else knows inasmuch as it reflects Its Knowing.
>
> (c) It is the only Blessedness—as in It there is no want. It comprehends all—is the essence of all.[148]

The Absolute is **Sat-Cit-Ānanda,** the absolute essence of being, consciousness, and bliss. "In the Vedānta, Sat-cit-ānanda (Existence-Knowledge-Bliss) is the highest concept of God."[149] **Sat-Cit-Ānanda** are not qualities or attributes of **Brahman.** They are the essence of the Absolute.[150] In fact "there is no difference between them and the soul. And the three are one; we see the one thing in three different aspects. They are beyond all relative knowledge."[151]

Brahman is **Tattvamasi**. "That thou art" is a realization of "the Reality in me, in thee, and in everything."[152] **Brahman is advaita.** "It has no parts, no attributes, neither pleasure nor pain, nor is it matter nor mind. It is the Supreme, Infinite, Impersonal Self in everything, the Infinite Ego of the Universe."[153] Thus the logic of the doctrine of the impersonal unity is completed. "It would be illogical to go from the Personal God to the Impersonal, and at the same time to leave man as a person. So the personal man is broken down, and man as principle is built up."[154] A poem of the **svāmī**, written in a light vein, stated:

> I never taught
> Such queer thought
> That all was God—unmeaning talking!

But this I say,
Remember pray,
That God is true, all else is **nothing,**
This world's a dream
Though true it seem,
And only truth is He the living!
The real **me** is none but He,
And never, never matter changing![155]

Therefore, all positive conceptions of **Nirguṇa Brahman** are intended to end in their own denial.[156]

Negatively and quite paradoxically then, even the affirmations concerning **Nirguṇa Brahman** as **Oṁ Tat Sat, Sat-Cit-Ānanda,** and **Tattvamasi**, must be denied. The **svāmī** saw himself going beyond Śaṁkara and returning to the pure teaching of the **Upanishads**.[157] "**Sachchiddānanda** is only an approximate definition, and Neti Neti is the essential definition."[158] The absolute (**nirvikalpa**), the undivided (**akhanda**), the undifferiented (**avyakta**), the one (**eka**), the eternal (**ānandi**), the immovable (**acala**), the only witness (**sākṣi**) is beyond all conceptualization. It remains beyond all that can be conceived by the mind. It is absolutely free. Finally one must just say "**neti neti**"—not this, not this! **Nirguṇa Brahman** is **avāngmanasogocharam**, "incapable of being grasped by word and mind."[159]

Brahman is completely satisfied, wanting nothing and causing nothing.[160] There are no waves; there is only the state of **nirvāṇa.**[161] The goal of absolute freedom (**mukti**) is already attained.

Summary of Vivekānanda's Eschatology. This summary will double as a summary for the **svāmī's** eschatology as well as the "Principles of the Religion Eternal." This is possible because the eschatology combines all of the components in the pattern of ultimacy.

When viewing the pattern of ultimacy from the vantage point of the solution, one is struck by its nearly perfect relationships. If it can be granted that Svāmī Vivekānanda was slightly ambiguous in his formulations about **Saguṇa** and **Nirguṇa Brahman,** even so the solution was eventually brought to the doctrine of **neti neti**, the absolute negation of formulations about the Absolute in categories limited by space, time and causation. Thus, each component of the pattern of ultimacy points to **advaita** (non-duality) or to **eka** (oneness). The epistemology of **Sanātana Dharma** was based upon the principle of unity which was found by the **ṛṣis** and **avatāras** to be the highest principle of knowledge. By it the relative value of sensate knowledge could be determined, and from it the structure of knowledge could be deduced. Thus, only data which proved unity are real data; all else (data which suggest multiplicity) must be understood in the light of the principle of unity. The psychology analyzed the process of perception and found that behind a radical split between the individual perceivers and the perceived was the one perceiver, the **Ātman**. The cosmology determined that the multiplicity of objects of perception was only apparent and that behind this illusion was the source of all objects, **Brahman**. Finally, the eschatology established that **Ātman** and **Brahman** are one and that beyond all qualities of space, time and causation is the perfect existence, consciousness and bliss of the inexpressible. The solution in the quest for ultimate meaning finally leaps from all categories of rational and sensate processes to the experience of the Absolute in **nirvikalpa samādhi** (changeless absorption in the One).

Except for placing the **Sanātana Dharma** on the epistemological foundation of personal experience judged by the principle of unity instead of the **Vedas,** Svāmī Vivekānanda's formulation offers little that has not already appeared in Indian thought. What is novel appears when the **svāmī** applied the eternal principles to the world of space, time and causation. He has attempted to glean from the inexpressible experience of **Nirguṇa Brahman** that which would provide direction and purpose on the plane of **vivarta** (the apparent reality of the cosmos).

Practical Vedānta

What is the relationship between the realization of the Absolute in **nirvikalpa samādhi** and the activity of an individual in the world of **deśa-kāla-nimitta**? Svāmī Vivekānanda recognized that it is this relationship that defines the nature of any application of the eternal principles to existential problems.

Svāmī Vivekānanda, in analyzing the problem of applying the **Sanātana Dharma** to activity in the world, abstracted principles from the Real, and applied these principles to the changing problems of the age.

The Problem

Vedānta teaches that the only Real is **Brahman,** and that Real is realized only in **nirvikalpa samādhi,** the changeless state of consciousness of Oneness. Limited existence (as **jīva**) is suffering, brought about by ignorance (**avidyā**). Ultimately it is illusion (**māyā**). Liberation from the bonds of suffering (**mukti**) is knowledge (**jñāna**) of one's true nature as the Unmanifested, who alone is beyond all activity. Since **Vedānta** teaches that **mukti** is not in the world, why should not the seeker of **Brahman** turn from all activity in the world to a life of contemplation (**dhyāna**) of the Real? But if this is done, what benefit will **Vedānta** be for the suffering masses of India and the world? Svāmī Vivekānanda concluded:

> As I have told you, theory is very good indeed, but how are we to carry it into practice? If it be absolutely impracticable, no theory is of any value whatever, except as intellectual gymnastics. The Vedanta, therefore, as a religion must be intensely practical. We

> must be able to carry it out in every part of our lives. And not only this, the fictitious differentiation between religion and the life of the world must vanish, for the Vedanta teaches oneness—one life throughout. The ideals of religion must cover the whole field of life, they must enter into all our thoughts, and more and more into practice.[162]

Does the realization of supreme truth, which is beyond all comprehension within the categories of time, space and causation, provide the answers for what should be done in the whole field of life, especially for the problems of suffering and evil? Or stated more pointedly in terms of Indian thought, does knowledge of the Absolute lead to action in the world, or does knowledge lead to inactivity in the Absolute? The **svāmī** did not have to tackle this dilemma explicity before his American and European audiences which were largely ignorant of the intra-mural battles among Indian philosphers. However, on one occasion in India (and unfortunately few of these are recorded) he seemed to advocate the supremacy or exclusivity of liberation by **jñāna**,[163] opposing it to **karma** (work or duty in the world). The **svāmi** was challenged by a listener:

> Sir, you said just now that knowledge and work are contradictory, that in the supreme knowledge there is no room at all for work, or in other words, that by means of work the realisation of Brahman cannot be attained. Why then do you now and then speak words calculated to awaken great Rajas (activity)? You were telling me the other day, "Work, work, work—there is no other way."[164]

Svāmī Vivekānanda answered the philosophical question with a practical observation: "Going round the whole world I find that people of this country are immersed in great Tamas (Inactivity), compared with people of other countries. On the outside, there is simulation of the Sattvika (calm and balanced) state, but inside—what work will be done in the world by such people? How long can such an inactive, lazy, and sensual people live in the world?"[165] The attack was upon a confusion of spirituality and inactivity. However, the **svāmī** well knew that the **guṇa** theory, to which he also subscribed, as well as the notion of **nirvikalpa samādhi**, necessitated the cessation of **karma** (actions producing more results) at the highest level of realization.

The philosophical dilemma posed by the apparent opposition of **jñāna** and **karma** could be solved in two steps. First, **Vedānta** had shown that relative truths are levels or stages (**avasthās**) in realizing the one Truth. These stages of interpreting the **Vedānta—dvaita** (dualism), **viśiṣṭādvaita** (qualified monism) and **advaita** (monism)—are complementary, fulfilling each other as one "stepping-stone to the other until the goal, the Advaita, the Tat Tvam Asi, is reached."[166] From the strict viewpoint of **advaita,** which is the highest stage of truth, there can be no duality. There is no doer or deed; there is no desire or attraction. There is only **Brahman.** However, this viewpoint is eschatological. While in the world of multiplicity, the **jīva** must act. Even thought is activity. Thus Svāmī Vivekānanda concluded: "The highest Advaitism cannot be brought down to practical life. Advaitism made practical works from the plane of Vishishtadvaitism."[167] It is on the relative level that practical accomplishments are demanded by the needs of the age. Viewed according to the stage of **viśiṣṭādvaita**, activity is real and plans can be made for the good of all beings. Second, since activity is inevitable in the world of multiplicity, the real problem concerns the binding effects of activity (**saṁsāra**). The **Bhagavad Gītā** has properly shown that the **jīva** is only bound to the results of its action (**karma**) if it is attached to them through egotism (**ahaṁkāra**) or desire.[168] By renouncing the fruits of its action, the **jīva** will be freed of the binding effects of **karma.** "To work without motive, to work unattached, brings the highest bliss and freedom."[169] Without regard to self (**jīva**), the actions can be given in the service of the Self (**Ātman**), the totality of all beings. The discipline of activity without selfish motives can also, therefore, lead to the attainment of liberation from **deśa-kāla-nimitta.** But more important, in this age of suffering (the **kali yuga**), **karma yoga** is the means by which **Vedānta** serves practically in the world.

What is the state of the world in this age that demands that **jñāna** (knowledge of the Absolute) become practical in **karma** (activity in the world)? The **svāmī** saw deplorable conditions both in India and in the West. In India, the home of the **Sanātana Dharma,** priests had turned their knowledge into privilege (**adhikārivāda**) for their own selfish interests.[170] Their spiritual tyranny had defiled the pure religion of the **Vedas** by mixing

> the real, eternal truths and the non-sensical prejudices of the people, and thus setting up the doctrine that Lokāchāras (customs of the people) and Deshācharas (customs of the country) must be adhered to. No compromise! No whitewashing! No covering of corpses beneath flowers! Throw away such texts as "**tathāpi lokācārah** yet the customs of the people have to be followed." Nonsense! The result of this sort of compromise is that the grand truths are soon buried under heaps of rubbish, . . . and the result is that the grandest scripture of the world is now made to yield many things which lead men astray.[171]

For their own gain the priests have squandered the knowledge of the **Vedas** and have perverted it into a religion of "Don't touchism."[172] Concerned with the protection of the privileges of his caste (**varṇa**) and with avoiding pollution from outcastes (especially the pollution of their food according to the doctrine of **aśraya-dośa**), the priest and members of the "Don't touch" party cry: " 'Don't touch, don't touch!' And so the whole country has been plunged to the utmost depths of meanness, cowardise, and ignorance."[173] The knowledge of these priests consists of disputes

> which are nonsensical in their very nature. Think of the last six hundred or seven hundred years of degradation when grown-up men by hundreds have been discussing for years whether we should drink a glass of water with the right hand or the left, whether the hand should be washed three times or four times, whether we should gargle five or six times. What can you expect from men who pass their lives in discussing such momentous questions as these and writing most learned philosophies on them! There is a danger of our religion getting into the kitchen. We are neither Vedantists, most of us now, nor Pauranics, nor Tantrics. We are just "Don't-touchists." Our religion is in the kitchen. Our God is the cooking-pot, and our religion is "don't touch me, I am holy."[174]

The **svāmī's** target was the regulations of the caste system (**varṇa-dharma**), which bound the masses in a system which allowed little social advance. Customs governed with whom they could eat or be joined in marriage—in fact, every aspect of their lives. In short, the results of this tyranny of the priesthood was a loss of spirituality and the onset of the **kali yuga** with its degradations of caste, of poverty, of abuse of women, and the accompanying technological and social backwardness and moral bankruptcy.[175]

As serious as the ills of India might have been, the West that the **svāmī** returned from in 1897 was judged to be in graver straits. It was founded upon materialism. Its prosperity and pleasure would soon "degrade and degenerate" because both were founded upon "competition and merciless cruelty."[176]

> The material tyranny is tremendous. The wealth and power of a country are in the hands of a few men who do not work but manipulate the work of millions of human beings. By this power they can deluge the whole earth with blood. Religion and all things are under their feet; they rule and stand supreme. The Western world is governed by a handful of Shylocks. All those things that you hear about—constitutional government, freedom, liberty, and parliament—are jokes.... The whole of Western civilisation will crumble to pieces in the next fifty years if there is no spiritual foundation. It is hopeless and perfectly useless to govern mankind with the sword.[177]

(Some of the **svāmi's** disciples take this as a prediction of the two world wars. 1897 + 50 = 1947.)

It is not surprising, then, that when Svāmī Vivekānanda wrote the prospectus for the **Advaita Aśrama** (which was to be the strictest **advaita** institution of the Order), he would stress making the **Sanātana Dharma** practical.

> Wherever there has been expansion in love or progress in well-being, of individuals or numbers, it has been through the perception, realisation, and the practicalisation of the Eternal

Truth —THE ONENESS OF ALL BEINGS.... Here will be taught and practised nothing but the Doctrine of Unity....[178]

The Principles

Svāmī Vivekānanda analyzed the problem of the apparent opposition of **jñāna** and **karma**. He found that the previous dilemma could be solved with reference to the stages (**avasthās**) of the perception of Truth and through use of mental renunciation of the fruit of one's action. With the consequent harmonization of **jñāna** and **karma**, the eternal principles of **Vedānta** could be applied to unselfish activity.

The realization of **Brahman**, brought down to the stage of **viśiṣṭādvaita** (qualified monism), provides the basis for the practical principles needed in the limited world of **deśa-kāla-nimitta**. The apparent projection (**sṛṣṭi**) of **Brahman** can therefore be taken seriously. This multiplicity is treated as if it were **Brahman** in manifested form and as if it can return to **Brahman** through its collective efforts. According to the **svāmī**, that is precisely the meaning of **karma**. Each person's destiny is controlled by "the fruits of what you yourselves worked for...."[179] The resources for help are within each person.[180] That which is within each person is the oneness of all beings. This realization provides the motivation for activity in the world. Underlying all this diversity is unity. This knowledge of the essential unity of all diversity is joined with the eschatological view of **Vedānta** that all diversity ends in unity. Thus, knowing the goal as unity, the **karma yogi** (worker for the good of others) can use the principle of oneness to judge all actions.

> To be able to use what we call Viveka (discrimination), to learn how in every moment of our lives, in every one of our actions, to discriminate between what is right and wrong, true or false, we shall have to know the test of truth, which is purity, oneness. Everything that makes for oneness is truth. Love is truth, and hatred is false, because hatred makes for multiplicity. . . .Therefore in all our actions we have to judge whether it is making for diversity or for oneness. If for diversity we have to give it up, but if it makes for oneness we are sure it is good.[181]

Svāmī Vivekānanda offered a number of corollaries to the major principle of practical **Vedānta, eka** (oneness). First, faith in the true Self (**Ātman**) teaches the divinity of man.

> In one word, the ideal of Vedānta is to know man as he really is, and this is its message, that if you cannot worship your brother man, the manifested God, how can you worship a God who is unmanifested?[182]

The oneness of all beings and the divinity of man leads directly to the second corollary—the strength within. Weakness connotes ignorance of one's true identity. Thus, all dualistic notions and activities will weaken, while monistic ones will strengthen because they point to the source of power within.[183] That is why **Vedānta** is called **puruṣakāra**, "manly endeavour."[184] **Vedānta** is a "man-making" religion since it teaches reliance upon the sources within and not upon help from above. Yet that source within is the oneness of all beings.[185] The last two corollaries are "extensity with intensity (universality without the loss of the faithfulness found in particularity)"[186] and "universal love."[187] Taken all together the principles of practical **Vedānta** include oneness, faith in the **Ātman**, strength, extensity with intensity, and universal love. Svāmī Vivekānanda was now armed with the principles necessary for "the practicalisation of the Eternal Truth—THE ONENESS OF ALL BEINGS."

The Plan

Svāmī Vivekānanda's plan of action involved all of life in the world. Therein practical **Vedānta** can both harmonize and revolutionize. It can produce "the new order of society."[188] It "can change the whole tendency of the world" by putting the forces which have become destructive in check.[189] Previous societies have been founded either on religion ("spirituality") or on social necessity ("materialism").[190] Both types of social life have become victims of the "exclusive claims" which have left power and privilege in the hands of a tyrannical few.[191] And both types of tyranny are headed fo their own destruction. Practical **Vedānta** can put society into a proper balance by applying its principles to life in the world.

The means of bringing in the new order is as important as the end. The end does not justify the means; that is fanaticism and tyranny. Social reform to remove tyranny is not achieved by tyranny. The few cannot dictate how others are to be reformed.

> The history of the world teaches us that wherever there have been fanatical reforms, the only result has been that they have defeated their own ends. No greater upheaval for the establishment of right and liberty can be imagined than the war for the abolition of slavery in America. You all know about it. What has been its results? The slaves are a hundred times worse off today than they were before the abolition. Before the abolition, these poor negroes were the property of somebody, and, as properties, they had to be looked after, so that they might not deteriorate. Today they are the property of nobody. Their lives are of no value; they are burnt alive on mere pretenses. They are shot down without any law for their

> murderers; for they are niggers; they are not human beings, they are not even animals; and that is the effect of such violent taking away of evil by law or by fanaticism. Such is the testimony of history against every fanatical movement, even for doing good.[192]

Attempting to dispose of evil by the external forces of law or of fanaticism (spiritual tyranny based on the authority of some scripture) will only end in failure by producing the grounds for more evil. Reform from without cannot bring the reform that is needed within.[193] Evil has been caused by limitation of the real Self, and the legislations of spiritual or materialistic societies cannot bring lasting and, therefore, radical reform.[194]

> The Vedantist says, the cause of all that is apparently evil is the limitation of the unlimited. The love which gets limited into little channels and seems to be evil eventually comes out at the other end and manifests itself as God. The Vedanta also says that the cause of all this apparent evil is in ourselves.[195]

For this reason true reform involves education—educating the masses concerning their true nature and the strength that lies within.[196]

Consequently, Svāmī Vivekānanda began his radical reform with education for the masses and constantly distinguished this reform from all others.[197]

Education for Unity. "Our work is to arouse knowledge of the real Self within in the masses."[198] Ignorance of the real Self within has brought weakness, suffering and evil.[199] Education about the potentiality within man will reverse the process of deterioration and begin the process of expansion toward men's true nature. The process of growth gradually develops the powers within until "Brahminhood" is reached.[200]

"Liberty is the first conditon of growth."[201] Society is not to be brought under another tyranny directed from above or beyond the self. Practical **Vedānta** does not come to rule by dictating what must be done. It comes only to serve by awakening knowledge of the real Self within.[202]

> The only service to be done for our lower classes is to give them education, **to develop their lost individuality.** That is the great task between our people and princes. Up to now nothing has been done in that direction. Priest-power and foreign conquest have trodden them down for centuries, and at last the poor of India have forgotten that they are human beings. They are to be given ideas; their eyes are to be opened to what is going on in the world around them; and then they will work out their own salvation. Every nation, every man, and every woman must work out their own salvation. Give them ideas—that is the only help they require, and then the rest must follow as the effect.[203]

Svāmī Vivekānanda tried to break the hold of superstition and "priestcraft" upon the masses by revealing the difference between customs and beliefs which are helpful under certain conditions and the eternal principles which alone apply to all conditions. These eternal principles are not the scriptures as such. While the eternal **Vedas** are absolute truth and therefore inerrant, the **Vedas** which have been written down are in the realm of relative knowledge bound by **deśa-kāla-nimitta.** The relative **Vedas** are a composite of two kinds of materials—**Karma Kānda** and **Jñāna Kānda.** The former deals with sacrificial and ceremonial methods which have already been discarded after the social conditons have changed from the particular age for which the **Karma Kānda** was intended. The **Jñāna Kānda** (or **Vedānta,** the end of the **Vedas**) is comprised of the **Upaniṣads**. But even they are not a body of scripture without change. The texts and the various schools of interpretation applied to them reflect the fact of the evolution of the perception of the Truth.[204] That is why each passage of scripture must be judged by the hermeneutical principle of reason—unity.[205] Reason as unity should be followed rather than any external authority, and that includes even the scriptures. The **svāmī** stated: "I believe in reason and follow reason having seen enough of the evils of authority, for I was born in a country where they have gone to the extreme of authority."[206] If there is any doubt about a scripture, a custom or a practice, Truth will be served by following unity, which leads to growth, strength and progress. Yet the best commentary of practical **Vedānta** is the **Bhagavad Gītā.**[207] Judged by reason (oneness, **eka**), the "Upanishads and the Gītā are the true scriptures," while the "Smritis and the Puranas are the productions of men of limited intelligence and are full of fallacies, errors, the feelings of class and malice. Only parts of them breathing broadness of spirit and love are acceptable, the rest are to be rejected."[208]

Once all scriptures are submitted to the principle of unity and the masses become aware that there is an evolution of ideas and practices in them toward unity, then the strangle hold of weakening superstitions and demeaning customs can be broken. The **svāmī** argued:

> I disagree with all those who are giving their superstitions back to my people. Like the Egyptologist's interest in Egypt, it is easy to feel an interest in India that is purely selfish. One may desire to see again the India of one's books, one's studies, one's dreams. **My** hope is to see again the strong points of that India, reinforced by the strong points of this age, only in a natural way. The new stage of things must be a **growth** from within.[209]

Neither relative scriptures, priests, nor foreign scholars are to be allowed to delude the masses with superstitions and customs which prevent the awakening of the strength of oneness which lies within them.

The education of the masses must begin where they are. The methods or religion of renunciation must not be forced upon them.

> Hitherto the great fault of our Indian religion has lain in its knowing only two words: renunciation and Mukti. Only Mukti here! Nothing for the householder! But these are the very people whom I want to help. For are not all souls of the same quality? Is not the goal of all the same? And so strength must come to the nation through education.[210]

First, the hungry are to be fed.[211] Then they must "have enough luxuries to enable them to enjoy life a little; and then gradually, true Vairāgya (dispassion) will come, and they will be fit and ready to realise religion in life."[212] One cannot know the true value of the material world and its folly until one has experienced it.[213] For this reason, India first needs scientific and material knowledge to raise its masses.[214] This must be obtained from the West. But the West needs India's spirituality as badly as India needs Western learning, so the exchange will be mutual.[215] And during this period of education and of great material activity, the masses must have adequate nourishment.

> About vegetarian diet I have to say this—first, my Master was a vegetarian; but if he was given meat offered to the Goddess, he used to hold it up to his head. The taking of life is undoubtedly sinful; but so long as vegetable food is not made suitable to the human system through progress in chemistry, there is no other alternative but meat-eating. So long as man shall have to live a Rājasika (active) life under circumstances like the present, there is no other way except through meat-eating . . .but the forcing of vegetarianism upon those who have to earn their bread by labouring day and night is one of the causes of the loss of our national freedom. Japan is an example of what good and nourishing food can do.[216]

Trained in the fiery **mantras** of the **Upaniṣads** and in the principles of practical **Vedānta,** the masses will be awakened to their strength. The radical reform of society, based upon a harmony of science and **Vedānta,** will have begun. Each man, woman and child will grow according to their own nature; none will need to rule them. The **svāmī** concluded: "They will solve their own problems. O tyrants, attempting to think that you can do anything for any one! Hands off! The Divine will look after all. Who are you to assume that you know everything?"[217]

Ethics of Unity. "The lessons of mildness, gentleness, forbearance, toleration, sympathy, and brotherhood, everyone may learn, whether man, woman, or child."[218] Svāmī Vivekānanda taught that there was a universal foundation for ethical standards. Not only did all religions point toward this foundation, but also all peoples could use it as the basis for judging their activity in the world.

> Taoists, Confucianists, Buddhists, Hindus, Jews, Mohammedans, Christians, and Zoroastrians, all preached the golden

> rule and in almost the same words; but only the Hindus have given the rationale, because they saw the reason: Man must love others because those others are himself. There is but One.[219]

Only **advaita** philosophy knows that all concern for others is founded "in the idea of the Impersonal God; you understand it when you learn that the whole world is one—the oneness of the universe—the solidarity of all life—that in hurting any one I am hurting myself, in loving any one I am loving myself."[220] Knowledge of the solidarity of the entire universe creates true brotherhood.[221] But **Vedānta** teaches more than mere brotherhood; it teaches "the solidarity of all life."[222] For these reasons the **svāmī** stated emphatically that

> . . .Advaita and Advaita alone explains morality. Every religion preaches that the essence of all morality is to do good to others. And why? Be unselfish. And why should I? Some God has said it? He is not for me. Some texts have declared it? Let them; that is nothing to me; let them all tell it. And if they do, what is it to me? Each one for himself, and somebody take the hindermost —that is all the morality in the world, at least with many. What is the reason that I should be moral? You cannot explain it except when you come to know the truth as given in the Gita: "He who sees everyone in himself, and himself in everyone, thus seeing the same God living in all, he, the sage, no more kills the Self by the self." Know through Advaita that whomsoever you hurt, you hurt yourself; they are all you.[223]

The ethics of unity are applicable for all people. Whenever anyone is unselfishly doing good for others, he is, consciously or unconsciously, acting in accord with practical **Vedānta**. The ethics of unity are not a body of rules and regulations but consist of principle for unselfish living. The twin principles, **vairāgya** (renunciation) and **jīvansevā** (service to all beings),[224] provide the basis for all activity in the world. They teach mankind to discover "their divinity, and how to make it manifest in every movement of life."[225]

Vairāgya is the giving up of all desires because of one's realization that pleasure in the world is finite, limited, and fleeting. It is self-abnegation (negation of individuality, **jīva**) and unselfishness. "Neither through wealth, nor through progeny, but by giving up alone immortality is reached," says the scripture.[226] This renunciation of the fruits of one's activity leads to freedom (**mukti**). One works and loves mankind without any desire for gain.

> A great landmark in the history of religion is here, the ideal of love for love's sake, work for work's sake, duty for duty's sake, and it for the first time fell from the lips of the greatest of Incarnations, Krishna, and for the first time in the history of humanity, upon the soil of India. The religions of fear and of temptations were gone forever, and in spite

> of the fear of hell and temptations of enjoyment in heaven, came the grandest of ideals, love for love's sake, duty for duty's sake, work for work's sake.[227]

Thus **vairāgya** leads to **seva** (service), without any desire on the part of the server that he benefit by his actions. The man who has renounced the effects of his actions "alone will have seen the real motive of doing good to others...."[228] The attutude is extremely important. "Look upon every man, woman, and every one as God. You cannot help anyone, you can only serve: serve the children of the Lord, serve the Lord Himself, if you have the privilege."[229] In this way **jīvansevā** purifies the mind and leads indirectly to **mukti.**[230] "Doing good to others out of compassion is good, but the Seva (service) of all beings in the spirit of the Lord is better."[231] **Sevā** should be without motive, or at the lower levels of **bhakti** (devotion) it should be dedicated to God (**Īśvara**). This "service for the good of others" awakens the powers within and becomes a means to **jīvanmukti.**[232]

But service for the good of others is also the activity of the **jīvanmukta** who

> sees the Self in all beings and in that consciousness devotes himself to service, so that any Karma that was yet left to be worked out through the body may exhaust itself. It is this state which has been described by the authors of the Shāstras (scriptures) as Jivanmukti, "Freedom while living."[233]

The **sevā** and **dayā** (doing good to others without any gain to oneself) of the **jīvanmukta** benefits others as **dānas** (gifts).

> What is meant by Dāna? The highest of gifts is the giving of spiritual knowledge, and the next is the saving of life, the last is giving food and drink. He who gives spiritual knowledge, saves the soul from many and many a birth. He who gives secular knowledge opens the eyes of human beings towards spiritual knowledge, and far below these rank all other gifts, even the saving of life. Therefore it is necessary that you learn this and note that all other kinds of work are of much less value than that of imparting spiritual knowledge.[234]

In this way the perfected soul, rather than retreating from the world in meditation, works for the good of others.

Besides the ethics of unity which are the principles for all unselfish action in the world, even to motivating perfected souls into activity for others, there is also in the teachings of Svāmī Vivekānanda an ethic of introspection for that stage of realization in which all mind-functions have been arrested and work ceases. Practical activity in the world, he has said, is not at the highest levels of **advaita** but at **viśiṣṭādvaita.**[235] But this ethic, while being for perfected souls in just ages (**yugas**) is not helpful when the world is suffering in the **kali yuga.**

Unity of All Paths. Because of the tendencies (**saṁskāras**) acquired by past **karma**, each person has his own spiritual nature and needs. Depending upon which of the **guṇas** (types of energy) predominates—**tamas** (inactivity), **rajas** (activity), or **sattva** (balance, equilibrium), particular religious capacities develop.

> Past lives have moulded our tendencies; give to the taught in accordance with his tendency. Intellectual, mystical, devotional, practical—make one the basis, but teach the others with it. Intellect must be balanced with love, the mystical nature with reason, while practice must form part of every method. Take every one where he stands and push him forward. Religious teaching must always be constructive, not destructive.
>
> Each tendency shows the life-work of the past, the line or radius along which that man must move. All radii lead to the centre. Never even attempt to disturb any one's tendencies; to do that puts back both teacher and taught.[236]

Svāmī Vivekānanda believed that **Vedānta** was the only religion that recognized that the religious capacities of man vary according to the tendencies.

The religious capacity of an individual must be channeled into the proper method or path (**yoga**). This allows each one to develop according to his "Svadharma, that is, one's own Dharma, or set of duties prescribed for man according to his capacity and position...."[237] But while the **yogas** offer diversity in the methods and preliminary goals, they are one in their ultimate goal, the realization of **Brahman.** Each **yoga** is "only a method leading indirectly to the realisation of the Absolute" and is not the goal itself.[238]

> The ultimate goal of all mankind, the aim and end of all religions, is but one—re-union with God, or, what amounts to the same, with the divinity which is every man's true nature. But while the aim is one, the method of attaining may vary with the different temperaments of men.
>
> Both the goal and the methods employed for reaching it are called Yoga, a word derived from the same Sanskrit root as the English "yoke," meaning "to join," to join us to our reality, God. There are various such Yogas, or methods of union—but the chief ones are—Karma-Yoga, Bhakti-Yoga, Rāja-Yoga, and Jnāna-Yoga.[239]

Svāmī Vivekānanda introduced his Western disciples to these **yogas** in a different order. **Rāja yoga** was first, followed by **karma, bhakti** and **jñāna yogas.** The **svāmī** found that each **yoga** began as diverse but ended in the One.

Rāja yoga as taught by Svāmī Vivekānanda is the typical method which develops **siddhis** (powers) to control the mind for the realization of **Brahman.** Of course this **yoga** adopts Hindu psychology's three levels of consciousness; subconsciousness, consciousness, and superconsciousness. The search for the Real turns inward. Direct perception of the Real is sought. Practice in control of the sense-producing organs **(indriyas)** leads to an experiental understanding of the process of "the very foundations of his mind, and it will be under his perfect control."[240] Different miraculous powers will come to the **yogi**, but if he is strong enough to reject them "he will attain to the goal of Yoga, the complete suppression of the waves in the ocean of the mind."[241] Having reached **samādhi**, real religion will have begun.

> Then the glory of the soul, undisturbed by the distractions of the mind, or motions of the body, will shine in its full effulgence; and the Yogi will find himself as he is and as he always was, the essence of knowledge, the immortal, the all-pervading.[242]

Rāja yoga will have brought one past the acquisition of **siddhis** to a realization of the Self.

> Each one of the steps to attain Samadhi has been reasoned out, properly adjusted, scientifically organised, and, when faithfully practised, will surely lead us to the desired end. Then will all sorrows cease, all miseries vanish; the seeds for actions will be burnt, and the soul will be free for ever.[243]

Karma yoga is the method of work by which one realizes "his own divinity through works and duty."[244] The word **karma** comes from the Sanskrit **kṛ** (to do) and should be taken in the sense of "work."[245] Since the goal of mankind is true knowledge and since knowledge "is inherent in man," work can be used to remove the veil of ignorance in a "process of uncovering."[246] The eternal law of **karma** teaches that

> We are responsible for what we are; and whatever we wish ourselves to be, we have the power to make ourselves. If what we are now has been the result of our own past actions, it certainly follows that whatever we wish to be in future can be produced by our present actions; so we have to know how to act.[247]

Since there can be no activity without a motive and since every action produces either good or bad **karma**, the secret of work is to renounce the fruits of work. When one is detached from one's action, the binding effects of that action are escaped. One becomes detached from the fruits of labor by working for others. There are three kinds of helping others: spiritual, intellectual, and physical, ranked in the order of the greatest help rendered.[248] "This is the one central idea in the Gita: work incessantly, but be not attached to it."[249] Purifying oneself in work, one learns self-abnegation—"Thy will be done."[250] "Unselfishness is God."[251] By giving up all attachments, the bondage of the law of cause and effect is broken.[252] Through complete unselfishness the self expands into the Absolute Self.[253] Buddha "is the ideal Karma-Yogi, acting entirely without motive, and the history of humanity shows him to have been the greatest man ever born...."[254] Thus, **karma yoga** is a "direct and independent means for the attainment of Moksha."[255]

Bhakti yoga as taught by the **svāmī** is the devotional method which manifests the true Self through devotion to a personal deity.

> The one great advantage of Bhakti is that it is the easiest and most natural way to reach the great divine end in view; its great disadvantage is that in its lower form it oftentimes degenerates into hideous fanaticism. The fanatical crew in Hinduism, or Mohammedanism, or Christianity, have always been almost exclusively recruited from these worshippers on the lower planes of Bhakti. That singleness of attachment (Nishthā) to a loved object, without which no genuine love can grow, is very often also the cause of the denunciation of everything else. All the weak and undeveloped minds in every religion or country have only one way of loving their own ideal, i.e. by hating every other ideal. [256]

There are two stages of **bhakti yoga: Gauni bhakti** (lower or preparatory devotion) and **Parā bhakti** (supreme devotion). **Gauni bhakti** "is a series or succession of mental efforts at religious realisation beginning with ordinary worship and ending in a supreme intensity of love for Ishvara."[257] **Īśvara** is the highest manifestation of Brahman, the unmanifested, and comes as a Personal God. **Gauni bhakti** provides many concrete helps for devotion—"mythological and symbological" pointers.[258] Each **Bhakta** (devotee) needs a **guru.** The **guru** knows "the spirit of the scriptures," is sinless, teaches out of love, and knows **Brahman.**[259] Higher than the **gurus** of **Īśvara** are the **avatāras.** "No man can really see God except through these human manifestations."[260] **Mantras**, images or substitutes (**pratimās** or **pratikas**), rituals, discrimination about food, control of the passions, and **ahiṁsā** (non-injury) are means of devotion of the lower stage. **Parā bhakti** is entered through renunciation. This renunciation leaves everything for the love of God. "Forms vanish, rituals fly away, books are superseded; images, temples, churches, religions and sects, countries and nationalities—all these limitations and bondages fall off by their own nature from him who knows this love of God."[261] His only attachment (**anurāga**) is to God.[262] This love manifests itself in reverence, **priti** (pleasure in God), **viraha** (intense misery due to the absence of the beloved), and **Tadiyatā** ("his-ness," the state of everything being sacred.[263] "The Bhakta wishes to realise that one generalised abstract Person, in loving whom he loves the whole universe."[264] The result of the universal love is **aprātikulya,** "the conviction that nothing that happens is against us."[265] In this state there is an "eternal sacrifice of the self unto the Beloved Lord" in which the self has no interests and "knows nothing that is opposed to it."[266] The human attempts to express this inexpressible experience of divine love, starting with the lowest form of **Parā bhakti, śānta. Śānta bhakti** is the peaceful devotion which has gone beyond forms and symbols but has not reached the first stages of madness for God.[267] Then follows **dāsya** (servantship),

sakhya friendship), **vātsalya** (loving God as one's child), and **madhura** (loving God as one's husband).[268]

> When this highest ideal of love is reached, philosophy is thrown away; who will then care for it? Freedom, Salvation, Nirvāna—all are thrown away; who cares to become free while in the enjoyment of divine love? ...To him God exists as all these, and the last point of his progress is reached when he feels that he has become absolutely merged in the object of his worship. We all begin with love for ourselves, and the unfair claims of the little self make even love selfish. At last, however, comes the full blaze of light, in which this little self is seen to have become one with the Infinite. Man himself is transfigured in the presence of this Light of Love, and he realises at last the beautiful and inspiring truth that Love, the Lover, and the Beloved are One.[269]

Jñāna yoga is the intellectual method which follows the path of knowledge to the realization of **Brahman.** "First, meditation should be of a negative nature. Think away everything."[270] The aspirant accomplishes this by practicing the following: **śama** (not allowing the mind to externalize), **dama** (checking the external instruments—the eyes, et cetera), **uparati** (not thinking of sense-object), **titikṣā** (forbearance—"Resist not evil"), **samādhāna** (constantly practicing, "holding the mind in God"), **mumukṣutva** (intense desire to be free), and **nityānitya-viveka** (discriminating between the true and the untrue).[271] This method of withdrawing from all sense-knowledge is necessary because "religion is beyond our senses, beyond even our consciousness."[272] The search for the absolute has led the aspirant to total renunciation (**vairāgya**).

> The Jnāna-Yogi has the harshest of all renunciation to go through, as he has to realise from the very first that the whole of this solid-looking nature is all an illusion. He has to know from the very start that all knowledge and all experience are in the soul and not in nature; so he has at once and by the sheer force of rational conviction to tear himself away from all bondage to nature. He lets nature and all that belongs to her go, he lets them vanish and tries to stand alone![273]

He practices "perfect self-abnegation," no longer having any idea of "me and mine" (**ahaṁkāra** and **mamatā**).[274] Then the **jñāni** is ready to realize his true nature, having escaped the bondage of **māyā**. In **samādhi** (objectless meditation) the true identity of the soul as **Brahman** is known. A special meditation is given as follows:

> Above, it is full of me; below, it is full of me; in the middle, it is full of me. I am in all beings, and all beings

> are in me. Om Tat Sat, I am It. I am existence above mind. I am the one Spirit of the universe. I am neither pleasure nor pain.
>
> The body drinks, eats, and so on. I am not the body. I am not mind. I am He.
>
> I am the witness. I look on. When health comes I am the witness. When disease comes I am the witness.
>
> I am Existence, Knowledge, Bliss.
>
> I am the essence and nectar of knowledge. Through eternity I change not. I am calm, resplendent, and unchanging.[275]

When this has been realized, the **jñāni** becomes a **jīvanmukta,** one no longer bound by **māyā**. "Then you will know the Truth because you have become the Truth."[276] **Jñāna** is the "creedless" path; by it one achieves direct experience of the Truth.[277]

The four **yogas** may be pursued singly,[278] together in a "harmonious development,"[279] or one after the other "through all the lower stages to reach the highest."[280] Some take longer than others.[281] **Vedānta** teaches "that we not only have to live the life of all past humanity, but also the future life of all humanity. The man who does the first is the educated man, the second is the Jivanmukta, for ever free (even while living)."[282] Thus, all the paths reach the ultimate goal, unity in **Brahman**.[283] "Jnāna, Bhakti, Yoga, and Karma—these are the four paths which lead to salvation. One must follow the path for which one is best suited; but in this age special stress should be laid on Karma-Yoga."[284]

The Unity of All Religions. All religions are but manifestations of the one eternal religion, the **Sanātana Dharma**. "Religion consists solely in realisation. Doctrines are methods, not religion. All the different religions are but applications of the one religion adapted to suit the requirements of different nations."[285] A Hindu hymn celebrates this fact:

> As the different streams having their sources in different places all mingle their water in the sea, so O Lord, the different tendencies, various though they appear, crooked or straight, all lead to Thee.[286]

Svāmī Vivekānanda held that "Comparative Religion" reveals that all religions reflect the evolution of the idea of God and of the soul. At the first stage of this evolution all religions taught the "eternity of the soul," that it was perfect and without beginning or end.[287] "Closely connected with these ideas is the doctrine—which was universal before the Europeans mutilated it—the doctrine of reincarnation."[288] They worshipped their ancestors and nature.[289] As men struggled "to transcend the limitations of the senses," the idea of God and of the soul expanded.[290] At the second stage, then, the ideas, which had been vague and diffuse, were shaped by a dualistic notion of a Personal God and many little souls.[291] Forms, symbols and dogmas were used at this stage. God was no longer a nature force or an ancestor but a tribal deity, often lifted above the universe to cosmic dimensions. At the highest stage of evolution all doctrines and dogmas are transcended in the monistic realization of "God in the soul."[292]

> The end of all religions is the realising of God in the soul. That is the one universal religion. If there is one universal truth in all religions, I place it here—in realising God. Ideals and methods may differ, but that is the central point. There may be a thousand different radii, but they all converge to the one centre, and that is the realisation of God: something behind this world of sense, this world of eternal eating and drinking and talking nonsense, this world of false shadows and selfishness.[293]

This evolution of the soul toward self-knowledge produced both weaknesses and strengths. The religions themselves can be typed as religions of fear and temptation—with doctrines about hell, religions of reward—with their shopkeeping ("I give you something; O Lord, you give me something in return"), and religions of love.[294] Dualistic religions like Christianity and Mohammedanism" are often fanatical, their followers believing their view to be the only true one.[295]

> Christianity is built upon the life of Jesus Christ, Mohammedanism upon Mohammed, Buddhism upon Buddha, Jainism upon the Jinas, and so on. It naturally follows that there must be in all these religions a good deal of fight about what they call the historical evidences of these great personalities.[296]

In fact, a great deal of misunderstanding has occurred about their teachings. The followers, who were operating at a lower stage of spirituality, usually distorted their masters' teachings. Some of Christ's teachings, for instance, were dualistic—"our Father who art in heaven." These were for the multitudes. However, his realization of his divinity as testified in the saying, "I and the Father are one," shows that his true message, properly understood, is the same as **advaita**.[297] He even taught reincarnation—"Before Abraham was, I am"—but was not understood.[298] Similarly, the Buddha was not properly understood by his disciples. They quickly perverted his pure teachings.

> The real Buddhism, I once thought, would yet do **much good**. But I have given up the idea entirely, and I clearly see the reason why Buddhism was driven out of India, and we will only be too glad if the Ceylonese carry off the remnant of this religion with its hideous idols and licentious rites.[299]

Thus, the great faith of the founder of a religion may degenerate in the hands of his followers into bigotry, fanaticism, and sectarianism.[300] The disciples were not able to distinguish the eternal principles discovered by the person from the (small) personality, thus distorting the personality and the ideas.[301]

Yet, Śrī Rāmakṛṣṇa discovered in all the religions an essential unity.[302] "In all religions the superconscious state is identical. Hindus, Christians, Mohammedans, Buddhists, and even those of no creed, all have the very same experience when they transcend the body."[303] **Vedānta** affirms that

> each one must have his own path, but the path is not the goal. The worship of a God in heaven and all these things are not bad, they are only steps towards the Truth and not the Truth itself. They are good and beautiful, and some wonderful ideas are there, but Vedanta says at every point, "My friend, Him whom you are worshipping as unknown and are seeking for, throughout the universe, has been with you all the time. You are living through Him, and He is the Eternal Witness of the universe."[304]

Despite the fact that the religions are but paths to the Truth, they are nevertheless important because they represent the cumulative effort of a race or nation in its striving toward the One. The particular contributions of the religions need to be assimilated in the future religion of mankind: the kingdom of God from Christianity, brotherhood from Mohammadanism (Islam), service for others from Buddhism, and spirituality from Hinduism.[305]

The Expectations for the Future of Unity. Svāmī Vivekānanda believed that the preaching of the **Vedānta** in all its phases would bring in the Golden Age, the **satya yuga** (age of truth). This world was now in the **kali yuga,** its darkest period of spirituality. Yet there were signs that the cycle was about to turn around. One of these was the coming of Śri Rāmakṛṣṇa Paramahaṁsa. In 1894 the **svāmī** proclaimed: "I believe that the Satya Yuga (Golden Age) will come when there will be one caste, one Veda, and peace and harmony. This idea of Satya Yuga is what would revivify India. Believe it."[306] When he first returned to India in 1897 he announced: "This cycle is turning round now, and I draw your attention to this fact."[307]

Besides this belief in the imminent approach of the Golden Age, the **svāmī** had a grand vision for the future of India and the world. He believed that practical **Vedānta's** principle of unity would create a new India. He saw the masses being liberated from dualistic customs and superstitions.[308] **Advaita** had never been allowed to come to the people. Now that it will come to them, the impersonal idea will gradually take "away all trade from the priests, churches, and temples."[309] True knowledge of the Self will gradually raise all to "Brahminhood."[310] The original nature of **varṇadharma** (division of society into four classes) will be recovered. All will become priests in their knowledge of the Self, the only Real. Outcastes and converts to Christianity and "Mohammadanism" will be won back to Indian spirituality.[311] The four classes (teachers, administrators, merchants, workers) will become functions in society, filled according to ability, not birth.[312] Caste privilege will have no place.[313] Intermarriage will strengthen the race.[314] Knowledge will "eliminate competition, both from the function of acquiring physical sustenance and of acquiring a mate."[315] Women will have the liberty to solve their own problems (education, child marriage, widow marriage, and social restrictions).[316] The masses will be taught the greatness of Indian culture in both Sanskrit and the vernaculars.[317] Western science and Indian spirituality will come together in a "life-building, man-making, character-making assimilation of ideas."[318] India will awaken and will recover its national tendency to lead the world through spirituality.[319]

The future of unity, according to the **svāmī**, will have a similar effect upon the world. Unlike the dualistic religions which are in conflict with modern science, **Vedānta** will assimilate this scientific knowledge through the rationale in the One.[320] **Vedānta** will guide in racial assimilation through universal toleration and brotherhood.[321] But most important, it will bring about the assimilation of all the religious achievements of mankind.

> As the human mind broadens, its spiritual steps broaden too. The time has already come when a man cannot record a thought without its reaching to all corners of the earth; by merely physical means, we have come into touch with the whole world; so the future religions of the world have to become as universal as wide.
>
> The religious ideals of the future must embrace all that exists in the world and is good and great, and, at the same time, have infinite scope for future development. All that was good in the past must be preserved; and the doors must be kept open for future additions to the already existing store. Religions must also be inclusive, and not look down with contempt upon one another, because their particular ideals of God are different.[322]

All sects will be allowed to live, for "Variation is the sign of life, and it must be there."[323] Yet there will be no sectarianism—the attitude that a particular sect has the whole Truth. "I believe that they are not contradictory; they are supplementary. Each religion, as it were, takes up one part of the great universal truth, and spends its whole force in embodying and typifying that part of the great truth."[324] So it can be said "that all these religions are different forces in the economy of God, working for the good of mankind....''[325] **Vedānta** not only accepts all the embodiments as parts of the truth, it also allows for all the religious types of men—the worker (**karma-yogi**), the emotional (**bhakti-yogi**), the mystic (**rāja-yogi**), and the philosopher (**jñāna-yogi**).[326] A universal religion must be ''equally acceptable to all minds; it must be equally philosophic, equally emotional, equally mystic, and equally conductive to action.''[327] **Vedānta** is the ''essence of all religions.''[328]

Able to assimilate the entire spiritual pilgrimage of mankind, **Vedānta** will be able to provide a rationale for being religious in the modern world.[329] In its spiritual bankruptcy, the West will turn to **Vedānta** and will be saved by ''the religion of the Upanishads.''[330] It will change ''the whole tendency of the world,'' bringing in the **satya yuga.**[331]

CHAPTER VI*

THE PLACE OF SVĀMĪ VIVEKĀNANDA IN THE RELIGIOUS HISTORY OF INDIA

> To the Hindu, man is not travelling from error to truth, but from truth to truth from lower to higher truth. To him all the religions, from the lowest fetishism to the highest absolutism mean so many attempts of the human soul to grasp and realize the infinite, each determined by the conditions of its birth and association, and each of these marks a stage of progress; and every soul is a young eagle soaring higher and higher, gathering more and more strength till it reaches the Glorious Sun.
>
> —Svāmī Vivekānanda, Chicago, 1893 [1]

The great motifs that were to be central in Svāmī Vivekānanda's quest for meaning rested as the lotus upon the primal ocean giving cataclysmic birth to a new age. The external events were not unrelated to his interiorization of this quest for meaning that knew both belief and doubt. They converged in intricate patterns of insight about that which could ultimately lay claim to life with the promise of joy and fulfillment or the requirement of sacrifice and suffering. But these patterns never captured the toality of meaning. His finite experience and conceptualizations touched upon the infinite but were as often burned crisp and dry by its fire. His quest, at least a popularized version of it, was to become the religious paradigm for millions of Indians. But its context was the personal nexus between dialectical contradictories as meaning and absurdity, life and death, infinite and finite, eternal and temporal. The dynamic character of personally appropriated meaning is that the nexus is maintained by the one who perceives. It is the decision "to make life meaningful for me" that transforms the givenness of existence into purposeful becoming. Each pattern of ultimacy held Vivekānanda's commitment only until a richer apperception became a new focus for ultimate concern.

Svāmī Vivekānanda's spiritual quest was not unique in the religious history of India. Spiritual giants like Rāmmohan Roy (1772-1883), Debendranath Tāgore (1817-1905), Keshab Chandra Sen

*This final chapter is evaluative and therefore introduces "outside" norms into the study. It should be viewed as a subjective postscript to a descriptive study.

(1838-1884), and Dayānanda Sarasvatī (1824-1883) already had faced the task of finding a viable religious perspective that would both affirm what was true of India's past but also make room for modern knowledge ("science") and greater ethical sensivity (developing a social concern for India's oppressed masses at least as deep as the one brought by Christian missionaries).

The difference in perspective with those who had led the reform for three-quarters of a century was inclusion of the entire Indian religious tradition. Previously, the humiliation of being "Indian" was made worse by that of being "Hindu." "Hinduism" had not yet been defended against pejorative associations deriving from the assumption that its social ills sprang from the evil soil of its religion. As a society that did not separate its religion from civil affairs Hindu social order was blamed for **sati** (widow-burning), **devadāsis** (temple prostitutes), marriage of girls before puberty, polygamy, idolatry, the caste system with its inhumane treatment of the outcastes, and numerous "Hindu" superstitutions and practices such as child-sacrifice to the turtles of the Ganges or human-sacrifice by **thagis** or sexual perversions (**vāmācari tantra**) justified as religious worship.

The Modern Period of Indian history is said to have begun in 1815 when Rāmmohan Roy initiated the reform movement that would transform Indian society. Yet the reformers of the **Brāhmo Samāj** like Rāmmohan implicity, if not explicitly, attacked Indian religious traditions as inferior and in decline. They argued against ritualized, externalized religious practice—"Hindu" orthopraxis. Their thinly-veiled Christian unitarianism and humanism substituted a more intellectualized belief system and its personal **Brahman** for what they perceived as idolatry and polytheism. They achieved a conjunction of new meanings and purpose for their small segment of society. But their interests in modern civilization and **their** place in it was far removed from the masses rooted in the Indian soil and identified with its symbols.

The right wing of the revitalization of Indian religious traditions was led by Svāmī Dayānanda Sarasvati. His slogan was "back to the **Vedas**." His pride in India's religious past was exhilarating but short-lived. The narrowness of his **brāhman** elitism excluded the vernacular traditions and their poets. And radical displacement of what had been experienced as worthy and purposeful, if not completely so, has always been rejected as spiritual tyranny.

These external forces have been treated often and from the vantage point of many disciplines. But the importance of the religious quest of Svāmī Vivekānanda seems to have been overstated or denied. To acquire a balanced view of Vivekānanda's contribution, we must look at the extremes.

Testimonies of no lesser figures than Gandhi and Nehru have been followed by a profusion of voices praising the influence of Svāmī

Vivekānanda's thought on modern India. Praise of his call for strength and self-reliance as well as his defense of Indian spirituality was considered a necessity in the past. This tendency to devote a few paragraphs or pages to the **svāmī's** achievement was continued in the prestigious **History and Culture of the Indian People:**

> To Hindus, Svāmījī has been a saviour and a reformer. The Rāmakṛishṇa Mission deserves great credit for placing Hinduism on a high pedestal and resisting the onslaughts of Christianity and Islam.[2]

> It will be hardly an exaggeration to say that Rāmakṛishṇa Missions are now functioning as the most important propaganda centres of the liberal form of Hinduism preached by Rāmakṛishṇa and Vivekānanda. They have not only elevated Hindu religion and placed it on the high pedestal of its pristine glory, but also enhanced its prestige in the world outside to a degree it has never reached during the last thousand years.[3]

The working assumption of these and hundreds of other like assessments is that the popularized reduction of Svāmī Vivekānanda's thought into simple pronouncements of Indian spiritual superiority exhaults the subject. It should be no surprise that a reaction had occurred by the beginning of the seventies.

The revisionist interpretation is quite complex and often justified. A more popular version of this negative reaction is captured in the sarcastic put-down: "Vivekānanda was only a **śakta** (a devotee of the Mother Goddess)!" Such a remark, coming from a fellow Bengali, would have been unpardonable. A scholarly version by Agehananda Bharati would place much of the blame for what went wrong in the revitalization of Indian civilization upon the **svāmī's** faulty vision. It is his thesis that the Hindu Renaissance has been "straitjacketed" by **sādhus**, the chief of whom is Vivekānanda.[4]

> Yet, all "modernites" overtly or covertly admire and venerate the "scientific," "modern" man who wears monastic robes: Swami Vivekananda is an undisputed culture-hero.... I shall go a step further: Modern Hindus derive their knowledge of Hinduism from Vivekananda, directly or indirectly. There are of course, competing schools within the Renaissance.... Yet it was Vivekananda and his latter day imitators, including the late Sivananda Sarasvati, who really created the diction and the style of the apologetic.[5]

Bharati sees this style as anti-scholarly, anti-intellectual, and even superficially grounded in the Indian religious tradition.[6]

The discovery of the richness of Svāmī Vivekānanda's spiritual quest may save him from being relegated to the fate of a simple-minded chauvinist—an apologete for the puritanical period of India's nationalistic infancy. The mystery and wonder that Vivekānanda felt as he opened himself to the possibility of ultimacy can now be seen. But it is not without doubt and human frailty. Narendranath Datta (Svāmī Vivekānanda) valued life from within matrices of meaning that ranged from theism to scepticism, to personal devotion for the Mother Goddess, to self-exertion in yoga, to monism. It even appears that his primary spiritual tendency at given periods underwent transformations from rational theism to devotionalism to service as worship to mysticism. His final spiritual tendency returned to the emotional, personal appropriation of the divine in **bhakti**.

The way he moved to the boundaries of the Hindu tradition, engaged in the paradoxical dynamics of the full tradition in a way no Indian prior to him had attempted, and transcended each spiritual perspective by exhausting its possibilities has established his stature as one of India's spiritual geniuses.

One final and general observation appears warranted. Despite the breadth and depth of his thought, Svāmī Vivekānanda's attempt to formulate the universal, scientific religion for the modern world had one major liability. The **svāmī's** thought is cosmological, reasoning from the nature of the Real (which is unknowable in categories of time, space and causation) to the implications for the finite.[7] The leap to an insight or intuition is not "unscientific" as such. However, if there is no procedure by which that insight can be falsified (and therefore the probabilitiy of its validity assessed), it bears no relationship to current perceptions of meaning which are generally referred to as scientific. This is not to suggest that Svāmī Vivekānanda's vision of ultimacy, or any other which is cosmologically derived, is irrelevant in the modern world. The poverty of meaning and the crisis in adequate valuing in the modern world are sufficient to recommend their study. It does suggest that the **svāmī's** attempt to find eternal and absolute knowledge is part of the human process of searching for meanings which can raise humanity to new vistas.

NOTES

LIST OF ABBREVIATIONS

CW **The Complete Works of Swami Vivekananda** (Calcutta: Advaita Ashrama, Sixth Edition, 1964), eight volumes.

BD Bhupendranath Datta, **Svami Vivekananda: Patriot-Prophet** (Calcutta: Nababharat Publishers, 1954).

GRK **The Gospel of Sri Ramakrishna,** recorded by Mahendranath Gupta and translated from Bengali into English by Swami Nikhilananda (New York: Ramakrishna-Vivekananda Center, 1969).

LVK **The Life of Swami Vivekananda,** by His Eastern and Western Disciples (Calcutta: Advaita Ashrama, 1965).

N Sister Nivedita, **The Master as I Saw Him** (Calcutta: Udbodhan Office, sixth edition, 1948).

Chapter I

1. Others crossed the "black water" from the "land of **Jambu**" in earlier centuries to spread Indian religions and culture to "Greater India." A few examples would include the Pandava Temple dedicated to Siva and Parvati on Java, the Besakih Temple on Bali, and the temple built for Siva in Cambodia by Suryavarman II from 1113-1148 A.D.

2. A. K. Majumdar (ed.), **The History and Culture of the Indian People** (Bombay: Bharatiya Vidya Bhavan, 195f).

3. Agehananda Bharati, "The Hindu Renaissance and Its Apologetic Patterns." **Journal of Asian Studies** (February 1970), p. 278, stated that "Swami Vivekananda is an undisputed culture-hero not simply of all modern Bengali Hindus" but further "Modern Hindus derive their knowledge of Hinduism from Vivekananda, directly or indirectly." We need not go that far in order to agree that the Svami is an important religious and cultural model.

4. Robert D. Baird, **Category Formation and the History of Religions** (The Hague: Mouton, 1971), pp. 1-16.

5. **Ibid.**, p. 2.

6. George M. Williams, "Understanding as the Goal of Some Historians of Religions," **The Journal of Religious Thought** (Autumn-Winter 1970), pp. 50-61.

7. Baird, **op. cit.,** pp. 11-14.

8. Michael Polanyi, **Science, Faith and Society** (Chicago: The University of Chicago Press, 1966, Phoenix Book), pp. 10ff. Intuition is used in modern science to gain new insights by leaping to a new "whole" view, a model which explains what other models have not. However, the critical use of models and the inductive method demands that the position not be absolutized. It is held only as long as it is **useful** in ordering the multiplicity of data; when it is brought into question, it is readily abandoned. When the phenomenologists learn to use their

[Notes for pages 3 to 11.]

intuited explanatory systems as useful models to be transcended with each advance of new knowledge, then phenomenology of religion will begin to approximate scientific methodology.

9. Wilfred Cantwell Smith, **The Meaning and End of Religion** (New York: Mentor Books, 1964).

10. **Ibid.**, especially Chapter Seven. 11. Baird, **op. cit.,** p. 5-14.

12. The openness of the term "religion" will become clear when Baird's usage of it as a **stipulative** term is presented on the following page.

13. "Religio-historical description" will be defined in the following section.

14. Paul Tillich, **Theology of Culture** (New York: Oxford University Press, 1959), pp. 7-8: "Religion, in the largest and most basic sense of the word, is ultimate concern," and **Christianity and the Encounter of the World Religions** (New York: Columbia University Press, 1963), p. 4: "Religion is the state of being grasped by an ultimate concern, a concern which qualifies all other concerns as preliminary and which itself contains the answer to the question of the meaning of life." Tillich presupposes the element of grace in his usage. He is further able to judge both Fascism and Communism "quasi-religious," pp. 5ff. and 18ff.

15. Frederick Ferre, "The Definition of Religion ," **Journal of the American Academy of Religion** (March 1970), pp. 3-16, argued that Tillich's definition was too inclusive and therefore unable to exclude "obsessional neurosis," (p. 12). Ferre's inability to use Tillich's definition as he has done is irrelevant to the point of logic that both are evaluating certain objects as "religious" or not "religious" from their normative definitions of "religion."

16. Baird. **op. cit.,** pp. 17-18. 17. **Ibid.**, especially p. 32.

18. **Ibid.**, p. 32. 19. **Ibid.**, p. 52. 20. **Ibid.**, p. 59.

21. **Ibid.,** p. 35.

22. Cf. CW, VI, p. 244, Ltr. XXXV; p. 245 Ltr. XXXVII; et cetera. In a letter dated April 26, 1971, this researcher attempted to obtain information from the Advaita Ashrama in Calcutta concerning these omissions and asked whether or not they would be made in the forthcoming seventh edition of **The Complete Works**. No response was received.

Chapter II

1. GRK, p. 727. 2. **Ibid.**, p. 394 and BD, p. 156-7.

3. BD, p. 259. 4. LVK, p. 28. 5. **Ibid.**, p. 22 and BD, p. 102.

6. CW, VII, pp. 466-7 (Sic.), (emphasis given). In the heat of controversy the Svami questioned the sincerity of Keshab Chandra Sen, although in every other extant remark he was remembered with the greatest respect. (CW, IV, pp. 280 and 417. VII, p. 16, etc.)

[Notes for pages 11 to 17.]

7. (3) CW, IV, pp. 411, 416-7; VI, p. 263; VIII, pp. 311, 373-4; and (4) CW, IV, pp. 280, 417, 462; V, p. 20; VII, p. 16.

8. John N. Farquhar, **Modern Religious Movements in India** (Delhi: Munshiram Manoharlal, 1967), p. 72, quoting the official belief as published in 1910.

9. GRK, pp. 505, 725-6, 733, 772, 962. 10. GRK, pp. 158, 508, 1018.

11. LVK, 64-5. 12. GRK, 219. 13. GRK, 225. 14. **Ibid.**

15. Farquhar, **op. cit.** p. 47 and GRK, pp. 145, 158, 508, 1018.

16. Keshab: GRK, pp. (49), 94, 111, 132ff, 178-9, 184, 188, 194, 239, 561, 565, 576-7, 689-90, 812, 972, 1009. Pratap: GRK, pp. (45), 94, 313, 450, 455, 457, 1009. Siva: GRK, pp. (44), 115-6, 145, 158, 312, 615, 1024, 1026. Vijay: GRK, pp. 132-3, 140-1, 158, 163, 167-8, 312-3, 538-9, 559-60, 577, 581, 661, 665ff, 934, 982.

17. Cf. GRK, p. 559. 18. GRK, pp. 219, 225, 505, 725-6, 772, 962.

19. Cf. fn. 6. 20. GRK, 157 and Farquhar, **op. cit.**, p. 55.

21. CW, III, pp. 208, 214-5.

22. GRK, p. 121. 23. BD, p. 102. 24. GRK, p. 127.

25. GRK, p. 198. 26. **Ibid.**

27. M. Sen, "Brahmo Samaj and Svami Vivekananda," **The Calcutta Review** (May, 1963), p. 159, quoting the **Kathamrita,** IV, p. 19.

28. BD, p. 154. 29. **Ibid.**, pp. 156-7. 30. LVK, p. 90.

31. BD, p. 109 (discussed further later).

32. BD, pp. 156-7 with the first sentence in parentheses contained in a footnote in the original. This author wrote the Belur Math but received no answer concerning this document.

33. "Freemasonry," James Hastings (ed.), **Encyclopaedia of Religion and Ethics** (New York: Charles Scribner's Sons, 1955 reprint), VI, pp. 118-20; "Freemasonry," **Encyclopaedia Britannica** (Chicago, 1960), Vol 9, pp. 732-7; Robert F. Gould, **A Concise History of Freemasonry** (London: Gala & Polden, Ltd., 1903), especially p. 398.

34. **Ibid.** 35. Brittanica, **op. cit.**, p. 735. 36. BD, **loc. cit.**

37. CW, IV, pp. 368-9 (emphasis given).

38. BD, p. 109 and LVK, p. 86. 39. LVK, p. 88.

40. GRK, pp. 219, 225; p. 278. 41. **Ibid.**, pp. 275ff.

42. **Ibid.**, p. 294.

43. **Ibid.**, 275-393. A negative argument entails the logical possibility that positive evidence may be found at some future date.

[Notes for pages 17 to 20.]

44. **Ibid.**, p. 393. Keshab died **January** 8, 1884. 45. BD, p. 107.

46. GRK, p. 1007. 47. BD, p. 156.

48. **Ibid.**, p. 157. Later Svami Vivekananda related: "By working in an attorney's office and translating a few books [Spencer?], I got just enough means to live from hand to mouth, but it was not permanent, and there was no fixed income to maintain my mother and brother." LVK, p. 94.

49. **Ibid.**, pp. 109-110. "Only when his eldest son [Narendra] after coming of age, began to inspect the papers, then some check was exercised on the clerks." p. 110.

50. GRK, p. 896 and BD, p. 110. 51. BD, p. 109.

52. GRK, p. 662.

53. BD, p. 153. 54. LVK, p. 24. 55. BD, **loc. cit.**

56. GRK, p. 733.

57. GRK, p. 735. 58. LVK, p. 76. 59. **Ibid.**, p. 77.

60. BD, p. 154. This book on "Education," published by Gurudas Chottopadhyaya, was not available; it might refer to **First Principles.**

61. CW, II, p. 342; III, p. 388; V, pp. 222, 339; VI, pp. 41, 104, 215, 437; VII, p. 375.

62. LVK, **op. cit.** 63. LVK, pp. 78-8. 64. **Ibid.**, p. 78.

65. **Ibid.** 66. **Ibid.** 67. **Ibid.**

68. LVK, p. 80: "He confessed that his intellect was conquered by the universal, his heart owned the allegiance of the individual Ego and complained that a pale bloodless reason, sovereign **de jure** but not **de facto**, could not hold out arms to save him in the hour of temptation. He wanted to know if my philosophy could satisfy his senses, could mediate bodily, as it were, for the soul's deliverance; in short, he wanted a flesh and blood reality visible in form and glory; above all, he cried out for a hand to save, to uplift, to protect, a Shakti or power outside himself which could cure him of his impotence and cover his nothingness with glory—a Guru or master who by embodying perfection in the flesh would still the commotion in his soul."

69. LVK, pp. 90-96. 70. CW, VI, p. 226.

71. CW, VIII, pp. 477-8.

72. GRK, p. 772. (May, 1885). 73. LVK, p. 64.

74. LVK, p. 92 ("So it was quite natural for me now to proceed to prove before the world that God was a myth, or that, even if He existed, to call upon Him was fruitless. Soon the report gained currency that I was an atheist and did not scruple to drink or even frequent houses of ill fame. This unmerited calumny hardened my heart still more." (It was at this time that Narendra began arguing for eating meat.)

75: LVK, p. 80: ". . .Vivekananda soon after betook himself to the ministers and missionaries of the Brahmo Samaj, asking Brahmos with an unconscious Socratic Irony for an ideal made real to sense, for truth made visible, for a power unto deliverance."

76. LVK, p. 30.

77. March: GRK, pp. 734, 987; June: GRK, pp. 797, 803, 834; LVK, pp. 95-6, 96-7; CW, VIII, pp. 263-4.

78. GRK, p. 987. 79. GRK, p. 734. 80. GRK, pp. 734-95.

Chapter III

1. This doctrine is known as **guruparampara** and was later taught by Svami Vivekananda. CW, VI, p. 265.

2. BD, p. 157. 3. LVK, pp. 158-9, 168. 4. GRK, p. 987.

5. Ramakrsna left no documents concerning his teachings and, specifically, his teachings to Narendra. The only contemporaneous documentation of these teachings are the verbatim accounts of Mahendranath Gupta (GRK). If we wish to know what can be documented as having been taught at that time, then contemporaneous documents must take precedence. The object of this chapter is not to establish the "true" teachings of Ramakrsna but to present what contemporaneous evidence can be brought forward.

6. GRK, p. 397 (March 2, 1884). 7. GRK, p. 734 (March, 1885).

8. GRK, pp. 456, 791, 804, 842-3. 9. GRK, pp. 238, 257, 359, 392, 447-8, 778-9, 801-2.

10. GRK, pp. 649, 901. 11. GRK, p. 359. 12. GRK, p. 801.

13. GRK, pp. 134, 277, 608, 634, 734.

14. GRK, p. 734; GRK, pp. 122, 198, 235, 394, 569, 692-8, 736, 806-8.

15. LVK, p. 93. 16. GRK, p. 255.

17. GRK, pp. 200, 255: "Too much study of the scriptures does more harm than good." 607, 625, 694, 729, 767, 772, 779-80, 882, 917.

18. GRK, p. 200. 19. GRK, p. 375.

20. GRK, p. 734. 21. GRK, pp. 772-3.

22. GRK, pp. 453, 629, 647, 851, 853, 899, 900.

23. GRK, pp. 88, 168, 470, 506, 560, 646, 700, 843. 24. GRK, p. 700

25. GRK, pp. 101, 104-5, 125-6, 166-7, 177, 179, 195, 246, 379, 410-1, 438, 502, 520, 612, 750, 769-70, 851, 944, 1014.

26. GRK, p. 88. 27. GRK, pp. 196, 364, 405.

[Notes for pages 25 to 26.]

28. GRK, p. 564.

29. GRK, pp. 985; 693; 695; 238, 693, 796, 812; 127, 279, 294, 662, 730; 279; 294, 811; 520, 549, 810; 127.

30. GRK, pp. 88, 691, 804. 31. GRK, pp. 88, 691.

32. GRK, p. 255.

33. GRK, pp. 104, 111-2, 128-9, 133, 135, 278, 306, 538, 559, 571, 700, 876.

34. GRK, pp. 134, 277, 608, 634, 734.

35. GRK, especially pp. 172, 584-5.

36. GRK, pp. 231, 717, 770, 841; LVK, p. 65.

37. LVK, pp. 93-4.

38. **Vivekananda: The Yogas and Other Works**, introduced by Svami Nikhilananda (New York: Ramakrishna-Vivekananda Center, 1953), p. 33 and GRK, p. 985.

39. GRK, p. 981; CW, VIII, pp. 139-40.

40. GRK, p. 985; CW, VII, pp. 206-7. 41. LVK, p. 153.

42. GRK, p. 231. 43. GRK, p. 7171. 44. GRK, p. 770.

45. LVK, pp. 65-6. "The magic touch of the Master that day immediately brought a wonderful change over my mind. I was stupefied to find that really there was nothing in the universe but God! I saw it quite clearly but kept silent, to see if the idea would last. But the impression did not abate in the course of the day. I returned home, but there too, everything I saw appeared to be Brahman. I sat down to take my meal, but found that everything—the food, the plate, the persons who served and even myself—was nothing but That. I ate a morsel or two and sat still. I was startled by my mother's words, 'Why do you sit still? finish your meal,' and began to eat again. But all the while, whether eating or lying down, or going to College, I had the same experience and felt myself always in a sort of comatose state.... This state of things continued for some days. When I became normal again, I realized that I must have had a glimpse of the Advaita state. Then it struck me that the words of the scriptures were not false. Thenceforth I could not deny the conclusions of the Advaita philosophy." Note that by foreshortening the time between this experience in early 1882 and his accepting Ramakrsna as his **guru** in 1885 the experience is reordered according to the values of the later belief system.

46. LVK, pp. 93-4. "The summer was over, and the rains set in! The search for a job still went on. One evening, after a whole day's fast and exposure to rain I was returning home with tired limbs and a jaded mind; overpowered with exhaustion and unable to move a step forward, I sank down on the outer plinth of a house on the roadside. I can't say whether I was insensible for a time or not. Various thoughts crowded in on my mind, and I was too weak to drive them off and fix my attention on a particular thing. Suddenly I felt as if by some divine power the coverings

of my soul were removed one after another. All my former doubts regarding the coexistence of divine justice and mercy, and the presence of misery in the creation of a blissful Providence, were automatically solved. By a deep introspection I found the meaning of it all and was satisfied. As I proceeded homewards I found there was no trace of fatigue in the body and the mind was refreshed with wonderful strength and peace. The night was well nigh over.

"... I began secretly to prepare myself to renounce the world like my grandfather...the Master was to come to Calcutta that very day... He pressed me hard to spend that night with him at Dakshineswar. . . . Then at night he dismissed others and calling me to his side said, 'I know you have come for the Mother's work, and won't be able to remain in the world. But for my sake, stay as long as I live.' Saying this he burst into tears again."

47. GRK, p. 985. 48. LVK, p. 135 and **Yogas, op. cit.,** p. 33.

49. CW, VII, pp. 206-7. Cf. LVK, pp. 147-8.

50. GRK, p. 981 (March 25, 1887).

51. CW, VIII, pp. 139-40 (1898). 52. GRK, p. 734.

53. LVK, p. 96. 54. LVK, pp. 96-7.

55. LVK, pp. 94-6 (emphasis given).

56. N, pp. 169-70 (omissions in the original); CW, VIII, pp. 263-4 (emphasis given).

57. GRK, pp. 797: "Narendra now believes these things." (July 13, 1885); 803: "At first Narendra used to say that these things were figments of my imagination, but now he accepts everything." (July 14, 1885); 834: "Narendra, too, sees forms of God nowadays." (August 10, 1885).

58. CW, VIII, p. 283: "I am praying to the Divine Mother. . ." (November, 1888); VI, p. 204; "Sri Durga be my Refuge." (June, 1889).

59. **Sakta kirtanas** sung by Narendra after 1885: GRK, pp. 806-9, 884, 897-9, 998, 1006; hymns to Siva: GRK, pp. 977-8, 990, 995, 1001; Ramakrsna **puja:** GRK, pp. 987, 991.

60. GRK, p. 807. Note the paradoxical nature of the belief.

61. GRK, p. 725.

62. GRK, p. 726. For Ramakrsna's **avatara** doctrine: GRK, pp. 186, 189, 226, 237, 243, 257, 271, 283, 308, 351, 353, 355, 359, 415-6, 432-3, 505, 522, 588, 640, 700, 717, 726, 773, 782-3, 789, 850-1, 853, 864, 883, 940, 942.

63. GRK, p. 733. 64. GRK, p. 771. 65. GRK, p. 773.

66. GRK, p. 904. 67. **Ibid .** 68. GRK, p. 906.

69. LVK, pp. 122ff. 70. GRK, pp. 935ff. 71. GRK, p. 972.

[Notes for pages 31 to 41.]

72. GRK, p. 945. 73. **Ibid.** 74. LVK, p. 148.

75. While the account may have been "devotionalized," the information that Narendra is moving toward a (**advaita**) Vedanta viewpoint should be noted.

76. GRK, pp. 987, 991. 77. GRK, pp. 986-8.

78. GRK, p. 987. 79. GRK, p. 988. 80. GRK, pp. 990ff.

81. GRK, pp. 250, 275, 276, 611.

82. GRK, pp. 456, 647, 804, 842, 843, 901.

83. GRK, p. 951. 84. GRK, p. 1004. 85. **Ibid.**,

86. GRK, pp. 772-3 (May 9, 1885). 87. GRK, p. 990.

88. CW, VI, pp. 202-3. 89. **Ibid.**, p. 206. 90. **Ibid.**, p. 208.

91. GRK, pp. 266, 274, 952, 990. 92. GRK, p. 266.

93. GRK, p. 952. (April, 1886). 94. GRK, pp. 417-8.

95. GRK, p. 593. 96. **Ibid.** 97. GRK, p. 939.

98. GRK, p. 936. 99. GRK, pp. 967-8. 100. GRK, pp. 996-1008.

101. GRK, p. 990. 102. LVK, pp. 159-60. 103. GRK, p. 991.

104. CW, VIII, 159-61. 105. GRK. p. 988 (May 7, 1887).

106. GRK, p. 999. 107. GRK, p. 903. 108. GRK, pp. 849-50.

109. GRK, p. 161.

Chapter IV

1. LVK, pp. 184-8. 2. CW, VI, p. 236. 3. CW, VI, p. 214.

4. CF. Chapter V on the "**Eternal Vedas.**"

5. These were the illnesses of **gurubhais** and the deaths of the chief supporters of the **math.**

6. CW, VI, pp. 208-9. (transliteration of **devanagari** made).

7. CW, VI, p. 208. 8. **Ibid.** 9. CW, VI, p. 209. 10. **Ibid.**

11. CW, VI, p. 210. If this letter is extant among the memorabilia of the Belur Math, it should be published, the author wrote concerning this and other materials directly relating to this period that might have been saved, but was not answered.

12. **Ibid.** (The "wrong idea" may have been a minor technicality, since the central concern of all four questions would be repeated as an introduction to the next series of twelve questions.)

13. **Ibid.** 14. **Ibid.**

15. CW, VI, p. 211. Each of the following numbered items come from this letter, pp. 211-3.

16. GRK, p. 963, **sic passim.** 17. CW, VI, pp. 213-4.

18. **Ibid.**, p. 214. 19. CW, VI, p. 215 (emphasis given).

20. CW, I, p. 6. ("...of the Vedanta philosophy, of which the latest discoveries of science seem like echoes.")

21. CW, V, p. 3. 22. CW, VI, p. 217. 23. **Ibid.**, pp. 216-7.

24. CW, VI, p. 219; VII, pp. 441-2.

25. CW, VI, p. 219. 26. **Ibid.**, p. 234. 27. **Ibid.**

28. CW, IV, p. 291. 29. CW, IV, p. 293. 30. CW, VIII, p. 224.

31. CW, IV, p. 287. 32. **Ibid.**, p. 288. 33. **Ibid.**, p. 289.

34. **Ibid.**, p. 290. 35. **Ibid.** 36. CW, VI, p. 221.

37. CW, IV, pp. 290-5. He finally offered himself as the supreme sacrifice, "the last oblation to his sacrificial fire." (p. 295) This tendency to practice literal self-sacrifice was not unknown and may account for his not allowing even Narendra to see him. His story of the criminal who founded a sect of noseless ascetics might well have referred analogically to an act of worship in which the ascetic cut off his nose in sacrifice. Such a conjecture would give new light to his conclusion to the story: "Thus a whole sect of nose-cut saints spread over the country. Do you want me to be the founder of another such?" (p. 293).

38. CW, VI, pp. 221-2. 39. **Ibid.**, p. 234. CW, VI, p. 236.

41. **Ibid.**

42. CW, VII, p. 243. The spiritual trauma through which he passed had an interesting sequel. The contemporaneous evidence spoke of Pavhari Baba as a **Raja yogi**, (CW, VI, p. 233)—a fact confirmed by later scholarship (LVK, p. 188). However, when Narendra's valuation was changed in subsequent patterns of belief, Pavhari Baba's **Raja yoga** was subordinated to the non-religious exercises of **Hatha yoga** (CW, VIII, p. 242; IV, p. 289 [practical **yoga**]).

In 1902 instead of being ready to leave Ghazipur as the contemporaneous accounts indicated (July 6, 1890—CW, VI, p. 242), Svami Vivekananda told rapt disciples: "I had heard that Pavhari Baba knew the science of Hatha-Yoga. So I thought I would learn the practices of Hatha-Yoga from him, and through them strengthen the body. You know, I have a dogged resolution, and whatever I set my heart on, I always carry out. One the eve of the day on which I was to take initiation, I was lying on a cot thinking; and just then I saw the form of Shri Ramakrishna standing on my right side, looking steadfastly at me, as if very much grieved. I had dedicated myself to him, and at the thought that I was taking another Guru I was much ashamed and kept looking at him. Thus perhaps two or three hours passed, but no words escaped from my mouth. Then he disappeared all of a sudden. My mind became upset seeing Shri Ramakrshna that night, so I postponed the idea of initiation from Pavhari Baba for the day. After a day or two again the idea of initiation from Pavhari Baba arose in the mind—and again in the night there was the appearance of Shri Ramakrishna as on the previous occasion. Thus when for several nights in succession I had the vision of Shri Ramakrishna, I gave up the idea of initiation altogether, thinking that as every time I resolved on it, I was getting such a vision, then no good but harm would come from it.'' It would seem more logical that initiation of religious significance was about to take place, and the evidence confirms this.

43. CW, VI, p. 236. 44. **Ibid.**, pp. 220-1 (emphasis given).

45. LVK, pp. 185-8. This account stressed Narendra's loyalty to Ramakrsna but used both contemporaneous and later sources with little sense of sequence to conclude that he had merely temporarily forgotten his earlier realizations, which finally came back to him with the reoccurring visions.

46. CW, VI, p. 233. 47. CW, VI, p. 230. 48 **Ibid.**, pp. 231-2.

49. **Ibid.**, p. 236. (''For some special reasons, I shall continue to stay in secret in a village some distance from this place....'')

50. CW, VI, p. 236.

51. **Ibid.**, p. 237. (''...the Babaji forbids me to [go]. I shall try to go on a few days' leave from him.); p. 238: ''Where shall I get that renunciation you speak of in your advice to me? It is for the sake of that very thing that I am out a tramp through the earth.''

52. **Ibid.**, pp. 242-3. This is positive evidence that no vision convinced him to return to the Order. It is contemporaneous with the events. The vision occurs in the discussion of the event twelve years later in 1902.

53. LVK, p. 200. 54. CW, VI, p. 239. 55. **Ibid.**, p. 241.

56. CW, VI, p. 209. 57. CW, VI, pp. 225-6. 58. **Ibid.**, p. 225

59. **Ibid.**, p. 226. 60. **Ibid.** 61. **Ibid.**, p. 227.

62. **Ibid.**, p. 225. 63. CW, V, p. 3.

Chapter V

1. LVK, p. 204. 2. **Ibid.**, p. 205. 3. **Ibid.**, p. 226.

4. **Ibid.**, pp. 226-7. 5. LVK, p. 184. 6. **Ibid.**, p. 227.

7. **Ibid.**, pp. 205, 281.

8. LVK, pp. 193-285; CW, VI, pp. 103-23; RSV, pp. 21-75, 105-21.

9. RSV, pp. 38-9.

10. LVK, pp. 210, 210-12, 215-7 and 279-83, 217-21, 223 and 231, 224-5,

225-6, 226, 229-30, 231, 241, 241-3 and 250, (RSV, pp. 64-6). (RSV, 65), 250-1, respectively.

11. This summary has been made from secondary later documents found in LVK, pp. 210-83; RSV, pp. 64-68.

12. LVK, p. 230. 13. RSV, p. 34. 14. **Ibid.**, p. 243.

15. CW, VI, pp. 254-6 (emphasis given).

16. LVK, p. 282. 17. LVK, p. 266. 18. IBid., p. 273.

19. **Ibid**. 20. CW, VIII, pp. 291-2.

21. LVK, p. 278 (emphasis given). 22. **Ibid**., p. 279.

23. When Svami Vivekananda delivered his first address in Madras after returning from America, he told how both groups tried to get him to join their group to be given a letter of introduction, and when that failed they opposed him. CW, III, pp. 207-16.

24. CW, V, p. 37. 25. CW, VI, p. 256.

26. LVK, pp. 348-9. Madame Marie Louise and Herr Leon Londsberg became **svamis** Abhayananda and Kripananda, respectively. Miss S.E. Waldo was the amanuensis. Cf RSV, pp. 122-70 and CW, I, pp. 119-313. The original **Raja-Yoga** was pirated by an English disciple, VIII 374-5, 453-4. So Vivekananda added an appendix (CW, I, pp. 304-13), which allowed Miss Waldo to publish the American edition as the complete and official version.

27. CW, I, pp. 25-118; II, pp. 55-288; III, pp. 29-100, respectively.

28. "The Message of Divine Wisdom" CW, V, pp. 428-35; "India's Message to the World," IV, pp. 308-16; and Fundamentals of Religion," IV, pp. 374-83.

29. CW, VIII, p. 326; VII, p. 464. 30. **Ibid**., p. 305.

31. CW, VI, p. 367. 32. CW, V, p. 29. 33. **Ibid**., p. 31.

34. CW, V, p. 46.

35. "Great works are to be done; what is this small success in comparison with what is to come? Believe, believe, the decree has gone forth, the fiat of the Lord has gone forth—India must rise, the masses and the poor are to be made happy." CW, V, p. 35. The struggle can be followed in the following letters: V, 25; V, 29; V, 31; V, 35; VIII, 310; V, 37; V, 40; V, 44; V, 46; V, 47; V, 50; IV, 367; "India is to be raised, the poor are to be fed, education is to be spread, and the evil of priestcraft is to be removed." (368); V, 52; V, 55; V, 57; V, 60; V, 64; V, 67; V, 74; V, 75; V, 77; V, 79; V, 82; V, 84; V, 91; V, 95; VIII, 371; V, 104; V, 105; V, 111; VIII, 408; VIII, 415; VIII, 419; VIII, 424; VIII, 464; VIII, 481.

36. His first (extant) letter to a member of the order was on March 19, 1894 (VI, 250). In it he told a brother how he planned to raise the masses in India; working in America to get the money, giving spirituality in return, depending "on no one in Hindusthan." If any of you help me in

[Notes for pages 61 to 62.]

my plans, all right, or Gurudeva will show me the way out." Shortly thereafter he wrote a scathing letter (VI, 263) which pointed out how they were failing him at the moment and had failed the masses for centuries. "If you want any good to come, just throw your ceremonials overboard and worship the Living God, the Man-God—every being that wears human form—God in His universal as well as individual aspect." Then he called upon them to renounce their personal goal of **mukti.** "It is only by doing good to others that one attains to one's own good, and it is by leading others to Bhakti and Mukti that one attains them oneself." He gradually drew some into famine relief work, goading them into practical service. But these were monks who had renounced the world to seek their own salvation through methods as **sadhanas, tapas, japas, puja, dhyana**—all designed to remove the **karma** already acquired from past actions. Now Vivekananda called them back into activity—organized activity at that! He reorganized the Math in April 1896 (VIII, 489-94), appointing its leaders for the next year. But even then he expected some resistance. "If you consider it wise to be guided by my ideas and if you follow these rules, then I shall supply on all necessary funds." For the struggle itself, read letters VI, 250; VI, 263; V, 33; V, 42; VI, 268; VI, 278; VI, 282; VI, 287; VI, 289; VII, 475; VII, 480; VII, 483; VI, 296; VI, 304; VI, 310; VI, 314; VI, 321; VI, 326; VI, 350; VI, 362; VI, 369; VI, 393; VII, 488; V, 111; VII, 503: "Everyone of you **must** be a **giant—must,** that is my word. Obedience, readiness and love for the cause—if you have these three, nothing can hold you back" (p. 505).

37. The replies to the resolutions: CW, IV, pp. 331-53. (Madras), pp. 365-6. (Calcutta), and pp. 322-30 (Khetri), and the requests for resolutions: V, 31; VII, 309 ("Thirdly, a year has rolled by, and our countrymen could not even do so much for me as to say to the American people that I was a real Sannyasin and no cheat, and that I represented the Hindu religion. Even this much, the expenditure of a few words, they could not do!") VII, pp. 310-14: "Boobies, who cannot get up a few meetings of 50 men each and send up a few empty **words** only to help me, talk big about influencing the world" (p. 312).

38. CW, VI, p. 476. 39. CW, VIII, pp. 489-90.

40. CW, VII, p. 366. 41. CW, VI, p. 432. 42. LVK, pp. 710-58.

43. The worship of Kali and of his **guru**, Sri Ramakrsna, at the end of his life necessitated a careful study to determine whether or not this constituted another pattern of ultimacy on the ideal level. On the ideal level Vivekananda had postulated a series of stages through which one progressed toward **nirvikalpa samadhi**, complete oneness with the Absolute (see below). Yet, on the actual level his last days did not follow these stages. He seemed to be worshiping as a **Sakta**—a devotee of Kali. (This emphasis on **puja** and occult powers would include: VII, 129ff.; V, 391ff.; VII, 139ff.; VIII, 252f.; VII, 230; VII, 264; VIII, 517; VI, 515ff.; N, 120-38, 162-73.) Was there another period with its own pattern of ultimacy? In weighing the probabilities the evidence would favor the conclusion that there was neither a changed pattern of ultimacy on the ideal level (even though there may have been another period on the actual level) nor an asystematic period which moved from one religious experience to another without a perceived unity, but there was within this pattern of ultimacy such latitude that growth and change could be tolerated without a reordering of the belief system. In between periods of Kali **puja** there were periods of strict **advaita**–denial of the duality necessary for worship.

44. CW, III, p. 121. 45. **Ibid.**, p. 111.

46. CW, V, p. 284. It is indisputable that Vivekananda intended a "rational system" of belief. He began several times to write it down but never got beyond the outline. Since he intended his pattern of belief to be systematic, then our task will be to bring the pieces together, see how they fit, and define any gaps. As the system emerges, a complex of levels and stages of truth can be seen. Vivekananda was primarily a teacher who was gauging his material to the appropriate level of spirituality he perceived in his students. Therefore, footnotes will indicate a source appropriate to the level or stage of truth being described.

47. The decision to value what comes from the senses as ultimately valueless is a decision against **bhoga** (enjoyment of anything in the phenomenal sphere) and for **mukti** (release from the sensate existences). This existential decision was made in relation to the death of his father) and became a continuity throughout the rest of his life.

48. Potter's designation of "leap philosophy" appears to apply. [Karl H. Potter, **Presuppositions of Indian Philosophies** (Englewood Cliffs: Prentice-Hall, 1963), pp. 236-56.] In Vivekananda's belief system the proposition of a knowable Absolute, the objectless witness and sole existent, indicates the direction of the "leap" from common knowledge to pure mystery.

49. The first question which had to be answered concerned authority: "Is the **Veda** your source of authority?" Those answering affirmatively "It is." **asti**) were known as **astika** philosophies, while those answering negatively ("It is not." **nasti**) were **nastika** philosophies (**darsanas**).

50. CW, VI, pp. 211-2. 51. **Ibid.,** p. 212.

52. CW, VII, pp. 196-7. 53. CW, III, pp. 422-3; VII, p. 120.

54. **Pratyaksa** points beyond the multiplicity of elements perceived by the senses to the one element (CW, I, p. 14). **Anumana** points beyond the multiplicity of inferences to the unity of Inference (II, 162). **Sruti** also points beyond itself to the One (V, 311).

55. CW, I, p. 320. 56. CW, V, p. 366.

57. CW, III, p. 354; VII, p. 9. 58. CW, VII, p. 142.

59. CW, I, p. 159; VI, pp. 463-4; VII, p. 254.

60. CW, VII, p. 140: "Shri Ramakrishna used to say that the Avataras alone can descend to the ordinary plane from that state of Samadhi, for the good of the world. Ordinary Jivas do not; immersed in that state, they remain alive for a period of twenty-one days; after that, their body drops like a sere leaf from the tree of Samsara (world) " (1898). When Svami Vivekananda first arrived back in India (1897), he maintained that he had not realized the absolute himself. (CW, V, p. 331: ". . .the few words I speak to you are only through the force of that current gained by coming in contact with them [mahatmas].") This was consistent with the previous systems of belief. He based his present teachings, not upon his own complete experience, but upon that of his **guru**. (V, 414: "All that I am, all that the world itself will some day be, is owning to my

Master Shri Ramakrishna, who incarnated and experienced and taught this wonderful unity which underlies everything, having discovered it alike in Hinduism, in Islam, and in Christianity." III, 268: "Only let me say now that if I have told you one word of truth, it was his and his alone...." III, 348: "Then came one whose life was the explanation, whose life was the working out of the harmony that is the background of all the different sects of India. I mean Ramakrishna Paramahamsa.") However, after some months in India he began to value two former experiences, not as partial realization, but as **nirvikalpa samadhi** (V, 391-3). Thus, the foundation which rested on personal experience was his own. It was then remembered that Ramakrsna had taken the memory of this experience from Vivekananda so that he could remain in the world. (Ramakrsna was remembered as saying: "If you remain day and night in that state, the work of the Divine Mother will not be accomplished; therefore you won't be able to induce that state again; when your work is finished, it will come again," VII, 140.) (The explanation does not attempt to suggest why, although not an **avatara**, Vivekananda's body did not fall away in 1898 when he came to know of his past realizations.)

61. The **svami** first used the term "Hinduism." This was later dropped for **Vedanta, sanatana dharma**, Religion Eternal, and Universal Religion which were used synonymously.

62. CW, III, p. 397. 63. CW VI, p. 519.

64. CW, V, pp. 519-520.

65. CW, I, p. 129. (No Sanskrit term was found as used by Vivekananda for "generalization" unless it would be **adhyasa** which he defines as "reflection, implication" [CW, II, p. 439].)

66. "Freedom of the Soul," **Prabuddha Bharata** (October 1897), p. 43.

67. CW, I, pp. 148-9. 68. CW, IV, p. 380. 69. CW, II, p. 304.

70. Vivekananda has used the English word "reason" in two ways: (1) as the activity of the mind, **anumana** (CW, VII, p. 91: inspiration is higher than reason) and (2) as the criterion of truth (CW, II, 335-6: reason is the universal authority; "I believe in reason and follow reason having seen enough of the evils of authority, for I was born in a country where they have gone to the extreme of authority." V, 315: "The Vedas, i.e. only those portions of them which agree with reason, are to be accepted as authority." V, 411: "Personally I take as much of the Vedas as agrees with reason.").

71. RVK, p. 396. 72. CW, VII, p. 120. 73. **Ibid**., p. 101.

74. **Ibid**., p. 9. The epistemological process works from sense-knowledge by "an ever-broadening generalization" (VIII, 347) to the very limit of sense-knowledge where it "leaps by **aparoksanubhuti** to direct perception of the One (Cf. CW, II, p. 61).

75. CW, III, p. 5. 76. CW, II, p. 455. 77. CW, I, p. 129.

78. CW, III, p. 418. 79. CW, II, p. 458.

80. CW, I, pp. 134-5, 250-1, 360-3, 394-6, 405; II, pp. 232-4, 264-7,

423-5, 433-9, 442-53, 454-62; III, pp. 5-7, 416; V, pp. 102-4, VII, pp. 408-9; VII, pp. 362-3. These presentations of **Samkhya** were made in different contexts and on different levels. That he was not fully satisfied with these presentations is seen in the following: "I want to work all this out carefully, but you will see at a glance that I am on the right track. It will take more study in physiology, on the relations between higher and lower centers to fill out the psychology of mind, chitta (mind-stuff), and buddhi (intellect), and so on!" (CW, V, 103-4.)

81. Cw, II, p. 438. 82. CW, V, p. 103. 83. CW, II, pp. 458-9.

84. CW, II, p. 461. 85. **Ibid**., p. 191.

86. **Ibid**., pp. 189-202, 226-262; II, pp. 318ff. 87. CW, III, p. 424.

88. CW, I, pp. 292, 327, 373, 449; II, pp. 74-5, 95-7, 107, 136-7, 174, 178, 207-8, 221, 227-31, 345-6, 354, 359, 427, 455, 478; III, pp. 111, 123, 218, 239, 281, 335, 343, 406-7; IV, pp. 126, 182, 189, 249, 271, 332, 334, 347; V, pp. 249, 255-6, 277-9, 298, 312, 419-20; VI, pp. 34, 45, 92, 103, 113, 378; VII, pp. 151-4, 311; VIII, pp. 237-8, 249, 362-3.

89. CW, III, p. 111. 90. CW, II, p. 207.

91. CW, I, p. 152. 92. CW, III, p. 407. 93. CW, II, p. 331.

94. CW, I, p. 14. The goal of science as unity is a logical extension of a "steady state"universe perceived as unity.

95. CW, II, p. 89; III, p. 111.

96. CW, I, p. 361; II, pp. 442-3, III, p. 122, **et. al.**

97. CW, I, p. 360; II, p. 239, **et al.**

98. CW, III, p. 299; VI, pp. 474-5; VII, p. 141.

99. CW, II, pp. 209-10.

100. CW, I, pp. 363-4; II, 88-9, 192; III, 11-2, 341-2, **et al.**

101. CW, II, p. 228. 102. CW, III, p. 343.

103. CW, III, p. 400. 104. **Ibid**., p. 343. 105. CW, VI, p. 215.

106. CW, III, p. 339. 107. **Ibid**., p. 407. 108. CW, II, p. 228.

109. CW, II, p. 427. 110. **Ibid.** 111. **Ibid**., pp. 120-1.

112. **Kalpa**: CW, I, pp. 147-8, 211, 223, 319; II, pp. 75, 207, 427, 435-6, 454; III, pp. 40, III, 124, 399; IV, p. 120; V, p. 101; VII, p. 192. **Yuga**: II, p. 72; III, pp. 111-2, 120-1, 133, 141, 167, 197, 222, 293, 350; IV, pp. 311, 318; V, p. 315 (This is the only extant quote which relegates the doctrine of four **yugas** to the status of "arbitrary assumptions of Pauranika times.").

113. CW, II, p. 255. 114. CW, I, p. 53. 115. CW, II, p. 255.

116. CW, I, pp. 399-400. 117. CW, II, p. 270.

[Notes for pages 76 to 80.]

118. CW, I, p. 292. 119. CW, II, p. 91. 120. CW, II, p. 254.

121. CW, VIII, p. 22. 122. CW, V, p. 276. 123. CW, II, p. 192.

124. CW, III, p. 13. 125. CW, VI, p. 44. 126. **Ibid.**, p. 45.

127. CW, I, pp. 363-4. 128. CW, VI, p. 44.

129. CW, II, p. 130 (emphasis given). 130. CW, III, p. 341.

131. CW, VI, p. 378.

132. Svami Vivekananda chose the term "eschatology" to describe the content of one chapter of a proposed book. "The eschatology will be explained from the Advaitic standpoint only. That is to say, the dualist claims that the soul after death passes on to the Solar sphere, thence to the Lunar sphere, thence to the Electric sphere. Thence he is accompanied by a Purusha to Brahmaloka. (Thence, says the Advaitist side, he goes to Nirvana.)

"Now on the Advaitic side, it is held that the soul neither comes nor goes, and that all these spheres or layers of the universe are only so many varying products of Akasha and Prana. That is to say, the lowest or most condensed is the Solar sphere, consisting of the visible universe, in which Prana appears as physical force, and Akasha as sensible matter. The next is called the Lunar sphere, which surrounds the Solar sphere. This is not the moon at all, but the habitation of the gods, that is to say, Prana appears in it as psychic forces, and Akasha as Tanmatras or fine particles. Beyond this is the Electric sphere, that is to say, a condition in which the Prana is almost inseparable from Akasha, and you can hardly tell whether Electricity is force or matter. Next is the Brahmaloka, where there is neither Prana nor Akasha, but both are merged in the mind-stuff, the primal energy. And here—there being neither Prana or Akasha—the Jiva contemplates the whole universe as Samashti or the sum total of Mahat or mind. This appears as a Purusha, an abstract universal **soul**, yet not the Absolute, for still there is multiplicity. From this the Jiva finds at last that Unity which is the end. Advaitism says that these are the visions which rise in succession before the Jiva, who himself niether goes nor comes, and that in the same way this present vision has been projected. The projection (Srishti) and dissolution must take place in the same order, only one means going backward, and the other coming out.

"Now as each individual can only see his **own** universe, that universe is created with his bondage and goes away with his liberation, although it remains for others who are in bondage. Now name and form constitute the universe. A wave in the ocean is a wave, only in so far as it is bound by name and form. If the wave subsides, it is the ocean, but those name and form have immediately vanished for ever. So though the name and form of wave could never be without the **water** that was fashioned into the wave by them, yet the name and form themselves were not the wave. They die as soon as ever it returns to water. But other names and forms live in relation to other waves. This name-and-form is called maya, and the water is Brahman. The wave was nothing but water all the time, yet as a wave it had the name and form. Again this name and form cannot remain for one moment separated from the wave, although the wave as water can remain eternally separate from name and form. But because the name and form can never be **separated** they can never be said to exist. Yet they are not **zero.** This is called Maya.

[Notes for pages 80 to 84.]

"I want to work all this out carefully, but you will see at a glance that I am on the right track." CW, V, pp. 102-3.

133. CW, V, p. 312. 134. CW, VIII, p. 26.

135. CW, V, p. 284. Cf. CW, I, p. 189; III, p. 411 (". . .the cessation of these wave forms is what is called Nirvana."); V, pp. 6, 147 (". . .that highest state—Mukti, or Nirvana, call it what you like.") pp. 206, 284.

136. CW, V, p. 317. 137. CW, V, p. 433. 138. CW, VIII, p. 158

139. CW, III, p. 336. 140. **Ibid** 141. **Ibid.**

142. CW, V, p. 433-4.

144. **Ibid.,** 436. 145. CW, V, p. 435. 146. CW, III, p. 336.

147. CW, V, pp. 428-34. 148. **Ibid.,** p. 432.

149. CW, I, p. 334. 150. CW, II, p. 459. 151. **Ibid.**

152. CW, V, p. 433. 153. **Ibid.** 154. CW, II, p. 191.

155. CW, VIII, p. 166.

156. CW, II, pp. 248-9: "What does the Advaitist declare? He says if there is a God that God must be both the material and the efficient cause of the universe. Not only is He the creator, but He is also the created. He Himself is this universe. How can that be? God, the pure, the spirit, has become the universe? Yes; apparently so. That which all ignorant people see as the universe does not really exist. What are you and I and all these things we see? Mere self-hypnotism; there is but one Existence, the Infinite, the Ever-blessed One. In that Existence we dream all these various dreams. It is the Atman beyond all, the Infinite, beyond the known beyond the knowable; in and through that we see the universe. It is the only Reality. It is this table; It is the audience before me; It is the wall; It is everything, minus the name and form. Take away the form of the table, take away the name; what remains is It: The Vedantist does not call It either He or She—these are fictions, delusions of the human brain—there is no sex in the soul. Everyone and everything is the Atman—the Self—the sexless, the pure, the ever-blessed. It is the name, the form, the body, which are material, and they make all this difference. If you take away these two differences of name and form, the whole universe is one; there are not two, but one everywhere. You and I are one. There is neither nature, nor god, nor the universe, only that one Infinite Existence, out of which, through name and form, all these are manufactured. How to know the Knower? It cannot be known. How can you see your own Self? You can only reflect yourself. So all this universe is the reflection of that One Eternal Being, the Atman, and as the reflection falls upon good or bad reflectors, so good or bad images are cast up. Thus in the murderer, the reflector is bad and not the Self. In the saint the reflector is pure. The Self—the Atman— is by Its own nature pure. It is the same, the one Existence of the universe that is reflecting Itself from the lowest worm to the highest and most perfect being. The whole of this universe is one Unity, one Existence, physically, mentally, morally and spiritually.

157. CW, III, p. 336. 158. CW, VIII, p. 362.

[Notes for pages 84 to 91.]

159. CW, V, p. 206. 160. CW, III, p. 348.

161. CW, V, p. 147: ". . .the cessation of these wave forms is what is called Nirvana." (CW, III, p. 411.)

162. CW, II, p. 291.

163. An Indian audience would have recognized this as an **advaita** claim. Dr. Anima Sen Gupta, in "The Karma-Yoga of Swami Vivekananda" (**Prabuddha Bharata,** May 1963, pp. 219-23), noted the **advaita** formula: **jnana-karmanoh sahayoga na ghatate** (Knowledge and work cannot join together.) She suggested that the **svami** "has offered us a unique interpretation of Advaita Vedanta..." (p. 219). She then attempted to offer an interpretation of Sankara's condemnation of **karma** which would make his teachings and the **svami's** compatible.

164. CW, VII, p. 181. 165. **Ibid.** 166. CW, III, p. 324.

167. CW, VI, p. 122.

168. CW, I, pp. 446-80; IV, pp. 102-10; V, pp. 239-42, 246-9; VI, pp. 83-4; VII, pp. 273-5 (note **svami** is being challenged on his particular usage of **karma yoga**); VIII, pp. 8-9, 484.

169. CW, V, p. 249. 170. **Ibid**. 171. CW, V, p. 264.

172. CW, III, pp. 167, 439; V, pp. 222, 226, 404, 480; VI, pp. 319-20; VII, pp. 108, 246, 484.

173. CW, V, p. 108. 174. CW, III, p. 167.

175. CW, III, pp. 157, 166-7, 199, 241, 246.

176. **Ibid**., p. 157. 177. **Ibid**., pp. 158, 159.

178. CW, V, pp. 435-6. 179. CW, II, p. 324.

180. **Ibid.,** III, p. 125. 181. CW, II, pp. 304-5.

182. **Ibid**., pp. 325-6. 183. **Ibid**., p. 300. 184. CW, VII, p. 126.

185. CW, III, p. 126. 186. **Ibid**., p. 174. 187. CW, II, p. 306.

188. CW, III, p. 161. 189. **Ibid**., pp. 158-9. 190. **Ibid**., p. 156.

191. **Ibid**., p. 157. 192. CW, III, p. 214. 193. **Ibid**., p. 214.

194. CW, II, p. 355; III, 216. 195. CW, II, p. 355.

196. **Ibid**., pp. 355-8.

197. CW, III, pp. 194: "Here naturally comes the difficult and the vexed question of caste and social reformation, which has been uppermost for centuries in the minds of our people. I must frankly tell you that I am neither a caste-breaker nor a mere social reformer. I have nothing to do directly with your castes or with your social reformation.... Personally, I have no fault to find with these reformers. Most of them are good, well-meaning men, and their aims too are very laudable on certain

points; but it is quite a patent fact that this one hundred years of social reform has produced no permanent and valuable result appreciable throughout the country."; 195: "I do not, therefore, want any reformation. My ideal is growth, expansion, development on national lines."; 196: "I am no preacher of any momentary social reform. I am not trying to remedy evils, I only ask you to go forward and to complete that has been laid out in the most perfect order by our ancestors. I only ask you to work to realise more and more the Vedantic ideal of the solidarity of man and his inborn divine nature."; 198: ". . .you must make progress without stopping, and that from the highest man to the lowest Pariah, every one in this country has to try and become the ideal Brahmin. His Vedantic idea is applicable not only here but over the whole world. Such is our ideal of caste as meant for raising all humanity slowly and gently towards the realisation of that great ideal of the spiritual man who is non-resisting, calm, steady, worshipful, pure, and meditative. In that ideal there is God."; 213: "To the reformers I will point out that I am a greater reformer than any one of them. They want to reform only little bits. I want root-and-branch reform. Where we differ is in the method. Theirs is the method of destruction, mine is that of construction. I do not believe in reform; I believe in growth. I do not dare to put myself in the position of God and dictate to our society, 'This way thou shouldst move and not that.' "; 214: "Thework against evil is more educational than actual, however big we may talk. This, first of all, is the idea of work against evil; and it ought to make us calmer, it ought to take fanaticism out of our blood."; 215: "That is where I differ entirely from these reform movements. For a hundred years they have been here. What good has been done except the creation of a most vituperative, a most condemnatory literature? Would to God it was not here! They have criticised, condemned, abused the orthodox, until the orthodox have caught their tone and paid them back in their own coin; and the result is the shame of the race, the shame of the country. Is this reform? Is this leading the nation to glory? Whose fault is this?"; 216: "The whole problem of social reform, therefore, resolves itself into this: where are those who want reform? Make them first. Where are the people? The tyranny of a minority is the worst tyranny that the world ever sees. A few men who think that certain things are evil will not make a nation move. Why does not the nation move? First educate the nation...You must go down to the basis of the thing, to the very root of the matter. That is what I call radical reform. Put the fire there and let it burn upwards and make an Indian nation. And the solution of the problem is not so easy, as it is a big and vast one. Be not in a hurry, this problem has been known several hundred years."

198. CW, II, p. 358. 199. CW, II, p. 355. 200. CW, III, p. 293.

200. **Ibid**., p. 246. 202. **Ibid**. 203. CW, IV, p. 362.

204. Cf. "Epistemology and Unity," pp. 65-7 in text.

205. CW, III, p. 304. 206. CW, II, p. 336. 207. CW, II, p. 292.

208. CW, VI, pp. 393-4. 209. CW, VIII, p. 266; N, p. 201.

210. CW, VIII, p. 267; N, p. 203. 211. CW, II, p. 292.

212. CW, V, p. 353. 213. CW, III, p. 150. 214. **Ibid**., p. 149.

215. **Ibid**., pp. 147-9.

[Notes for pages 93 to 98.]

216. CW, IV, pp. 486, 487. CW, III, p. 174: "There was a time in this very India when, without eating beef, no Brahmin could remain a Brahmin...."

217. CW, III, p. 246. 218. CW, III, p. 115.

219. CW, VII, p. 96. 220. CW, III, p. 129. 221. **Ibid.**, p. 240.

222. CW, II, p. 252; III, pp. 240-1, 269. 223. CW, III, p. 425.

224. CW, II, p. 285; V, p. 228. 225. CW, VII, p. 498.

226. CW, III, p. 343. 227. CW, III, p. 258.

228. CW, V, p. 285. 229. CW, III, p. 246. 230. CW, V, p. 325.

231. **Ibid.** 232. CW, V, p. 382; VII, pp. 110, 112-3.

333. CW, VII, p. 113. 234. CW, III, p. 133.

235. CW, I, p. 188; II, pp. 98, 137: "Change is always subjective. All through evolution you find that the conquest of nature comes by change in the subject. Apply this to religion and morality, and you will find that the conquest of evil comes by the change in the subjective alone.That is how the Advaita system gets its whole force, on the subjective side of man. To talk of evil and misery is nonsense, because they do not exist outside."; III, pp. 14-5: "True freedom cannot exist in the midst of this delusion, this hallucination, this nonsense of the world, this universe of the senses, body, and mind."; V, pp. 274: "The real Existence is without manifestation. . . .We are the Self, eternally at rest and at peace.", 281: "If we can stop all thought, then we know that we are beyond thought.", 359; VII, pp. 54: "No action can give you freedom; only knowledge can make you free. Knowledge is irresistible; the mind cannot take it or reject it. When it comes the mind has to accept it; so it is not a work of the mind; only, its expression comes in the mind.";74: "Sit down and let all things melt away, they are but dreams."; 81, 140-1.

236. CW, VII, p. 98. 237. CW, V, p. 455.

238. CW, VIII, p. 152. 239. CW, V, p. 292. 240. CW, I, p. 188

241. **Ibid.** 242. **Ibid.** 243. CW, I, p. 188.

244. CW, V, p. 292. 245. CW, I, p. 27. 246. **Ibid.**, p. 28.

247. CW, I, p. 31. 248. **Ibid.**, p. 52. 249. **Ibid.**, p. 53.

250. **Ibid.**, p. 87. 251. **Ibid.** 252. **Ibid.**, p. 98.

253. **Ibid.**, p. 109. 254. **Ibid.**, p. 117. 255. **Ibid.**, p. 93.

256. CW, III, p. 32. 257. **Ibid.**, p. 36.

258. **Ibid.**, p. 43; IV, pp. 40-7. 259. **Ibid.**, pp. 48-51.

260. **Ibid.**, p. 53. 261. CW, III, p. 72. 262. **Ibid.**, p. 76.

[Notes for pages 98 to 103.]

263. **Ibid.**, pp. 79-80. 264. **Ibid.**, p. 81. 265. **Ibid.**, p. 82.

266. **Ibid.**, pp. 84-5. 267. **Ibid.**, p. 93. 268. CW, III, pp. 94-9.

269. **Ibid.**, p. 100. 270. CW, VI, p. 91

271. CW, I, pp. 405-12. 272. **Ibid.**, p. 415. 273. CW, III, p. 71.

274. CW, II, p. 83. 275. CW, VI, pp. 91-2. 276. CW, II, p. 165

277. CW, V, p. 272. 278. CW, I, p. 93.

279. CW, VII, pp. 87, 98. 280. **Ibid.**, p. 97. 281. **Ibid.**, p. 62.

282. **Ibid.**

283. CW, III, pp. 281, 422-3; V, pp. 336-7, 384-5, 393: VII, pp. 62, 96-8, 277; VIII, pp. 152-4.

284. CW, V, p. 414. 285. CW, VII, p. 96. 286. CW, I, p. 3.

287. CW, I, pp. 318-22.

288. **Ibid.**, p. 319. 289. CW, II, pp. 58-9. 290. **Ibid.**, p. 59.

291. CW, I, p. 323. 292. **Ibid.**, p. 324. 293. **Ibid.**, pp. 324-5.

294. CW, III, pp. 258-9. 295. **Ibid.**, p. 32. 296. **Ibid.**, p. 249.

297. CW, II, p. 353; VIII, p. 141. 298. CW, I, p. 321.

299. CW, VII, p. 502. 300. CW, V, p. 425.

301. **Ibid.**, p. 68 302. **Ibid.**, p. 414. 303. CW, VII, p. 43.

304. CW, II, p. 321. 305. CW, II, pp. 371-2; III, pp. 108-9.

306. CW, V, p. 31. 307. CW, III, p. 198.

308. **Ibid.**, pp. 225, 263-5, 279.

309. CW, II, p. 320; II, 303: "You know in your inmost heart that many of your limited ideas, this humbling of yourself and praying and weeping to imaginary beings, are superstitions."

310 CW, III, p. 293. 310 CW, IV, pp. 382-3. 312. **Ibid**.

313. **Ibid.**, p. 294. 314. CW, V, p. 334. 315. CW, I, p. 192.

316. CW, III, p. 246. 317. **Ibid.**, p. 240.

318. **Ibid.**, p. 302; V, p. 111.

319. CW, III, pp. 108, 219-20, 285; IV, 399, 438, 488; V, 225ff.

320. CW, III, pp. 110-11. 321. CW, IV, pp. 308-11.

322. CW, II, p. 67. 323. **Ibid.**, p. 364. 324. **Ibid.**, p. 365.

[Notes for pages 104 to 108.]

325. CW, II, p. 366. 326. **Ibid.**, pp. 385-6. 327. **Ibid.**, p. 387.

328. CW, V, p. 306. 329. CW, IV, p. 482.

330. CW. III, p. 159.

331. CW, III, pp. 159, 197-8, 293-304; V, 31; VII, 95.

Chapter VI

1. CW, I, p. 17.

2. R. C. Majumdar (ed.), **History, op. cit.,** X, p. 131.

3. **Ibid.**, XI, p. 986.

4. Agehananda Bharati, **Journal of Asian Studies** (February, 1970), pp. 267-87.

5. **Ibid.**, p. 278. 6. **Ibid.**, p. 272.

7. This accounts for most of the discrepancies in his thought. For example, when he sought an answer to the question about whether the Dravidians are Aryans, he used intuition to arrive at an answer. Over a period of fifteen years what he "saw" as an answer varied greatly. CW, III, p. 242ff; IV, pp. 68,70, 327; VII, p. 395; **LVK**, p. 250.

APPENDIX A

CHRONOLOGICAL SURVEY OF DOCUMENTATION

Appendix A is a compilation in chronological order of the types of documentation used in this study. This survey is necessitated by the general disregard for chronology in **The Complete Works** and the need of this study to know what he believed and when. This compilation will facilitate future researchers so that when new materials may be found, their influence upon the findings of this study may be more easily assessed.

References in this survey will omit the designation "CW" for **The Complete Works** but will designate it simply by volume and page numbers. Other references will be designated as they have been throughout the study (cf. "The List of Abbreviations"). Each reference will include the date, place, type of documentation, and source. The types of documentation used in this study were discussed in the introduction under the heading, "The Object of Study." **Primary contemporaneous** documentation will include letters (Ltr.) and speeches or articles (their titles will be given), while **secondary contemporaneous** (sc) documentation and **secondary later** (sl) documentation, both of which are not by the **svāmī**, will not be broken down into smaller categories.

Once the documents were arranged chronologically, it became possible to ask "what was Svāmī Vivekānanda's pattern of ultimate concern and when was it believed?" In this way the changes in his belief system could be accurately dated and periods of belief could be deduced.

1881

Nov. —S.N. Mitra's House. sc. LVK, 30.

1882

Jan. —Choudhury's House. sc. GRK, 1019f.
Mar. —Dakshineswar. sc. GRK, 83-90, 90-2.
Oct. 16—Dakshineswar. sc. GRK, 117-26.
Oct. 22—Dakshineswar. sl. GRK, 126f.
Oct. 27—Home of S. Mitra. sl. GRK, 144.
Nov. 16—Calcutta Brahmo Temple. sl. GRK, 156.

1883

Feb. 18—Calcutta. sl. GRK, 181f.
Apr. 7—Balaram's home. sl. GRK, 198f.
Aug. 11—Dakshineswar. sl. GRK, 275f.

1884

Mar. 2—Dakshineswar. sl. GRK, 393f.
Jun. 25—Calcutta. Ishan's. sl GRK, 462f.
Sep. 6—Adhar's parlor. sl. GRK, 508f.
Sep. 14—Dakshineswar. sl. GRK, 522f.
Sep. 28—Adhar's home. sl. GRK, 562f.
Sep. 29—Dakshineswar. sl. GRK, 567f.
Oct. 1—Dakshineswar. sl. GRK, 581.

1885

Feb. 22—Dakshineswar. sc. GRK, 691f.
Feb. 25—Star Theatre. sc. GRK, 704f.
Mar. 1—Dakshineswar. sc. GRK, 707f.
Mar. 11—Calcutta. Balaram's. sc. GRK, 724f.
Apr. 24—Balaram's. sc. GRK, 761f.
May 9—Balaram's. sc. GRK, 768f.
May 23—Ram's. sc. GRK, 778f.
Jun. 13—Dakshineswar.sc. GRK, 795.

RĀMAKṚṢṆA'S DISCIPLE

Jul. 14—Dakshineswar. sc. GRK, 804f.
Sep. 1—Dakshineswar. sc. GRK, 840f.
Oct. 18—Syampukur House. sc. GRK, 848f.
Oct. 24—Syampukur House. sc. GRK, 876f.
Oct. 25—Syampukur House. sc. GRK, 879f.
Oct. 26—Syampukur House. sc. GRK, 886f.
Oct. 27—Syampukur House. sc. GRK, 895f.
Oct. 30—Syampukur House. sc. GRK, 915f.
Oct. 31—Syampukur House. sc. GRK, 920f.
Dec. 11—RK moved to Cossipore.
Dec. 23—Cossipore. sc. GRK, 931f.

1886

Jan. 4—Cossipore. sc. GRK, 935f.

Jan. 5—Cossipore. sc. GRK, 937f.
Mar. 11—Cossipore. sc. GRK, 939f.
Mar. 14—Cossipore. sc. GRK, 940f.
Mar. 15—Cossipore. sc. GRK, 941f.
Apr. 9—Cossipore. sc. GRK, 947f.
Apr. 12—Cossipore. sc. GRK, 950.
Apr. 13—Cossipore. sc. GRK, 950f.
Apr. 16—Cossipore. sc. GRK, 954f.
Apr. 17—Cossipore. sc. GRK, 959f.
Apr. 21—Cossipore. sc. GRK, 962f.
Apr. 22—Cossipore. sc. GRK, 963f.
Apr. 23—Cossipore. sc. GRK, 970f.
Aug. 15—Death of RK. sc. GRK, 72.
Dec. 24—Samnyasa. Pilgrimage. sl. LVK, 158-9, 168.
Undated document, 1886—"Hymn of Samadhi." IV, 498.

1887

Feb. 21—Baranagore Math. sc. GRK, 977f.
Mar. 25—Baranagore Math. sc. GRK, 980f.
Apr. 8—Baranagore Math. sc. GRK, 983f.
Apr. 9—Baranagore Math. sc. GRK, 984f.
May 7—Baranagore Math. sc. GRK, 987f.
May 8—Baranagore Math. sc. GRK, 990f.
May 9—Baranagore Math. sc. GRK, 1000f.

1888

Aug. 12—Vridaban. Ltr. VI, 201.
Aug. 12—Vridaban. 2nd Ltr. VI, 201.
Nov. 19—Baranagore Math. Ltr. VI, 202.
Nov. 28—Baghbazar. Ltr. VIII, 283.

1889

Feb. 4—Baranagore. Ltr. VI, 203.
Feb. 7—Auntpur. Ltr. VI, 204.
Feb. 22—Baranagore. Ltr. VIII, 283.
Mar. 21—Baghbazar. Ltr. VIII, 284.
n.d. —n.p. "A Preface to the Initiation of Christ." VIII, 259-61.
Jun. 26—Baranagore. Ltr. VI, 204.
Jul. 4—Baghbazar. Ltr. VI, 205.
Jul. 14—Simla (Calcutta). Ltr. VIII, 284.

THE SEARCH

Aug. 7—Baranagore. Ltr. VI, 208.
Aug. 17—Baranagore. Ltr. VI, 209.
Sep. 2—Baghbazar. Ltr. VI, 214.
Dec. 3—Baghbazar. Ltr. VI, 214.
Dec. 13—Baghbazar. Ltr. VI, 215.
Dec. 25—Baidyanath. Ltr. VII, 439.
Dec. 26—Baidyanath. Ltr. VI, 216.
Dec. 30—Allahabad. Ltr. VI, 216; VII, 441.

1890

Jan. 8—Allahabad. Ltr. V, 3; VI, 217.
Jan. 21—Ghazipur. Ltr. VI, 219.
Jan. 30—Ghazipur. Ltr. VII, 441.
Jan. 31—Ghazipur. Ltr. VI, 220.
Feb. 4—Ghazipur. Ltr. VI, 220.
Feb. 7—Ghazipur. Ltr. VI, 221.
Feb. 13—Ghazipur. Ltr. VI, 222.
Feb. 14—Ghazipur. Ltr. VI, 223.
Feb. 19—Ghazipur. Ltr. VI, 223.
n.d. —Ghazipur. Ltr. VI, 224.
Feb. 23—Ghazipur. Ltr. VI, 229.
Mar. 3—Ghazipur. Ltr. VI, 229.
Mar. 8—Ghazipur. Ltr. VI, 232.
n.d. —Ghazipur. Ltr. VI, 233.
n.d. —Ghazipur. Ltr. VI, 234.
Mar. 31—Ghazipur. Ltr. VI, 236.
Apr. 2—Ghazipur. Ltr. VI, 237.
Apr. 2—Ghazipur. Ltr. VI, 238.
May 10—Baranagore. Ltr. VI, 238.

THE RELIGION ETERNAL

May 26—Baghbazar. Ltr. VI, 239.
Jun. 4—Baghbazar. Ltr. VIII, 285.
Jul. 6—Baghbazar. Ltr. VI, 242.
n.d. —Pilgrimage with Svami Akhandananda. sl. LVK, 193-204.

1891

Jan. —Delhi. sl. LVK, 205.
Feb. —Alwar. sl. LVK, 207-14.
Apr. —Pandupol. sl. LVK, 215.
Apr. —Tahla, Narayan. sl. LVK, 215.
Apr. —Jaipur. sl. LVK, 215-17.
Apr. 14—Ajmer. Ltr. VI, 244.
Apr. 30—Mount Abo. Ltr. VI, 224.
n.d. —Mount Abo. Ltr. VI, 245.
n.d. —Khetri. sl. LVK, 217-21.
n.d. —Ahmedabad. sl. LVK, 222.
n.d. —Wedhwan, Limbdi. sl. LVK, 222.
n.d. —Bhavnagar, Shilore. sl. LVK, 222.
n.d. —Junagad. sl. LVK, 223.
n.d. —Junagad. sl LVK, 223.
n.d. —Bhooj. sl. LVK, 224.
n.d. —Somnath or Prabhas. sl. LVK, 225-6.
n.d. —Junagad. sl. LVK, 226.
n.d. —Porbandar. sl. LVK, 226-8.

1892

Apr. 26—Baroda. Ltr. VIII, 286.
May —Khandua. LVK, 229.
Jun. 14—Poona. Ltr. VIII, 287.
Aug. 22—Bombay. Ltr. VIII, 287.
Aug. 22—Bombay. Ltr. VIII, 288.
Sep. 20—Bombay. Ltr. V, 4.
Oct. —Belgaum. sl. LVK, 231-40.
Oct. —Bangalore. sl. LVK, 241-4.
Oct —Trichur, Travancore, Madurai, Rameswaran. sl. LVK, 251.
Dec. —Kanyakumari (Cape Comorio). sl. LVK, 251-5.

1893

n.d. —Margaon. Ltr. VIII, 290.
Feb. 10—Arrive Hyderabad. sl. LVK, 273.
Feb. 11—Hyderabad. Ltr. VIII, 291.
Feb 13—"My Mission to the West." sl. LVK, 275.
Feb 17—Left Hyderabad.
n.d. —Madras. VI, 203-23.
Apr. 23—Khetri. Ltr. VI, 245. Ltr. VIII, 292.
May —Khetri. VIII, 293.
May 22—Bombay. Ltr. VIII, 296.
May 23—Bombay. Ltr. IV, 354.
May 24—Bombay. Ltr. VI, 246.
May 31—Left Bombay by steamer "Peninsdar."
Jul. 10—Hong Kong, Canton, Nagasaki, Kobe, Osake, Kyoto, Yokahama. Ltr. V, 5.
n.d. —Vancouver, B.C. sl. LVK, 292.
n.d. —Arrive Chicago, Ill.
n.d. —Leave Parliament of Religions, rest until Sept.
n.d. —Leave Chicago for Boston, Mass. sl. LVK, 295.
n.d. —Metcalf, Mass. Lodged in Miss Kate Sanborn's "Breezy Meadow." sl. LVK, 295.
Aug. 20—Metcalf. Ltr. V, 11.
Aug. 28—Sunday. Annisquam, Mass. Annisquam Episcopal Church. Prof. Wright. III, 469.
Aug. 28—Annisquam. Talk. VII, 278-82.
Aug. 28—Salem, Mass. Thought & Work Club. "Religion of the Hindus." III, 465.
Aug. 30—Salem. Ltr. VIII, 447.
Sept. 4—Salem. Ltr. VIII, 447.
Sep. 4—Salem. East Church. "Religion in India." III, 468-70.
Sep. 5—Saratoga, N.Y. "Mohammedan Rule in India." III, 470.
Sep. 6—Saratoga. "Use of Silver in India." III, 470.
Sep. 11—Opening Meeting of Parliament of Religions.
Sep. 11—Chicago. Extemporaneous address. I, 3.
Sep. 15—Chicago. "Why We Disagree." I, 4.
Sep. 19—"Hinduism." I, 6.
Sep. 20—Chicago. "Religion Not Crying Need of India." I, 20.
Sep. 22—Chicago. "Orthodox Hinduism and the Vedanta Philosophy." VIII, 199fn.
Sep. 22—Chicago. "Modern Religions of India." In scientific section, not extant.
Sep. 23—Sep. 23—Chicago. Same topic and "Women o East." VIII, 198.

Sep. 24—Chicago. Third Unit. Ch. Chicago. "The Love of God." Sermon. VIII, 200.
Sep. 25—Chicago. "The Essence of the Hindu Religion." Not extant.
Sep. 26—Chicago. "Buddhism, the Fulfillment of Hinduism." I, 21.
Sep. 27—Chicago. "Address at the Final Session." I, 27.
Sep. 27—Begin tour for a Lyceum Lecture Bureau.
Sep. 30—Evanston, Ill. Cong. Ch. III, 478.
Oct. 2—Chicago. Ltr. VII, 451.
Oct. 3—Evanston. III, 478.
Oct. 5—Evanston. Cong. Ch. "Reincarnation." III, 478.
Oct. 7—Streator, Ill. "Hindu Civilisation." III, 480.
Oct. 10—Chicago. Ltr. VII, 454.
Oct. 26—Chicago. Ltr. VII, 455.
Nov. 2—Chicago. Ltr. V, 19.
Nov. 15—Chicago. Ltr. VIII, 325.
Nov. 19—Chicago. Ltr. VII, 456.
Nov. 20—Madison, Wisc. Cong. Ch. "The Religions of India." III, 481.
Nov. 24—Minneapolis, Minn. 1st Unit. Ch. "Brahminism." III, 481.
Nov. 26—Minneapolis. 1st Unit. Ch. "Mercenaries in Religion." III, 482; VII, 414.
Nov. 27—Des Moines, Iowa. "Hindu Religion." III, 482.
Dec. 28—Chicago. Ltr. V, 25.
Undated document, 1893—n.p. VIII, 328.
Newspaper accounts, 1893—III, 465-84.

1894

Jan. 13—Memphis, Tenn. Lecture to 19th Century Club. V, 183.
Jan. 16—Memphis. "Hindooism." III, 454-5.
Jan. 17—Memphis. "The Destiny of Man." VIII, 417.
Jan. 19—Memphis. "Reincarnation." VII, 421.
Jan. 20—Memphis. "Manners and Customs in India." III, 488.
Jan. 21—Memphis. VII, 282-6. "Comparative Theology." VII, 423.
Jan. 24—Chicago. Ltr. V, 27.
Jan. 29—Chicago. Ltr. VIII, 297.
Feb. 14—Detroit, Mich. Newspaper interview. VII, 286. "Manners and Customs of India." III, 490.
Feb. 15—Detroit. "Hindoo Philosophy." III, 492; VIII, 204.
n.d. —Detroit. Newspaper interview. III, 495.
Feb. 17—Detroit. "The Divinity of Man." III, 496.
Feb. 20—Detroit. "The Love of God." III, 503. VIII, 201.
Feb. 21—Detroit. "Hindus and Christians." VIII, 209.
Feb. 22—Detroit. "The Divinity of Man." II, 477.
Mar. 3—Detroit. Ltr. IV, 356.
Mar. 11—Detroit. "Christianity in India." VIII, 214.
Mar. 12—Detroit. Ltr. VIII, 300.
Mar. 15—Detroit. Ltr. VIII, 301.
Mar. 17—Detroit. Interview. VII, 291. Ltr. VII, 475.
Mar. 18—Detroit. Ltr. VIII, 303.
Mar. 19—Chicago (sic.). Ltr. VI, 250. Detroit. "Buddhism." VII, 427.
Mar. 20—Saginaw, Mich. "Different Religions of India." II, 479.
Mar. 21—Saginaw. "The Harmony of Religions." II, 482-4.
Mar. 24—Detroit. "The Women of India." III, 505. "Is India a Benighted Country?" IV, 198.
Mar. 29—Detroit. Ltr. VII, 458.
Mar. 30—Detroit. Ltr. VIII, 304.
Apr. 9—New York, N.Y. Ltr. V, 30.
Apr. 10—New York. Ltr. VIII, 334.
Apr. 14—Northampton, N.Y. "Customs of the Hindus." II, 486.
Apr. 25—New York. Ltr. VII, 459.
Apr. 26—New York. Ltr. VII, 460.
May 1—New York. Ltr. VII, 462.
May 4—New York. Ltr. VII, 463.
May 6—Boston. Ltr. VII, 464.
May 7—Boston. Lecture at Women's Club. Not extant.
May 15—Boston. "The Manners and Customs of India." II, 488.
May 16—Boston. "The Religions of India." II, 490-1.
May 20—Boston. Ltr. V, 33.
May 24—Chicago. Ltr. VII, 465.
May 28—Chicago. Ltr. V, 33.
Jun. 18—Chicago. Ltr. VII, 467.
Jun. 20—Chicago. Ltr. VIII, 305.
Jun. 23—Chicago. Ltr. IV, 361; VI, 256.
Jun. 26—Chicago. Ltr. VI, 257.
Jun. 28—Chicago. Ltr. VIII, 310.
Jul. 11—n.p. Ltr. V, 37.
n.d. —Fishkill Landing, N.Y. Ltr. VIII, 314.
Jul. 26—Swampscott. Ltr. VIII, 316.
Jul. 31—Greenacre Inn, Elliot, Me. Ltr. VI, 259.
Aug. —n.p. Ltr. VI, 263.
Aug. 11—Greenacre. Ltr. VIII, 318. (Mentions "Sympathy of Religions." Lecture at Plymouth.)
Aug. 20—Annisquam, N.Y. Ltr. V, 38.
Aug. 31—Annisquam. Ltr. V, 40. Ltr. VIII, 319.
Sep. 5—Annisquam. Ltr. VII, 469.
Sep. 9—New York. Ltr. VIII, 316.
Sep. 13—Boston. Ltr. VIII, 320-1.
Sep. 19—Boston. Ltr. VI, 267.
Sep. 21—Boston. Ltr. V, 45.
Sep. 25—New York (sic.). Ltr. VI, 268.
Sep. 26—Boston. Ltr. V, 45.
Sep. 27—Boston. Ltr. V, 46.
Sep. 29—Boston. Ltr. V, 47.
n.d. —Chicago (sic.). Ltr. VIII, 322.
Oct. 15—Baltimore. "Less Doctrine and More Bread." II, 492.
n.d. —Baltimore. Ltr. VIII, 323.
Oct. 21—Baltimore. "The Religion of the Buddha." II, 494.
Oct. 22—Baltimore. Ltr. VI, 278.
Oct. 23—Washington. Ltr. V, 48.
Oct. 26—Washington. Ltr. V, 49.
Oct. 27—Washington. Ltr. V, 50; VI, 279.
Oct. 28—Washington. "The Aryan Race." II, 497.
Oct. 30—Washington. Ltr. VI, 279.
Nov. —Washington. Ltr. VIII, 324.
Nov. 18—New York. IV, 365.
Nov. 19—New York. Ltr. IV, 367.
Nov. 30—New York. Ltr. V, 52, 54.
Dec. 8—Cambridge, Mass. Ltr. VIII, 331-2.
Dec. 21—Cambridge. Ltr. VIII, 333.
Dec. 26—Cambridge. Ltr. V, 55.
Dec. 28—Brooklyn, N.Y. Ltr. VI, 295.
Dec. 30—Brooklyn. "The Hindu Religion." I, 329. II, 494.
Dec. 31—Brooklyn. Lecture. sl. RVK, 1246.
Undated documents, 1894—III, 495, 506; V, 525; VI, 282, 287, 289; VII, 475, 480, 483; VIII, 36ff.

1895

Jan. 3—Ltr. to Justice Iyer. IV, 371.
Jan. 3—Ltr. to Mrs. Bell. Chicago. V, 63.
Jan. 11—Chicago. Ltr. V, 64.
Jan. 12—Chicago. Ltr. V, 66.
Jan. 17—New York. Ltr. VI, 296.
Jan. 20—Brooklyn. Ltr. V, 68.
Jan. 20—Brooklyn. "Ideals of Womanhood." II, 503.
Jan. 24—New York. Ltr. VIII, 333.
Feb. 1—New York. Ltr. V, 70.
Feb. 4—Brooklyn. "True Buddhism." II, 507.
Feb. 9—New York. Ltr. V, 74; VI, 298.
Feb. 15—New York. Ltr. & poem. VIII, 162.
Feb. 25—New York. Ltr. V, 74.
Feb. 26—Brooklyn. "India's Gift to the World." II, 510, 513.
Mar 6—New York. Ltr. V, 75.
n.d. —Brooklyn Ethical Assoc. "Indian Religious Thought." IV, 188.
Mar. 21—New York. Ltr. VI, 301.
Mar. —New York. "Reincarnation." IV, 257.
Mar. 27—New York. Ltr. V, 75.
Apr. 4—New York. Ltr. V, 77.
Apr. 7—Brooklyn Ethical Assoc. "Some Customs of the Hindus." II, 515.
Apr 10—New York. Ltr. V, 78.
Apr 11—New York. Ltr. VI, 302, 304.
Apr. 24—New York. Ltr. VIII, 335.
Apr. 25—New York. Ltr. VI, 306.
May 2—New York. Ltr. V, 79.
May 5—New York. Ltr. VIII, 337.
May 6—New york. Ltr. V, 80.
May 7—New York. Ltr. VI, 308. (Mentions "The Science of Religion" and "The

Rationale of Yoga.")
May 14—New York. Ltr. V, 84.
n.d. —New York. Ltr. VI, 308; VII, 486.
May 16—"No One to Blame." Poem. VIII, 175.
May 28—New York. Ltr. VIII, 338.
n.d. —New York. Ltr. VIII, 338.
Jun 7—Percy, N.H. Ltr. VI, 309.
Jun 17—Percy. Ltr. VIII, 339. Completed **Raja Yoga.**
n.d. —New York. Ltr. VI, 309.
Jun 18—Thousand Island Park, N.Y. Ltr. V, 85.
Jun 19—Retreat to Thousand Island Park. "Talks." VII, 3ff. (cf. RVK, 126.)
Jun. 22—(Thousand Island Park,) N.Y. Ltr. V, 85; VIII, 340.
Jun. 26—Thousand Island Park. Ltr. VIII, 342, 344.
Jul. 1—Thousand Island Park. Ltr. V, 86.
Jul. 7—Thousand Island Park. Ltr. V, 90.
Jul. 8—(Thousand Island Park,) N.Y. Ltr. VI, 313.
Jul. 9—Thousand Island Park. Ltr. V, 91.
n.d. —Thousand Island Park. "The Song of the Sannyasin." II, 392.
Jul. 18—Toronto, Canada. Parliament of Religions. sl. RVK, 174.
n.d. —Thousand Island Park. Ltr. V, 88.
Jul. 29—Thousand Island Park. Ltr. V, 87.
Jul. 31—Thousand Island Park. Ltrs. V, 92-3.
Aug. 2—New York. Ltr. VIII, 346.
Aug. 7—End of Thousand Island Park Retreat.
Aug. 9—New York. Ltr. VIII, 347.
Aug. 15—Sails from New York.
Aug. 26—Paris. Ltr. V, 94.
Sep. 5—Paris.Ltr. VIII, 350.
Sep. 9—Paris. Ltr. V, 95.
Sep. 10—Leave for London.
Sep. 17—Caversham. Ltr. VI, 342.
Sep. 24—Reading, Caversham. Ltr. VI, 343.
n.d. —Reading. Ltr. VIII, 351.
n.d. —Reading. Ltr. VIII, 352.
Oct. 4—Reading. Ltr. VI, 344-5.
n.d. —Caversham, Eng. VI, 343; VIII, 354.
Oct. 6—Caversham, Eng. Ltr. VI, 348.
Oct. 13—London. Ltr. VI, 348.
Oct. 20—Reading. Ltr. VIII, 354.
Oct. 22—Piccadilly, Prince's Hall. "Self Knowledge." Not extant.
Oct. 23—Westminster. Interview. V, 185.
Oct. 24—London. Ltr. V, 96.
Oct. 31—Chelsea. Ltr. VIII, 355-6.
Nov. 1—Chelsea. Ltr. VIII, 357. (Mentions "Indian Philosophy.")
Nov. 2—Chelsea. Ltr. VIII, 358.
Nov. 16—London. "The Religion of Love." VIII, 220.
Nov. 18—London. Ltr. V, 97.
Nov. 21—London. Ltr. VI, 350.
Nov. 23—London. "Jnana and Bhakti." VIII, 225.
Nov. 27—Sail from London on "Britannic."
Dec. 5—Aboard Ship. Ltr. VI, 351.
n.d. —Ltr. VIII, 358.
Dec. 6—Arrive at New York.
Dec. 8—New York. Ltr. VI, 352; VIII, 359-60.
Dec. 10—New York. Ltr. VI, 353.
Dec. 16—New York. Ltr. VIII, 363.
Dec. 20—New York. Ltr. V, 98.
Dec. 23—New York. Ltr. VIII, 365.
Dec. 29—New York. Ltr. VI, 354; VIII, 367.
Undated documents, 1895—VI, 310, 321, 336-7; VII, 484; VIII, 361.

1896

Jan. 3—New York. VIII, 169.
Jan. 5—New York. Ltr. VI, 355.
Jan. 5—New York. "Unity the Goal of Religion." III, 1. (Same as "Claims of Religion." IV, 203.) Ltr. VI, 355.
Jan. 9—New York. Ltr. VIII, 368.
n.d. —New York. "The Free Soul." III, 6.
n.d. —New York. "One Existence Appearing as Many." III, 19.
Jan. 16—New York. Ltr. VIII, 370.
Jan. 19—New York. "The Cosmos: The Macrocosm." II, 203.
Jan. 23—New York. Ltr. VIII, 371.
Jan. 24—New York. Ltr. VI, 356.
Jan. 25—New York. Ltr. VI, 357.
Jan 26—New York. "The Cosmos: The Microcosm." II, 212.
n.d. —n.p. Ltr. VI, 355.
Feb. 10—New York. Ltr. V, 99.
Feb. 13—New York. Ltr. V, 100. (c.f. VIII, 277-8, 363.)
Feb. 17—New York. Ltr. V, 104.
Feb. 17—Organized Vedanta Society of New York.
Feb. 24—Madison Sq. Garden. "My Master." IV, 154. (cf. RVK, 135.)
Feb. 24—**Karma Yoga** published.
Feb. 29—New York. Ltr. VIII, 372.
Lectures probably given to classes in February: "Immortality," II, 226; "The Atman," II, 238; "The Atman: Bondage and Freedom," II, 254; "The Real & the Apparent Man," II, 263; "Bhakti-Yoga," III, 31-100; "Addresses on "Bhakti-Yoga," IV, 3-60; "Notes on Lectures on Jnana-yoga," VIII, 3-35.
Mar. 2—Boston. Ltr. VI, 359.
Mar. 17—New York. Ltr. VIII, 374.
Mar. 22—Boston. Talk. V, 277f.
Mar. 23—Boston. Ltr. V, 105.
Mar. 24—Boston. Talk. V, 277f.
Mar. 25—Harvard. "Philosophy of the Vedanta." I, 357. Discussion. V, 297.
Apr. 6—Chicago. Ltr. VI, 360.
Apr. 14—New York. Ltr. V, 107; VI, 361; VIII, 376.
Apr. 15—Sailed for England. "Germanic."
Apr. 20—Reading. Ltr. VIII, 377.
Apr. 27—Reading. Ltr. VII, 488.
n.d. —Reading. Ltr. VII, 496.
May —London. Ltr. VII, 495.
May 16—London. Ltr. VII, 497.
May 28—Visit with Prof. Max Muller.
May 30—London. Ltr. VI, 362; VIII, 378.
Jun. 3—London. Ltr. VI, 363.
Jun. 6—London. Ltr. IV, 278.
Jun. 7—London. Ltr. VII, 498.
Jun. 24—London. Ltr. VI, 364.
Jul. 3—Reading. Ltr. VI, 364.
Jul. 6—London. Ltr. VI, 365.
Jul. 7—London. Ltr. VIII, 379.
Jul. 8—London. Ltr. VI, 367.
Jul 14—England. Ltr. V, 108.
Jul 18—London. Hindu Assoc. "The Hindus and their Needs." Not extant.
n.d. —Ridgeway Gardens, Eng. "Vedanta as a Factor in Civilisation." I, 383.
Jul 28—Saas-Grund, Switzerland. Ltr. VI, 369.
Aug. 5—Switzerland. Ltr. VIII, 380.
Aug. 6—Switzerland. Ltr. V, 109.
Aug. 8—Switzerland. Ltr. V, 110; VIII, 383, 386.
Aug. 12—Switzerland. Ltr. VIII, 387.
Aug. 23—Lucerne. Ltr. V, 112, VI, 369-70.
Aug. 26—Switzerland. Ltr. V, 113.
Sep. 10—Kiel. Ltr. VIII, 388.
Sep. 10—Westminster. Ltr. V, 116.
Sep. 17—Wimbledon. Ltr. VI, 272; VIII, 389.
Sep 22—Wimbledon. Ltr. V, 114.
Oct. 7—Wimbledon. Ltr. VI, 373.
Oct. 8—Wimbledon. Ltr. VI, 376-7.
n.d. —Wimbledon. "Maya and Illusion." II, 88.
Oct. 20—Wimbledon. "Maya and the Evolution of the Conception of God." II, 105.
Oct. 22—London. "Maya and Freedom." II, 118.
Oct. 27—"God in Everything." II, 144.
Oct. 28—London. Ltr. V, 119-20.
Oct. 29—London. "Realisation." II, 155.
Nov 1—London. Ltr. VI, 378.
Nov 3—London. "Unity in Diversity." II, 175.
Nov 5—London. "The Freedom of the Soul." II, 189.
Nov 10—London. "Practical Vedanta—Part 1." II, 291.
Nov 11—Westminster. Ltr. V, 121.
Nov 12—Westminster. "Practical Vedanta—Part II." II, 309.
Nov. 13—Westminster. Ltr. VI, 382.
Nov. 14—Westminster. "Practical Vedanta—Part III." II, 328.
Nov. 18—Westminster. "Practical Vedanta—Part IV." II, 341.
Nov. 20—London. Ltr. V, 122.
Nov. 21—London. Ltr. VI, 383.
Nov. 28—London. Ltr. VI, 384.
Dec. 3—London. Ltr. VI, 385. Ltr. VIII, 392.
Dec. 9—London. Ltr. VI, 386.
Dec. 10—London. "Advaita Vedanta." sl. LVK, 439.

Dec. 13—London. Ltr. V, 124; Ltr. VI, 386.
Dec. 16—Leaves London for Naples.
Dec. 20—Florence. Ltr. VI, 387; VIII, 393.
Dec. 30—Leaves Naples for Ceylon.
Undated documents, 1896—"Vedanta and Privilege," I, 417. Ltr. VI, 383; VIII, 376, 380-1.

1897

Jan. 3—Aboard "Prinz-Regent Leopold." Ltr. VIII, 394.
Jan. 16—Colombo Address. III, 104.
Jan. 25—Jeffna. "Vedantism." III, 116.
Jan. 26—Pamban. III, 136.
Jan. 27—Rameswaram. "Worship," III, 141; "Reply," III, 155ff.
n.d. —Kumba Konam. "The Mission of Vedanta." III, 176.
Jan. 30—Ramnad. Ltr. VI, 387.
Jan. 30—Ramnad. "Reply." III, 144.
Feb. 12—Madras. Ltr. VIII, 396.
n.d. —Madras addresses: "Welcome," III, 200; "My Plan," III, 207; "Vedanta in its Application," III, 228; "The Sages of India," III, 248; "The Work Before Us," III, 269; "The Future of India," III, 285; "On Charity," III, 305.
Feb. 15—Left by steamer for Calcutta.
Feb. 20—Calcutta. Conversation. VI, 465.
Feb. 25—Calcutta. Ltr. VI, 388.
Feb. 28—Calcutta. Special reception. "Reply." III, 306.
Mar. 1—Calcutta. "The Vedanta in All Its Phases." III, 322.
n.d. —Alambazar. Conversation. VI, 465.
Mar. 19—Darjeeling. Ltr. VII, 500.
Apr. 6—Darjeeling. Ltr. V, 125.
Apr. 20—Darjeeling. Ltr. VIII, 397.
Apr. 24—Darjeeling. Ltr. IV, 481.
Apr. 28—Darjeeling. Ltr. VI, 389.
May 1—Alambazar. Talk. VI, 476.
May 1—Founding of Ramakrishna Mission. LVK, 500f.
May 5—Alambazar Math. Ltr. VII, 501; VIII, 399.
n.d. —Alambazar. Talk. VI, 471.
n.d. —Left Calcutta for Almora.
May 13—Almora. III, 350.
May 20—Almora. Ltr. VIII, 400, 403.
May 29—Almora. Ltr. V, 127.
May 30—Almora. Ltr. VI, 392.
Jun. 1—Almora. Ltr. V, 129; VI, 396.
Jun. 2—Almora. Ltr. VIII, 403.
Jun. 3—Almora. Ltr. VI, 398.
Jun. 14—Almora. Ltr. VI, 399.
Jun. 15—Almora. Ltr. VI, 400.
Jun. 20—Almora. Ltr. VI, 401; VIII, 405.
Jul. 3—Almora. Ltr. V, 131.
Jul. 4—Almora. Ltr. VIII, 407.
Jul. 9—Almora. Ltr. V, 133; VI, 402. Ltr. poem. VIII, 169.
Jul. 10—Almora. Ltr. VIII, 408.
Jul. 11—Almora. Ltr. VII, 502.
Jul. 13—Almora. Ltr. VIII, 410.
Jul. 23—Almora. Ltr. VII, 506.
Jul. 24—Almora. Ltr. VI, 404.
Jul. 25—Almora. Ltr. VIII, 412.
Jul. 28—Almora. Ltr. V, 137.
Jul. 29—Almora. Ltr. VIII, 416.
Jul. 30—Almora. Ltr. VI, 405.
Aug. 11—Belur. Ltr. V, 138; VII, 507.
Aug. 19—Ambala. Ltr. VI, 407; VIII, 417.
Sep. 2—Amritsar. Ltr. VIII, 418.
Sep. 13—Srinagar, Kashmir. Ltr. VIII, 419.
Sep. 15—Srinagar, Kashmir. Ltr. VIII, 422-3.
Sep. 30—Srinagar. Ltr. VIII, 424, 426-7.
Oct. 1—Srinagar. Ltr. VIII, 428.
Oct. 10—Murree. Ltr. VI, 409, 411.
Oct. 11—Murree. Ltr. V, 138; VIII, 430.
Oct. 12—Murree. Ltr. VIII, 433.
Nov. 3—Jammu. Ltr. VIII, 434.
Nov. 9—Lahore. "Bhakti." III, 383.
Nov. 11—Lahore. Ltr. VIII, 435.
Nov. 13—Lahore. Ltr . VI, 413; VIII, 436.
Nov. 24—Behra Dun. Ltr. V, 139; VI, 414; VIII, 437.
Nov. 30—Delhi. Ltr. VIII, 437.
Dec. 8—Delhi. Ltr. VIII, 438.
Dec. 14—Khetri. Ltr. VIII, 440.
Dec. 20—Khetri. Ltr. III, 434.
Dec. 27—Jaipur. Ltr. VIII, 440.

1898

Jan. 22—Calcutta. Conversation. V, 332.
Jan. 23—Calcutta. Conversation. V, 334.
Jan. 24—Calcutta. Conversation. V, 339, 344.
Feb. 6—Howrah. Conversation. VI, 512.
Feb. 25—Belur Math. Ltr. VIII, 441-2.
Mar. 2—Belur. Ltr. VIII, 445, 447.
Mar. 11—Calcutta. "The Influence of Indian Spiritual Thought in England." III, 440.
Mar. 16—Belur. Ltr. VIII, 461.
Mar. 20—Calcutta. "Work Without Motive." V, 246.
Apr. 11—Math. Ltr. VI, 418.
Apr. 18—Darjeeling. Ltr. VIII, 448.
Apr. 23—Darjeeling. Ltr. VIII, 449.
Apr. 29—Darjeeling. Ltr. VIII, 450.
May 11—Leaves for Almora.
May 20—Almora. Ltr. VI, 415; VIII, 451.
Jun. 9—Almora. Ltr. V, 139.
Jun. 10—Leaves for Kashmir. Ltr. VI, 415.
Jul. 3—Kashmir. Ltr. VIII, 453.
Jul. 4—Kashmir. Poem. I, 439.
n.d. —Belur. Talks. V, 349-61, 361f. (The disciple appears to have remembered the wrong data.)
Jul. 17—Srinagar. Ltr. VIII, 454.
Jul. 27—Arrive Islamabad.
Aug. 1—Srinagar. Ltr. VIII, 456.
Aug. 2—Amarnath. sl. LVK, 589-95.
Aug. 25—Kashmir. Ltr. VI, 416.
Aug. 28—Srinagar, Kashmir. Article for **Prabuddha Bharata,** "To the Awakened India," IV, 387. "Requiescat in Pace," IV, 389. Ltr. VIII, 457.
Sep. 17—Kashmir. Ltr. V, 140; VIII, 459.
Sep. 30—Left for Kshir Bhowani. N, 115.
Oct. 6—Kshir Bhowani. Kali worship described. N, 115, 131.
Oct. 11—Left for Baramulla. N, 134.
Oct. 16—Lahore. Ltr. V, 141; VIII, 460.
Oct. 18—Arrives in Calcutta.
Oct. 26—Howrah Dist., Bengal. Ltr. V, 142.
Nov. —Howrah Dist. Ltr. V, 142.
Nov. 12—Calcutta. Ltr. VIII, 461.
Nov. 13—Baghbazar. Opening of Sister Nivedita Girls' School.
Nov. 15—Belur. "Angels Unawares." Poem. IV, 385. Ltr. V, 143.
Dec. 9—Belur. Consecration of Ramakrishna Math.
Dec. 15—Belur. Ltr. VI, 417.
Dec. 19—Leaves for Vaidyanath.
Dec. 23—Vaidyanath. Ltr. IV, 488.
Dec. 29—Deoghar. Ltr. VI, 417.
Undated documents, 1898—"Talks at Belur Math," VII, 107. Interviews, V, 225, 228.

1899

Jan. 3—Deoghar. Ltr. V, 143.
Jan. 14—Deoghar. "The Problem of Modern India and its Solution." IV, 399.
Jan. 30—Returns to Belur.
Feb. 2—Belur. Ltr. V, 147.
Feb. 12—Article: "Knowledge: Its Source and Acquirement." IV, 430.
Mar. 14—Review Article, IV, 409. "Modern India," IV, 438.
Mar. 19—Mayavati purchased.
Apr. 16—Belur Math. Ltr. VII, 509.
Jun. 14—Alambazar. Ltr. V, 148.
Jun. 19—Belur Math. "Sannyasa: Its Ideals and Practice." III, 446.
Jun. 20—Sails from Calcutta.
Jun. 28—Colombo, Ceylon.
Jul. 14—Reached Suez. Port Said. Ltr. VIII, 463.
Jul. 31—Arrived in London. Article: "Memoirs of European Travel." VII, 297-372.
Aug. 3—Wimbledon. Ltr. VIII, 464, 466.
Aug. 10—London. Ltr. VIII, 468.
Aug. 16—Sails for New York.
Aug. 26—Goes to Ridgely Manor, N.Y., until Nov. 5.
Sep. 2—Ridgely. Ltr. V, 149.
Sep. 4—Ridgely. Ltr. VI, 418; VIII, 470.
Sep. 14—Ridgely. Ltr. VIII, 470.

n.d. —Ridgely. Ltr. VIII, 472.
Sep. 21—Ridgely. Ltr. LVK, insert between pp. 660 and 661.
Oct. 3—Ridgely. Ltr. VIII, 475.
Oct. 30—Ridgely. Ltr. VIII, 475.
Nov. 1—Ridgely. Ltr. VI, 419.
Nov. 3—Leaves Ridgely.
Nov. 8—New York. Presides over Society Meeting.
n.d. —New York. Ltr. VII, 511.
Nov. 15—New York. Ltr. VI, 419; VIII, 479.
Nov. 20—New York. Ltr. VIII, 480, 482.
Nov. 21—New York. Ltr. VIII, 482.
Nov. 22—Leaves for California.
Nov. 26—Chicago. Ltr. VII, 516.
Nov. 30—Chicago. Ltr. VII, 516.
Dec. 6—Los Angeles, Calif. Ltr. VII, 517.
Dec. 8—Los Angeles. "Vedanta Philosophy." LVK, 663.
Dec. 12—Los Angeles. Ltr. VI, 419.
Dec. 22—Los Angeles. Ltr. VIII, 483.
Dec. 23—Los Angeles. Ltr. VI, 421.
Dec. 27—Los Angeles. Ltr. VIII, 485, 487.
Undated documents, 1899—Article in Bengali, "A Preface to the Imitation of Christ," VIII, 159f. "Talks at Belur Math," VII, 186-200. Prospectus, "The Advaita Ashrama," V, 435. Interview, V, 233. "Talk at Belur Math," VII, 271-7. Ltr. VIII, 478. Poems, IV, 395; VIII, 170.

1900

Jan. 4—Los Angeles. "Work and Its Secret." II, 1.
Jan. 8—Los Angeles. "Powers of the Mind." II, 10.
Jan. 5—Los Angeles. "The Open Secret." II, 397.
Jan. 17—Los Angeles. Ltr. VIII, 489.
Jan. 18—Pasadena, Calif. Ltr. VIII, 53.
Jan. 24—Los Angeles. Ltr. VI, 422.
Jan. 27—Pasadena. "My Life and Mission." VIII, 73.
Jan. 28—Pasadena. "The Way to Realization." II, 359.
n.d. —Los Angeles. "Hints of Practical Spirituality." II, 24.
Jan. 31—Pasadena. "The Ramayana." IV, 63.
Feb. 1—Pasadena. "The Mahabharata." IV, 78.
Feb. 2—Pasadena. "Buddhistic India." III, 511.
Feb. 3—Pasadena. "The Great Teachers of the World." IV, 120.
n.d. —Pasadena. "The Story of Jada Bharata." IV, 111.
n.d. —Pasadena."The Story of Prahlada." IV, 115.
Feb. 15—Los Angeles. Ltr. VI, 423. Pasadena. Ltr. VIII, 491.
Feb. 20—Pasadena. Ltr. VIII, 492.
Feb. 21—Pasadena. Ltr. VI, 425.
Feb. 25—Oakland. "The Claims of Vedanta on the Modern World." VIII, 231.
Feb. 28—Oakland. "The Vedanta and Christianity." VI, 46.
Mar. 2—San Francisco. Ltr. VII, 493.
Mar. 4—San Francisco. Ltr. VI, 428; VIII, 494.
Mar. 7—Oakland. "The Laws of Life and Death." VIII, 235. San Francisco. Ltrs. VIII, 495, 498.
Mar. 8—Oakland. "The Reality and the Shadow," VIII, 237.
Mar. 12—Oakland. "Way to Salvation." VIII, 239. San Francisco. Ltr. VIII, 499, 500-1.
Mar. 16—San Francisco. "Concentration." IV 218.
Mar. 17—San Francisco. Ltr. VII, 518-9.
Mar. 18—San Francisco. "Buddha's Message to the World." VIII, 92.
Mar. 19—Oakland. "The People of India." VIII, 241.
Mar. 20—San Francisco. "I Am That I Am." VIII, 244.
Mar. 22—San Francisco. Ltr. VIII, 502.
Mar. 23—San Francisco. "The Soul and God." I, 489.
Mar. 25—San Francisco. "Mohammed." Ltr. I, 481; VI, 429.
Mar. 27—San Francisco. "The Goal." II, 463.
Mar. 28—San Francisco. "Breathing." I, 502. Ltr. VI, 430; VIII, 503.
Mar. 29—San Francisco. "Discipleship." VIII, 106.
n.d. —San Francisco. Ltr. VIII, 505.
Mar. 30—San Francisco. Ltr. VIII, 506.
Apr. 1—San Francisco. "Krishna." I, 437. Ltr. VIII, 510.
Apr. 3—San Francisco "Meditation." IV, 227.
n.d. —San Francisco. Ltr. VIII, 508.
Apr. 5—San Francisco. "Practical Religion: Breathing & Meditation." I, 513.
Apr. 6—San Francisco. Ltr. VIII, 512.
Apr. 7—San Francisco. Ltr. VII, 520; VIII, 513.
Apr. 8—San Francisco. "Is Vedanta the Future Religion?" VIII, 122, 513.
Apr. 9—San Francisco. "Worshipper and Worshipped." VI, 49.
Apr. 10—San Francisco. "Formal Worship." VI, 59. Ltr. VIII, 515.
Apr. 12—San Francisco. "Divine Love." V, 70. Alameda, Calif. Ltr. VIII, 517.
Apr. 13—Alameda. "The Science of Yoga." VII, 428.
Apr. 16—Alameda. "Concentration and Breathing." LVK, 667.
Apr. 17—Alameda. Ltr. VII, 521.
Apr. 18—Alameda. "Practice of Religion," IV, 238; VI, 101 (inc.). Ltr. VI, 431.
Apr. 20—Alameda. Ltr. VIII, 518.
Apr. 23—Alameda. Ltr. VIII, 519.
Apr. 30—Alameda. Ltr. VIII, 520.
May 2—Alameda. Ltr. VII, 522; VIII, 521.
May —Retreat to Camp Taylor, 3 weeks.
May 24—San Francisco. "Questions and Answers." V, 320. Guest of Dr. W. Forster.
May 26—San Francisco. "Gita I." I, 446. Ltr. VIII, 522.
May 28—San Francisco. "Gita II." I, 459.
May 29—San Francisco. "Gita III." I, 467.
Jun. 9—Arrive N.Y. LVK, 672.
n.d. —New York. "Unity." VIII, 250.
Jun. 10—New York. "Vedanta Philosophy." LVK, 673.
Jun. 16—New York. "What is Religion?" Not extant. LVK, 673.
Jun. 17—Los Angeles. (sic.) Ltr. VIII, 522. (The date or place is wrong.)
Jun. 17—New York. "What is Religion?" N, xv.
Jun. 20—New York. Ltr. VI, 433.
Jun. 23—New York. Ltr. III, 525.
Jun. 24—"Mother Worship." VI, 145; VIII, 292; N, xix.
n.d. —New York. "Worship of the Divine Mother." VIII, 252.
Jul. 1—New York. "Source of Religion." Not extant. LVK, 673.
Jul. 2—New York. Ltr. VI, 433.
Jul. 3—Left for Detroit; Detroit until July 10.
Jul. 10—Returned to New York.
Jul. 11—New York. Ltr. VIII, 526.
Jul. 18—New York. Ltr. VIII, 527.
Jul. 20—Sailed for Paris. N.Y. Ltr. VIII, 527.
Jul. 24—New York. (sic.). Ltr. VIII, 528. (Date or place is wrong.)
Jul. 25—New York. (sic.) Ltr. VIII, 529. (Date or place is wrong.)
Aug. 1—Arrived in Paris.
Aug. —New York. (sic.) Ltr. VIII, 529. (Date or place is wrong.)
Aug. 13—Paris. Ltr. VIII, 530.
Aug. 14—Paris. Ltr. VIII, 531.
Aug. —Paris. Ltr. VIII, 532.
Aug. 17—Poems. VIII, 168.
Aug. 17—Paris. "The East and the West." Article. V, 441.
Aug. 25—Paris. Ltr. VI, 434.
Aug. 28—Paris. Ltr. VI, 435.
Sep. 1—Paris. Ltr. VIII, 533.
Sep. —Paris. Ltr. VIII, 535.
Sep. 2—Paris. Ltr. VI, 436.
Sep. 10—Paris. Ltr. VI, 439.
Sep. 22—Bretagne. Ltr. VII, 523.
Oct. —Paris. Ltr. VIII, 536.
Oct. 14—Paris. Ltr. VIII, 537.
Oct. 14—Paris. Ltr. VIII, 537.
Oct. 24—Left Paris.
Oct. 25—Arrived in Vienna.
Oct. 30—Arrived in Constantinople.
Nov. 26—Port Tewfick. Ltr. VIII, 539.
Dec. 9—Arrived at Belur Math.
Dec. 11—Belur. Ltr. VI, 439.
Dec. 15—Belur. Ltr. VIII, 540.
Dec. 19—Belur. Ltr. VI, 440.
Dec. 26—Belur. Ltr. V, 149; VI, 440; VIII, 168.
Undated documents, 1900—"Memoirs of European Travels, Oct. 23-30, 1900." VII, 372f.

1901

Jan. 3—Arrived at Mayavati.
Jan. 6—Mayavati. Ltr. V, 150.
Jan. 15—Mayavati. Ltr. V, 152.
Jan. 24—Belur Math.
Jan. 26—Belur. Ltr. V, 153.
Feb. —Belur. Ltr. V, 154.
Feb. 2—Belur. Ltr. V, 154.
Feb. 14—Belur. Ltr. V, 155.
Feb. 17—Belur. Ltr. V, 156.
Mar. 18—Left Calcutta for Dacca.
Mar. 19—Dacca. "What Have I Learnt?" III, 449.
Mar. 29—Dacca. Ltr. V, 156.
Mar. 31—Dacca. "The Religion We Are Born In." III, 454.
May 15—Belur. Ltr. V, 158.
May 18—Belur. Ltr. V, 158.
Jun. 3—Belur. Ltr. V, 159.
Jun. 14—Belur. Ltr. V, 161.
Jun. 18—Belur. Ltr. V, 163.
Jun. —Belur. Ltr. V, 163.
Jul. 5—Belur. Ltr. V, 164.
Jul. 6—Belur. Ltr. V, 165.
Aug. 27—Belur. Ltr. V, 165.
Aug. 29—Belur. Ltr. V, 168.
Sep. 7—Belur. V, 169; VI, 42.
Nov. 8—Belur. Ltr. V, 170.

1902

Jan. —Trip to Buddha Gaya. LVK, 728; N, 396.
Feb. 10—Varanasi. Ltr. V, 172.
Feb. 12—Varanasi. Ltr. V, 174-5.
Feb. 18—Varanasi. Ltr. V, 176.
Feb. 21—Varanasi. Ltr. V, 177.
Feb. 24—Varanasi. Ltr. V, 177.
Mar. —Returned to Belur Math.
Apr. 21—Belur. Ltr. V, 178.
May 15—Belur. Ltr. V, 179.
Jun. 14—Belur. Ltr. V, 179.
Jul. 4—Death. sl. LVK, 747f.
Jul. 5—Cremation. sl. LVK, 755f.
Jul. 6—Collection of relics. sl. LVK, 756.

APPENDIX B

The following selected linguistic equivalents appear as used by Svāmī Vivekānanda in **The Complete Works** (CW) and are referred to by volume number and page, e.g., III, 453. (Some diacritical marks have been added to the **svāmī's** spellings for clarity.)

SANSKRIT-ENGLISH

abhyāsa—constant meditation on chosen ideal (III, 453)
achārā—custom (III, 173); cleanliness (V, 473)
achit—(not-consciousness); nature (VIII, 54)
adhikārabheda—doctrine of breaking authority (III, 397)
adhikāravāda—special rights and privileges (V, 267)
adhyāsa—superimposition (VII, 33)
advaitavāda—non-dualism, monism (V, 318)
ahaṁ brahmāsmi—I am **Brahman** (VIII, 47)
ahaṁkāra—egoism (V, 258); third part of mind
āhāra—food; objects of senses (V, 403); thought collected in mind (III, 338)
āhāra-shuddhi—pure food (III, 337)
ahiṁsā—non-injury
ākāsha—primal matter (II, 265), ether (VIII, 192); one external element (II, 435)
akhanda-sachchidānanda—undivided absolute (III, 58)
ānanda—bliss
anavasāda—strength
anubhuti—realization (III, 377)
anurāga—attachment to God (III, 76)
anuraki—attachment after knowledge of God (III, 36)
antarjyotis—inner light (VII, 63)
antaryāmin—omnipresent one (III, 376), inner ruler (III, 60)
aparokṣānubhūti—supersensuous perception (VI, 475), transcendent perception (VII, 142)
aprātikulya—state of mind without interests (III, 85)
āptas—those who have sensed religion (VII, 64)
avaraṇa—veil over Atman (III, 335)
avasthā—stage (V, 53)
avatāra—incarnation of God

bhāva—divine vision (V, 336)
bhiksha—begging (V, 262)
bhoga—enjoyment (V, 353)
brahmachārin—one with full control over passions (V, 524)
brahmachārya—chastity (I, 190)
brahmaloka—highest heaven (II, 184)
Brahman—Absolute, Impersonal God, God
brahmavidyā—knowledge of **Brahman** (VII, 42)

chaitānya—bodyless (III, 421), spirit (III, 414)
chandāla—outcaste
chārvākas—materialists (II, 115)
chidākāsa—knowledge space (I, 162)
chit—man (VII, 54), consciousness
chitta—mind stuff (II, 256), floor of mind
chittashuddhi—purification of the heart (III, 301)

dāna—gift
daridra nārāyana—service of God in the poor (VII, 245)
darshaṇas—six schools of philosophy (III, 396)
dāshya-bhakti—devotion through service (VI, 209)
daya—doing good to others without any gain to one's self (III, 67)
deshāchāras—customs of the country (V, 264)
desha-kāla-nimitta—space, time, causation (I, 95)
devayāna—way to God (II, 271)
dharaṇa—fixing the mind (I, 191)
dharma—seeking happiness here and hereafter (V, 446)
dhyāna—meditation (I, 191)

drishṭisaukaryam—"help to the vision" of God, image (III, 61)
dvijāti—twice-born (VII, 107)

ekāgranishṭhā—one-pointed devotion (V, 387)
ekāgratā—one-pointedness (faith) (V, 387)
eka—one, oneness (III, 384)

guṇas—qualities (**satva, rajas, tamas**) (I, 377); equilibrium, activity, inertness (I, 36)
guru-griha-vāsa—living with Guru (V, 364)
guru-paraṁparā—unbroken chain of discipleship (initiation) (V, 322)

indriyas—sense organs (II, 233)
ishṭa-nishṭā—"steadfast devotion to a chosen ideal" (III, 62) (VII, 63)
ishṭāpurta—work for God (III, 44)
Īshvara—personal God (V, 269)

jada—inert (jada-karma) (III, 414)
jagat (n.)—world; humanity; universe (III, 459)
japa—repetition of **mantras** (V, 324); repeating Holy Name (VII, 37)
jāti—birth (III, 409)
jīva—soul, individual (II, 348)
jīvanmuktas—free souls (III, 55)
jīva-sevā—service to beings (V, 325)
jñāna—knowledge
jñāna kānda—portion of Vedas dealing with knowledge (III, 228)
jñāni—one who aims at wholeness of things (III, 81)

kaivalya—freedom (V, 239)
kāla—time (I, 95)
kalpa—cycle (II, 207)
kāma—lust (V, 261)
kānchana—greed; wealth (V, 261)
karma—act, deed (II, 348); ritual (I, 72); devotion to duty (I, 72); causation (V, 434)
karma-bhumi—sphere of **karma** (II, 270); earth, place where liberation is attained (III, 127)
karma-kānda—portion of Vedas dealing in sacrifice (III, 324); ritualistic karma (III, 60)
karma-yoga—concentration in action (V, 247)
kriyā—activity (VII, 56)

linga sharīra—astral body, one assumed between death and rebirth (V, 304)
lokāchāras—customs of the people (V, 264)

madhura-bhāva—worshipping God as husband or lover (V, 344)
mahākāsha—ordinary space (I, 162)
mahāpralaya—final dissolution (VII, 140)
mahat—mind (II, 265); intelligence (II, 7); the great principle (II, 443)
manas—mind (III, 354), cognating faculty (VIII, 39)
mantra-drashṭās—the expiration of the mantras (III, 375); "seer of thought"
manushyatva—human birth (III, 451)
māyā—ignorance (II, 254); illusion (II, 251); delusion (VIII, 22); fact of contingency, mind (VIII, 143)
māyāvāda—teaching of maya (III, 325)

moksha—liberation (III, 43)
mukti—freedom (III,127); disembodiedness (VII, 52)
mumukshutā—realization of God (III, 451)
mumukshutva—desire for moksha (III, 451)

nāmarupa—name and form (II, 112); devotion to one ideal (VII, 87)
nārāyaṇa—God manifest (VII, 245)
nāstika—"It is not." Vedas are not authority (III, 333)
nimitta—causation (I, 95)
nirvāṇa—realization of the Self (V, 284); death of the body forever; mukti (VII, 94); annihilation (M, 413)
nirvikalpa—"absolute"
nivritti—circling inward (II, 108); self abnegation (I, 85); dragging from attachment (VII, 102); no desire (VIII, 146); turning from world (VII, 17)

paṇḍit—a scholar, learned in scriptures
paramātman—God (III, 410)
pariṇāma—evolution (III, 407)
pariṇāmavāda—evolution by real modification (VI, 215)
parivrājaka—the stage of solitary wandering
prakriti—nature, world (III, 122), (VII, 66)
pralaya—creation (III, 437); involution (III, 407); law of cycles (III, 123)
prāṇa—energy (II, 265); primal force (VIII, 193); sources of motion (VII, 62)
prāṇāyāma—controlling the **prāṇa** (VIII, 42)
prasāda—consecrated food (V, 375); grace, graciousness, favor, help by the Lord
prasthānas—three systems of **Vedānta**: **advaita, dvaita**, and **vishishtādvaita**
pratikas—substitutes for God; "Going towards"
pratimas—images (III, 61)
pratyaksha—direct perception (III, 253)
prema—love (V, 345)
priti—pleasure in God (II, 79)
pūjā—worship (III, 301)
pūjārī—one who performs ritualistic worship, a priest
purushakāra—personal exertion
purusha—soul (I, 135)

rajas—activity (I, 36); humanity (VII, 94); repulsion (II, 433)

sādhanās—austerities for realization (V, 268); worship (V, 388)
sādhāraṇa dharma—universal religion
sādhu—holy man
sākshi—witness (III, 418)
samādhi—one wave, one-formedness (I, 191), superconsciousness (I, 180)
samashti—"Collected" as synonum for personal God (V, 269), (III, 188), (IV, 488)
saṁsāra—cycle of birth and rebirths (II, 259); continuous motion (III, 416)
saṁakāra—impressions (II, 255), tendencies (VII, 240)
saṁyama—three forms of meditation: dharaṇa, dhyāna, samādhi (I, 186)
sanātana dharma—everlasting, eternal
sānkhya—darshana which is fountainhead of all Indians
sannyāsa—renunciation (V, 260)
sat—"isness," truth (VII, 57)
sat-chit-ānanda Brahman—existence, knowledge, bliss absolute (III, 453)

sattva—equilibrium (I, 36); divinity (VII, 94); balance (II, 433)
sāttvika—introspective (VII, 12); quality of Brahminhood (V, 377)
sāttvika—quality of Brahminhood (V, 377)
satya—truthfulness (III, 67)
sevā—service
shraddhā—faith; faith in yourself (the Ātman)
siddha—one who has realised the Truth (V, 319)
siddhis—perfections (III, 335); powers (VII, 65)
smaraṇa—rememberance, the meaning of service to the Lord (V, 318)
smriti—Vedas (III, 120)
srishṭi—creation (V, 338); projection (III, 399)
sukshma sharīra—the fine body, the mind (III, 401)
sutra—sacred thread (VII, 37)
svadharma—natural duty (V, 448), duty according to capacity and position (V, 455)
svargas—heavens (II, 176)

tamas—inertness (I, 36); brutality (VII, 94); attraction (II, 433)
tāmasas—the bound (VII, 12)
tāmasika—bondage to tamas (VIII, 29)
tanha, tissā—grasping
tanmātras—subtle matter (I, 135)
tapas—austerities, penance, "to burn," heat (VII, 25)
tapasyā—course of austerities (V, 319)
tattva—element (II, 454)
thākur—Lord (VII, 109)
tirthas—pilgrimages
titikshā—forbearance (III, 17)
trishnā—thirst after life (I, 97)
tyāgis—men of renunciation (V, 369)

upāsanā—dualistic teaching (III, 398)
utsava—celebration (VI, 466)

vaidantika—Vedantist
vairāgya—non-attachment, renunciation (V, 306)
vāmāchari—left-handed (III, 388)
varṇa-sāṁkarya—mixture of castes (V, 456)
varṇāshrama—caste system
Vedānta—advaita, vishishtādvaita, shuddhāvaita, dvaita, etc. (III, 323)
Vedas—karma kānda, jñāna kānda
vibhu—omnipresent (III, 416)
vidyā—science (III, 60)
vijñāna—all-knowingness (II, 459) real knowledge (VIII, 23) (consciousness)
vikāsha—expansion of the soul (III, 337)
viraha—intense misery in absence of beloved (III, 79)
virāt—universe (III, 301); all-pervading spirit in form of universe (pantheism) (BD, 84)
vishishṭa—differentiation (VII, 56)
vishishṭādvaita—qualified non-dual **Vedānta**
viveka—discrimination (II, 304)
vyashṭi—finite (III, 416)
vyatireki—process of reasoning from phenomenal existence to the Absolute (V, 391)

yajña—sacrifice
yugas—satya yuga, treta yuga, dwapara yuga, kali yuga (III, 121)

ENGLISH—SANSKRIT

absolute—**nirvikalpa**
action—**karma, karmabhumi**
activity—**kriyā**
all-knowingness—**vijñāna**
astral body—**linga sharīra**
attachment to God—**anurāga, anuraki, [nishtas]**
austerities—**sādhanās, tapas, tapasyā**
authority, breaking of—**adhikārabheda**
authority question—**nāstika, astika**

begging—**bhikshā, mādhukari**
birth—**manushyatra, mumukshutva, mumukshutā, jati**
bound—**tāmasas, baddhas**
Buddhist, crypto—**Prachchhanna Bauddha**

caste—**varṇāshrama, chāturvarya, varna-sāmkarya**
causation—**nimitta, karma**
celebration—**utsava**
circling inward—**nivritti**; outward—**pravritti**
compassion(pity)—**kripā**
creation—**srishṭi, [pralaya], nihsritam**
customs—**lokāchāras, deshāchāras, āchāra**
cycle of ages—**yugas, kalpa, pralaya** (law of)
cycles of birth and rebirth—**saṁsāra**

desire—**pravitti**
devotion—**bhakti, ishta-nishtā, parābhakti, gaunibhakti**
devotee—**bhakta**
differentiation—**vishishṭa**
discrimination—**viveka**
dissolution—**mahāpralaya**
divine vision—**bhāva**
dualistic teaching—**upāsanā, dvaita**
doing good—**dayā**

egotism—**ahaṁkāra**
energy—**prāṇa, shakti**
enjoyment—**bhoga**
evolution—**pariṇāma [mahāpralaya]**

faith—**shraddhā, ekāgratā, ekāgranishthā**
finite—**vyashti**
freedom—**kaivalya, mukti, moksha**

gift—**dāna**
God—**Ishvara, Brahman; Nirguṇa Brahman; Saguna Brahman; avatāra, deva, paramātman, virāt** (pantheistic), **Samashti, ekaṁ, Nārāyana, Thākur**
grace—**prasāda**
greed—**kānchana**

heart, purification of—**chittashuddhi**
heavens—**Brahmaloka, Gandharva, svargas, Vaikuntha**

images—**drishtisankaryam, pratikas, pratimas**
impressions—**saṁskāras**
introspection—**sāttvikas**
involution—**pralaya**

joy—**rasāsvādana**

knowledge—**jñāna, Brahmavidyā, Brahmavit**

left-handed—**vāmāchari**
life, thirst after—**trishna**
love of God—**madhura-bhāva; Rādhā-prema; bhakti; parābhakti, prema, rāgānugā, ānanda**
lust—**kāma**

man—**manusha, chit**
materialism—**chārvāka**
matter—**akāsha, tanmātras**
meditation—**dhyāna, samyana, abhyāsa**
mental processes—**stambhāva, uchchātana, vashikāraṇa, mārana**

mind—**Mahat, chitta, sukshma sharīra, manas, antahkāraṇa**
Mother—**Kālī, Jagadambā**

name and form—**nāmarupa**
nature—**prakriti, achit**
non-attachment—**vairāgya**
non-desire—**nivritti**
non-dualism—**advaitavāda**
non-injury—**ahiṁsā, [ahiṁsākas]**

offering—**prasāda**
omnipresent—**vibhu, antaryāmin**
oneness—**ekaṁ**
outcaste—**chandāla**

particular—**vyashti**
paths to God—**devayāna, pritiyāna**
perception—**buddhi, pratyāksha, aparokshānubhūti, samādhi**
pleasure in God—**priti**
postures—**āsana**
power—**shakti, bala**
preparatory—**guani**
privilege—**adhikārivāda**
projection—**srishti, [nihsritam], [adhyāsa**—superimposition]

qualities—**guṇas, tattvas**

realization—**mumukshutā, nirvikalpa samādhi, anubhuti**
realizer—**siddha, āptas**
reason—**[anumāna], [aparoksha]**
remembrance—**smaraṇa**
renouncer—**tyāgis**
renunciation—**sannyāsa, vairāgya, [nivritti]**
repetition—**japa**
revelation—**mantra-drashtās**

sacred word—**Oṁ, Pranava**
sacrifice—**yajña, panchamahāyajña, rājasvya**
science—**vidyā**
sense-organs—**indriyas**
service—**jīva-sevā, sevā, [dayā], daridra nārāyana**
soul—**jīva; vyashti; Ātman, purusha, sankuchita, siddhis**
space—**Akāsha, Mahākāsha, Chittākāsha, Chidākāsha, desha-kāla-nimitta, desha**
spirit—**chaitanya**
strength—**anavasāda, ojas**
study—**svādhyāya**
superimposition—**adhyāsa**

teacher—**guru, siddha-guru**
time—**kāla, [yuga]**
truth—**sat** (existence)
truthfulness—**satya**
twice-born—**dvijāti**

undivided—**akhanda**
unity—**[advaita], eka**
universal—**samashti**
universe—**virāt, Brahmā, Hiranyagarbha**
unselfish—**apratikulya**

veil—**āvarana**
vibration—**spandana**

ways to God—**devayāna, pitriyāna**
witness—**sākshi**
word—**sphota, oṁ, vāc, shabda, nāda, Brahmā**
work—**karman** (n); **grantha** (m); **ishtapurta**
world—**loka**(n); **jagat**(n); **bhuvana**(n); **virāt, karma bhumi, prakriti, Brahmā, Hiranyagarbha**
worship—**puja, sevā** (service), **sādhanā**

BIBLIOGRAPHY

Sources

The Complete Works of Swami Vivekananda. Volumes 1-8. Sixth Edition. Calcutta: Advaita Ashrama, 1964.

Datta, Bhupendranath. **Swami Vivekananda: Patriot-Prophet.** Calcutta: Nababharat Publishers, 1954.

Eastern and Western Disciples. **The Life of Swami Vivekananda.** Calcutta: Advaita Ashrama, 1965.

Gupta, Mahendranath. **The Gospel of Sri Ramakrishna.** Translated from Bengali into English by Swami Nikhilananda New York: Ramakrishna-Vivekananda Center, 1969.

Nivedita, Sister. **The Master as I Saw Him.** Sixth Edition. Calcutta: Udbodhan Office, 1948.

SELECTED INTERPRETIVE WORKS IN ENGLISH

Books

Abhedananda, Swami. **Swami Vivekananda and His Work.** Third Edition. Calcutta: Ramakrishna-Vedanta Math, 1950.

Aroa, V.K. **The Social and Political Philosophy of Swami Vivekananda.** Calcutta: Punthi Pustak, 1968.

Avineshilingam, T.S. **Vivekananda and Gandhi.** Coimbatore: Sri Ramakrishna Mission Vidyalaya, 1962.

Barrows, Rev. J.H. **Introduction to the Parliament Papers.** Chicago: n.d.

——————— **World's Parliament of Religions.** Chicago: n.d.

Basu, Sankari Prasad (ed.). **Vivekananda in Indian Newspapers, 1893-1902.** Calcutta: Basu Bhattacharyya, 1969.

Bhattacharya, Bejoy Chandra. **Karl Marx and Vivekananda.** Calcutta: 1953.

Bose, Narayan. **Social Thinking of Vivekananda.** Lucknow: Bina Bose, 1963.

Burke, Marie Louise. **Swami Vivekananda in America: New Discoveries.** Calcutta: Advaita Ashrama, 1958.

Centenary Publications, Swami Vivekananda. **Worldwide Celebrations of Swami Vivekananda Centenary.** Calcutta: Sri Gouranga Press Ltd., 1965.

Centenary Committee, Swami Vivekananda. **Parliament of Religions — Swami Vivekananda Centenary.** Calcutta: Sree Saraswaty Press Ltd., 1965.

Chakraborty, Tarini Sankar. **Patriot-Saint Vivekananda.** Allahabad: R.K. Mission Sevashram, 1963.

Chaudhuri, Sanjib Kumar. **Visions of Vivekananda.** Calcutta: n.p., 1962.

Christine, Sister. **The Memoirs.** n.p., n.d.

Das, Trilochan. **Social Philosophy of Swami Vivekananda.** Calcutta: Co-operative Book Depot, 1949.

Datta, Bhupendranath. **Swami Vivekananda, the Socialist.** Calcutta: n.p., 1926.

Devdas, Nalini. **Svami Vivekananda.** Bangalore: Christian Institute for the Study of Religion and Society, 1968.

Eastern and Western Admirers. **Reminiscences of Swami Vivekananda.** Calcutta: Advaita Ashrama, 1964.

Farquhar, J. N. **Modern Religious Movements in India.** New York: Macmillan, 1919.

Gambhirananda, Swami. **The Apostles of Ramakrishna.** Calcutta: Advaita Ashrama, 1967.

Ganguli, Manmohan. **Swami Vivekananda, A Study.** Calcutta: Lalchand Dutta, 1907.

Herbert, Jean. **Swami Vivekananda: Bibliographie.** Paris: Advien Maisonneuve, 1938.

Isherwood, Christopher. **Ramakrishna and His Disciples.** New York: Simon & Schuster, 1959.

Majumdar, Ramesk C. **Swami Vivekananda, a Historical Review.** Calcutta: General Printers & Publishers, 1965.

———————(ed.). **Swami Vivekananda Centenary Memorial Volume.** Calcutta: Swami Vivekananda Centenary, 1963.

Nehru, Jawaharlal. **Sri Ramakrishna and Swami Vivekananda.** Mayavati: Advaita Ashrama, 1949.

Naravane, V.S. **Modern Indian Thought.** New York: Asia Publishing House, 1964.

Nikhilananda, Swami. **Vivekananda, a Biography.** New York: Ramakrishna-Vivekananda Center, 1953.

Prabhavananda, Swami. (ed.) **A Ramakrishna-Vedanta Wordbook.** Hollywood: Vedanta Press, 1962.

Rai Chaudhuri, S.K. **Swami Vivekananda, the Man and His Mission.** Calcutta: Scientific Book Agency, 1966.

Rolland, Romain. **Life of Swami Vivekananda and the Universal Gospel.** Translated into English by E.F. Malcolm-Smith. Sixth Edition. Calcutta: Advaita Ashrama, 1965.

Roy, Binoy K. **Socio-political Views of Vivekananda**. New Delhi: People's Publishing House, 1970.

Seminar on Swami Vivekananda's Teachings: May 1 to May 7, 1964. Coimbatore: Sri Ramakrishna Mission Vidyalaya, 1965.

Articles

Atulananda, Swami. "Swami Vivekananda in the West," **Prabuddha Bharata** (April, 1945), pp. 89-92 and (May, 1945), pp. 119-23.

———————."What Did Swami Vivekananda Teach in America?" **Prabuddha Bharata** (February, 1945), pp. 42-6.

Bharati, Agehananda. "The Hindu Renaissance and its Apologetic Patterns," **Journal of Asian Studies 39**, No. 2 (February 1970), pp. 267-287.

Chari, C.T.K. "On the Dialectic of Swami Vivekananda and Soren Kierkegaard: an 'Existential' Approach to Indian Philosophy," **La Revue Internationale de Philosophie,** 37, pp. 315-31.

Deshmukh, C.D. "Swami Vivekananda and his Contributions to Vedanta," **Vedanta Keseri**, 50 (October 1963), pp. 391-95.

Elenjimittam, Anthony. "Contributions of Swami Vivekananda to Hinduism," **Vedanta Keseri**, 50 (August 1963), pp. 265-68.

Goswami, Braj Lal. "Vivekananda and the Indian Renaissance," **Prabuddha Bharata**, 68 (October 1963), pp. 512-14.

Gupta, Anima Sen. "The Karma-Yoga of Swami Vivekananda," **Prabuddha Bharata**, 68 (May 1963), pp. 219-23.

Hussian, Zakir. "Swami Vivekananda and the Present Indian Context," **Vedanta Keseri**, 50 (September 1967), pp. 378-84.

Rajagopala, Sastri. "Swami Vivekananda's Contribution to Hinduism," **Vedanta Keseri**, 50 (August 1963), pp. 269-74.

Sarkar, Benoy Kumar. "The Legacies of Vivekananda," **Prabuddha Bharata**, (June 1945), pp. 151-2.

Sarkar, Indira Palit. "Swami Vivekananda's Concept of God," **Calcutta Review**, 169 (December 1963), pp. 295-7.

Sen, M. "Brahmo Samaj and Swami Vivekananda," **Calcutta Review**, 167 (May 1963), pp. 156-60.

Srinivasachari, P.N. "The Pure Advaita of Swami Vivekananda," **Journal of Oriental Institute of Baroda**, 13 (September 1963), pp. 31-47.

INDEX

absolute--20,23,32,78-86,96, 97,99.
adhikārivāda--87.
Advaita Vedānta--12,25,32,35, 36,39-47,51,52,70,74,79, 125,126.
arguments--18,45,52.
āryan--1,130.
aśramadharma [ashrama-dharma--24.
atheism--23.
ātman--25,73,80,85,87,89,90, 125.
authority--39-47,91.

Bābā--see Pavhāri Bābā.
Baird, Robert--2-5.
Bhagavad Gītā--34,87,92,94, 97.
bhakta--34,36,98.
bhakti--13,25,37,44,49,51,52, 62,95,96,98-100,120.
Bhakti Yoga--see **Yoga, Bhakti.**
bliss--71,83,100.
Brahman--12,23,28,29,33,35, 41,43,64,66,79-86,96-100, 106.
Brāhmo Samāj--10-15,20,106.
Brāhmo Samāji--10-15.
Buddha--37,52,97,101.
Buddhism--52-3,101,102.
Buddhist--43,52-53,93,102.

caste--14,25,39-42,52,60,88, 102-103,106,126-7.
Chaitanya--16,37,42.
Christ--36-37,52,101.
Christian--10-11,36,52,57,93, 102-106.
Christian Scientists--60.
Christianity--98,101-103,107, 122.
consciousness, levels of--19, 26-27,96-97,102.
cosmology--67,73-79.

darśaṇa [darshaṇa]--35,67,121.
dāsya--52,98.
Datta, Bhupendranath (brother)--10,17.
Datta, Bisvanath (father)--17-18.
Datta, Narendranath--1,10-53, 107.
dayā--95.
dhyāna--54,62.
dīksā [**dīkshā**]--49.
divinity of man--89,96,101.
documentation, contemporaneous--7,10; later--8; secondary later--8-9,10.
Durgā--23,44.

education of masses--90,93, 103.
epistemology--63,64-67,80, 122.
eschatology--80-85,124.
ethics--52,74,93-95.
evil--91,128.
evolution--19,46,68,75,92,100, 101,128.

fanaticism--90,91,98,102,127.
Freemason--10,15-16.

geruā--22.
Gītā--see **Bhagavad Gītā.**
Gospel of Sri Ramakrishna--8, 9,14,33.
grace--33,38,48,52.
guṇa--42,86,96.
gurubhāis--22,32,38,47-49,51, 54,60,119-120.

harmony of all views--39,96-104.
Hatha Yoga--see **Yoga, Hatha.**
hell--101.

Hinduism--vii-viii,56,60,61,98, 102,106,107,121.

idol worship--12,13.
intermarriage--103.
involution--75.
Islam--see Mohammedanism.
Īśvara [**Ishvara**]--81-82,95,98.

jīva--70-73,76,79,85,87,94,124.
jīvansevā--95.
jñāna--45,49,51,62,86,87,89.
Jñāna-kānda--40,41,45,92.
Jñāna Yoga--see **Yoga, Jñāna.**
Judaism--52.

Kālī--10,13,16,20-24,27-30, 33-35,55,62,120.
Kali yuga--25,37,44,45,75,87-88,95,102.
kalpas--75-76.
kāminikānchan--24-25,32-33, 56. See also money and women.
Kapila--68.
karma--32,46,52,62,76,80,86-89,96-97.
Karma-kanda--40-41,45,92.
Karma Yoga--see **Yoga, Karma.**
kṣatriya [**kshatriya**]--1.

līlā--23.
love--13,66,81,89,98,99.

marriage--16,18,88,103.
materialism--88,90.
māyā--54,74,77-81,85,99-100, 124.
meditation--21,54,61,99.
methodology:definitional problem--2-5; descriptive procedure--5-7; type and understanding--7; object of study--7; norms of religion studied as heuristically true--5.
methods, spiritual--96-100.
Mill, John Stuart--19.
Mohammedan--57,94,102.
Mohammedanism (Islam)--98, 102,103,107,122.
money--24,25,32,33,56,58-60. See also **kāminikānchan.**
mukti--42,61,80,84,85,93,94, 120,121,125.
multiplicity--66,68,73,74,79, 80,84.

names, monastic--55.
Narendra--see Datta, Narendranath.
nationalism--60.
Nirguṇa Brahman--80,82-85.
nirvāṇa--35,36,42,52,80,84,99.
nirvikalpa samādhi--32,65,85-86,120,122.

organization--60.

parabrahman--19.
paradox--63,78.
pariṇāma--46,75-79.
parivrājaka--38,48.
Parliament of Religions--1,46, 56-61.
Pavhāri Bābā--14,38,47-52.
peace--60,102,128.
perception--63,65-73,84,97, 109.
Plato--68.
Prabuddha Bharata--56.
pralaya--75-76.
prasāda--48,52.
prayer--13,21,28-29,129.
priest-power--91.
privilege--87,103.
projection--63,67,73-79,89.
psychology--67-73,84.
pūjāri--16,22.
Purāṇas--92.
puruṣakāra [**purushakāra**]--38, 48,52,90.
Pythagoras--68.

Rājas--55-56.
Rāja Yoga--see **Yoga, Rāja.**
Ramakrishna Mission--1,54, 61,107.
Ramakrishna Order--52.
Rāmakṛṣṇa [Rāmakrishna]--1, 10,12,19,20-38,43,45,47, 49-55,59,61,65,102,107, 121,122.
Rāmānuja--16,48.
realization--32,36,51,63,82,83, 86,95-96,100,101,127.
renunciation--24,25,32,33,36, 50,52,61,93-95,99.

śabda [**shabda**]--44.
scared remains--51.
sādhanās--25,32,34.
Sādhāran Brāhmo Samāj--12, 13,16.
sādhu--48,49,107.
samādhi--32,49,52,65,85,86, 97,99,120.
Saguṇa Grahman--80-82.
śakti [**shakti**]--23,28-31,44,52, 82.
Śaṁkara [Shankara]--16,36,40-46,52,61,74,84,126.
Saṁkhya [**Sankhya**]--43,67-70, 74,79-80,123.
saṁkīrtaṇa [**sankīrtaṇa**]--13, 14.
saṁnyāsa [**sannyāsa**]--9,22,25, 27,36,37,44,60,61.
saṁnyāsin [**sannyāsin**]--1,9,22, 25,26,36,37,48,56,57.
saṁsāra--76,87.
Sanātana Dharma--1,38,45,60, 85,87-88,100,122.
Śastras [**Shastras**]--1.
Satya Yuga--60,75,102,104.
sceptic--vii,10,16-21,24.
science--46,64,73,74,94,103, 105,108.
scientific Advaitism--46.
Scottish Church College--18.
scriptures--24,33-35,39-46,49, 51,88,91-93.
sectarian--82,102,104.
Sen, Keshab Chandra--11-14, 17,105.
sevā--see **jīvansevā**.
Shelly--19.
siddhis--97.
sister-iii,14,61.
Śiva [Shiva]--30.
Smith, Wilfred Cantwell--4.
spellings--9.
Spencer--18-19.
śudras [**shudras**]--40-42.
suffering--14,17,18,28,47,61, 86,87,96.
superstition--92,93,103,128.
śūnyatā [**shūnyatā**]--43.
svadharma--38,56.

Tantras--33,53,106.
Tillich, Paul--5.
Totapuri--22.
transliterations--9.
truth--5,12,66,67,69,82,89,90, 92,100,102,104,121.

ultimate concern--5-6.
Ultimate Reality--19.
unity--15,66,74,75,80,82,89, 91-96,100-103.
Universal Reason--19-20.

vairāgya--52.
varṇa dharma--25,39,88,103.
Vedānta, practical--11,20,54, 60-104.
Vedas--39-46,52,60,64,67,85, 87,88,92,103.
vegetarian--14,93.
viśiṣṭādvaita [**Vishishtādvaita**] --82,83,87,89,96.
vivarta--46,64,75,78,80,85.
viveka--90.
Vyāsa--45.

weakness--90,101.
women--14,24-25,32,33,56,88,
103.
word study--9,142-144
(Appendix B).
worship of Rāmakṛṣṇa--32,51.

yajñas--41.
Yoga, Bhakti--60,97-100,104.
Yoga, Hatha--49,117.
Yoga, Jñana--60,97,99-100,
104.
Yoga, Karma--37,60,87,97,
100,104,126.
Yoga, practical--48-52. See
Rāja Yoga.
Yoga, Rāja--60,97,99,100,104.
yogas--25,32.
yugas--75-76,123.

DEC 15 1993			
JUN 24 1998			
JUN 18			